MW00559615

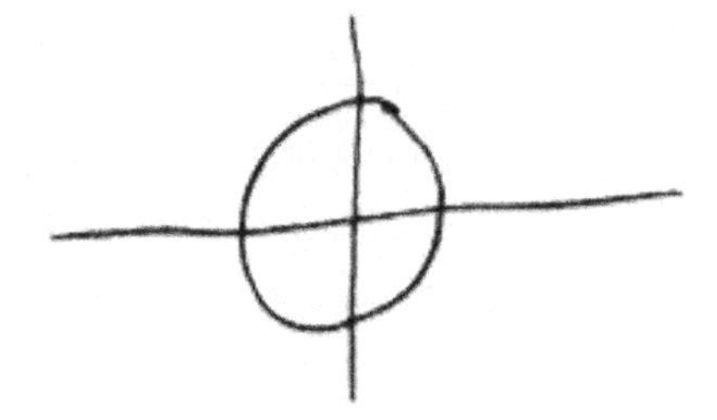

In one of his last taunting letters to the news media, Zodiac claimed he had 37 victims to show for his five years of terrorizing the San Francisco Bay Area. However, he was only linked conclusively to eight victims.

This list of victims (and subsequent police reports) is in chronological order of when they were killed, and not necessarily when they were conclusively determined by law enforcement to be Zodiac victims.

DISCLAIMER

In order to preserve the history of the original documents many misspellings and typos have been left as is. Some corrections have been made when they impacted the utility of the index of this book.

ZODIAC KILLER

just the facts

TOM VOIGT

Brainjar Media

109 N Main Ave #202

Gresham, OR 97030

www.BrainjarMedia.com

Ordering Information:

Quantity sales. Special discounts are available on quantity purchases by corporations, associations, and others. For details, contact ZodiacKiller.com

Orders by U.S. trade bookstores and wholesalers. Please contact Author at info@zodiackiller.com

Printed in the United States of America

ISBN 978-1-7370981-0-2

First Edition

Front and back cover design by Guy Edwards and Brainjar Media

TABLE OF CONTENTS

WANTED 1

Cheri Josephine Bates..3

David Arthur Faraday And Betty Lou Jensen 9

Darlene Elizabeth Ferrin and Michael Renault Mageau.....................86

Cecelia Ann Shepard and Bryan Calvin Hartnell..............................203

Paul Lee Stine 276

Zodiac Killer Case Overview Prepared by California DOJ................281

TOP SECRET REPORT...321

ZODIAC KILLER CIPHERS...333

WING WALKER SHOE PHOTOS 335

WANTED

SAN FRANCISCO POLICE DEPARTMENT

No. 90-69	<u>WANTED FOR MURDER</u>	OCTOBER 18, 1969

ORIGINAL DRAWING

AMENDED DRAWING

Supplementing our Bulletin 87-69 of October 13, 1969. Additional information has developed the above amended drawing of murder suspect known as "ZODIAC".

WMA, 35-45 Years, approximately 5'8", Heavy Build, Short Brown Hair, possibly with Red Tint, Wears Glasses. Armed with 9 MM Automatic.

Available for comparison: Slugs, Casings, Latents, Handwriting.

ANY INFORMATION:

Inspectors Armstrong & Toschi

Homicide Detail

CASE NO. 696314

THOMAS J. CAHILL

CHIEF OF POLICE

Cheri Josephine Bates

Killed: Between 9:23 PM Oct. 30. (Sunday) and

12:23 AM Oct. 31, 1966 (Monday)

~~~~~~

Case number: 352-481

Place of attack: An alley on the campus of Riverside City College, Riverside, Calif.

Method of attack: A 1966 graduate of Riverside's Ramona High School, 18-year-old Cheri Jo Bates was beaten and stabbed multiple times with a short-bladed knife. Her throat was also cut. There was no evidence of robbery or sexual molestation. There were no witnesses.

(Miss Bates was not suspected of being a Zodiac victim until October 1969. In November 1970, investigators added her to the official list of Zodiac victims.)

See more at:

https://zodiackiller.com/zodiac-killer-victim-cheri-jo-bates/

Here is the Oct. 20, 1969 three-page report detailing the Bates murder. It was sent from the Riverside Police Department to the Napa County Sheriff's Department. The purpose of the report was to make Napa County authorities aware that their "Zodiac" killer may have started his murder spree several years earlier in Riverside. By late November 1970, at a task-force meeting of Zodiac detectives, the Bates/Zodiac connection was made official. More on that to come –
~~~~~~

DEPARTMENT OF POLICE

L T KINKEAD

CHIEF

RADIO STATION KMB 401

October 20, 1969

REF: 352-481

Earl Randol

Sheriff of Napa County

Napa, California 94558

Attention Captain Donald A. Townsend

Dear Sir:

This letter is in reference to our telephone conversation of 10-17-69 regarding the similar M.O. of your "Zodiac" suspect and the suspect of our homicide File No. 352-481.

It may aid you to have a brief synopsis of our homicide. It is as follows:

On October 30, 1966, Cheri Jo Bates, a college student at Riverside City College, was brutally murdered. Our investigation revealed that the victim had gone to the city college campus to obtain some books from the library (the library was open on Sunday for the students' benefit). It was established that she had entered the library and checked out three books at approximately 6:00 PM. She returned to her vehicle, which was parked on a city street a short distance from the library, placed her books in the vehicle, and attempted to start her vehicle. The vehicle had been tampered with so it would not start. This was evidently done by the suspect to keep the victim near her vehicle so that the suspect could make his approach.

Our victim then left her vehicle, accompanied by the suspect, and walked approximately 200 feet from her vehicle into a dirt driveway between two houses. These houses were vacant and a part of the school property, having recently been purchased by the city college. While in this driveway area, our victim was attacked with a knife and stabbed numerous times in the chest. She was also stabbed once in the back, and her throat was severly cut, almost to the extent where she was decapitated. In addition to the stab wounds, our victim had been beaten about the

10-24-69 [UNREADABLE]

ADDRESS ALL COMMUNICATIONS TO THE CHIEF OF POLICE – BOX [UNREADABLE]

face and had been choked. There was no evidence that the victim had been sexually attacked, as she was fully clothed and the clothing was not disarranged. There was nothing to indicate a motive of robbery, as our victim's purse and its contents were intact. From all indications, the knife used by the suspect was one of approximately a 1/2-inch width blade by 3-1/2 inches long.

One month after the homicide, letters were received at the Press and our department written by the suspect of our homicide. The suspect used a black felt pen to address the envelopes and had used upper case print. The confession letter was typed. There are numerous errors in spelling, punctuation, etc., as you will notice.

The person who wrote the confession letter is aware of facts about the homicide that only the killer would know. There is no doubt that the person who wrote the confession letter is out homicide suspect.

The original of this letter was evidently destroyed or kept by the suspect, as the Press and our department received a carbon copy of the original. These carbon copies were a fourth or fifth copy and difficult to read. A photograph of this letter and the envelopes is attached. It should be noted that the copies received by the Press and our department were on plain white paper of poor quality. Width of the paper is 8 inches. The length of the paper is unknown, as the suspect (a peculiarity) tore off the bottom and top of the paper. (Refer to the photographs.)

It might be worthwhile to note that just outside the city limits of Riverside is located March Air Force Base, a SAC base. Physical evidence found at the scene of our crime indicated that heel prints found near the body were made by a heel that was manufactured for military and other government agencies, including prisons.

We were able to lift some latent fingerprints from the victim's vehicle. These prints were not identified. Our unidentified prints are on file with the FBI under the FBI File No. 32-27195, Latent Case No. 73096.

Copies of the latent lifts from your homicide were obtained from CII and sent to the FBI for comparison with the latent lifts of our investigation.

There are numerous similarities in your homicide and our Inv. 352-481. I thought you should be aware that we are working a similar-type homicide investigation. If you are able to determine by handwriting comparison or by any other means that your homicide suspect is the same as ours, please advise. I will notify you of the results in comparing your latent lifts with ours as soon as I hear from the FBI.

I hope this information may aid you in your investigation. Please be assured of our complete cooperation in all matters of mutual interest.

Yours very truly,

L. T. KINKEAD

Chief of Police

H L Homsher

H.L. Homsher, Sergeant

Detective Division

HLH: seb

Attachments:

1. Two reproductions of the confession letter.

2. Photograph of the envelope received by the Press.

3. A photograph of the envelope received by our department.

4. Two Xerox copies of envelopes received (after having been processed for fingerprints).

Cy to: Chief of Police, San Francisco Police Department

David Arthur Faraday And Betty Lou Jensen

Killed: Dec. 20, 1968 (Friday)

~~~~~~

Case number: V-25564

Time of attack: Approximately 11:15 p.m.

Place of attack: A gravel parking area along remote Lake Herman Road on the eastern outskirts of Vallejo, Calif.

Method of attack: David Faraday, age 17, was shot once in the head at point-blank range and died within minutes. Betty Lou Jensen, age 16, was shot five times in the back and killed instantly. The weapon was a .22 caliber semi-automatic pistol. The ammunition was Winchester Western Super X copper-coated long rifle. There was no indication of robbery or sexual molestation. While there were no witnesses, several vehicles were seen in the area just prior to local resident Stella Borges discovering the crime scene.

(As a result of the Zodiac providing authorities with written proof he was their killer, in the summer of 1969 Faraday and Jensen were placed on the list of confirmed Zodiac victims.)

See more at:

https://zodiackiller.com/zodiac-killer-victims-david-faraday-and-lou-jensen/

Here is the extensive, 60-page report prepared by the Solano County Sheriff's Department pertaining to the homicides of David Faraday and Betty Jensen –
~~~~~~

OFFENSE REPORT

OFFICE OF SHERIFF

County of Solano, California

OFFENSE 187 P.C. MURDER CASE NO V25564

LOCATION Lake Herman Road, Entrance to Benicia's Water Pumping Station

REPORTED BY CAPTAIN PITTA ADDRESS Benicia P.D. PHONE

RECEIVED BY Sgt. Cunningham DATE 12/20/68 TIME 11:52PM

( ) LETTER ( ) DESK (X) PHONE ( ) TELETYPE ( ) RADIO

DESCRIPTION OF PROPERTY	
	Suspect No. 1 UNKNOWN
(1)	Sex Descent
(2)	Height Weight Age
(3)	Hair color Eye color
(4)	Marks/scars
(5)	
	Occupation
	Disguise or dress
	Arrested: Identification No.
TOTAL VALUE	(Yes or No)

RO: BUTTERBACH & WATERMAN

On arrival at the above location RO's observed several Benicia Police units. RO's contacted Captain Pitta, Lt. Little and Officer Varner and a reporter from the Fairfield Daily Republic, Thomas D. Balmer. There was a 1961 Rambler 4-door S/W, two-tone dark tan over light tan, California license DTL-962, no registration. The station wagon was parked in the entrance way into the pumping station. The front of the station wagon was pointing in an Easterly direction. Approximately ten feet behind the station wagon was the body of a young lady (BETTY LOU JENSEN, WFJ 16 years, DOB 7-21-52, of 123 Ridgewood Ct., Vallejo) The body was partially covered with a wool gray blanket. The face and head was covered with blood. There was a large pool of blood where the body was lying. There was a chalk outline of a man's body on the ground (DAVID ARTHUR FARADAY, WMJ 17 years, DOB 10-2-51, of 1930 Sereno Drive, Vallejo) By the right front door of the station wagon where the man's head was outlined, there was a very large pool of blood. Several

APB Date INV Officer Date

SHERIFF'S OFFICE -	SOLANO COUNTY	Time	11:52PM	Date	12/20/68 V25564
Nature of Complaint:	MURDER			Location	Lake Herman Road
Complainant:	CAPTAIN PITTA			Address	Benicia P.D

Received by: Sgt. Cunningham ( ) Letter ( ) Desk ( ) Phone ( ) Teletype ( ) Radio

small caliber casings were on the ground in the area. There was a white fur type ladies' coat laying on the left side of the rear seat of the station wagon. There was what appeared to be a bullet hole in the rear window, right side just above the chrome stripping on the lower part of the window just off center to the rear of window. RO requested the reporter stay out of the area until Detective Sgt. Lundblad and the coroner arrived and gave him their permission to enter the area.

12:05AM 12/21/68 Det/Sgt. Lundblad arrived at the scene. Sgt. Lundblad requested RO's go to Vallejo Hospital to try to get a statement from the boy (FARADAY) 12:23AM 987 Vallejo General Hospital. Contacted nurse, Mrs. Barbara Lowe, 321 Cypress Street. RO requested permission to see FARADAY. Mrs Lowe stated FARADAY was dead on arrival at the hospital. He was pronounced as dead at 12:05AM by Dr. Siebert. RO checked FARADAY. He had been shot in the upper portion of the left ear by a small caliber bullet which penetrated the ear and head. There was what appeared to be powder burns on the left ear where the bullet had entered. There was a large lump on his right cheek and his hair on the left side of his head was matted with blood. There was also blood on his hands and the sleeves of his shirt. He was wearing a light blue long sleeve shirt, brown corduroy pants-levi type, black socks, tan leather shoes-rough texture. He had a Timex wrist watch, chrome case and band, on his left wrist, 85¢ (3-quarters and one dime) in his left front pants pocket, a black comb in his left hip pocket, a white handerchief and small bottle of breath drops (Binaca) in his right front pants pocket. There was

SHERIFF'S OFFICE -	SOLANO COUNTY	Time	11:52PM	Date	12/20/68 V25564
Nature of Complaint:	MURDER			Location	Lake Herman Road
Complainant:	CAPTAIN PITTA			Address	Benicia P.D
Received by:	Sgt. Cunningham	( ) Letter	( ) Desk	( ) Phone	( ) Teletype ( ) Radio

RO: BUTTERBACH & WATERMAN PAGE 2

nothing in his right hip pocket. He held a class ring by the tips of the ring and middle fingers of his left hand. The ring in yellow metal with a red stone. The wallet he had was given to RO by Mrs. Lowe. It contained several I.D. cards, social security card and driver's license. The wallet is a small son's valet, black in color. He was also wearing a brown leather belt.

RO called Sgt. Cunningham to have someone come to the hospital to take pictures. Pictures taken by Deputy J.R. Wilson.

1:36AM 987-c enroute to Colonial Chapel. 1:38AM 987 Colonial Chapel. 4:30AM 987-c.

(Butterbach & Waterman) ab

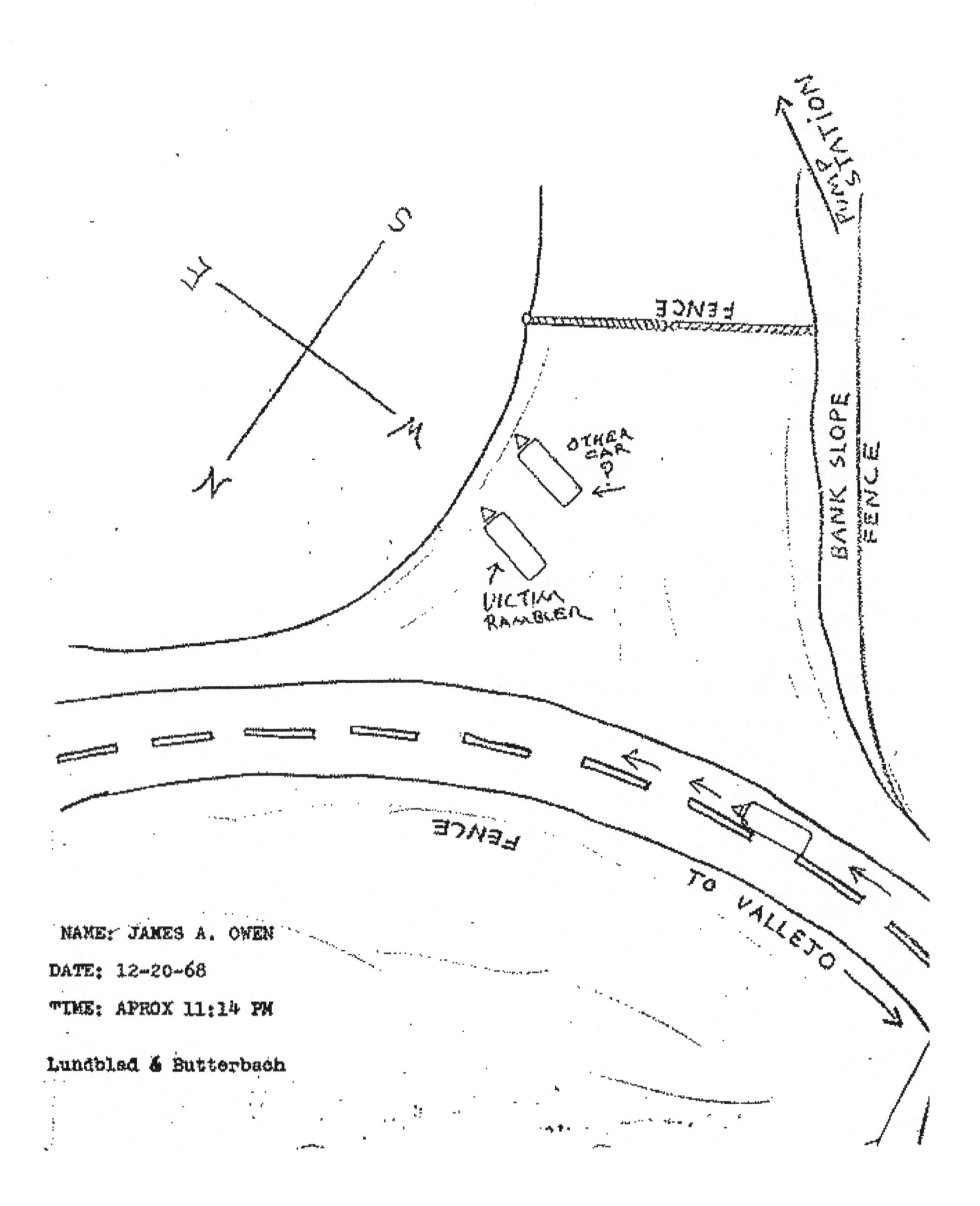
PUMP STATION
S
E
W
N
FENCE
OTHER CAR ?
VICTIM RAMBLER
BANK SLOPE
FENCE
FENCE
TO VALLEJO
NAME: JAMES A. OWEN
DATE: 12-20-68
TIME: APROX 11:14 PM
Lundblad & Butterbach

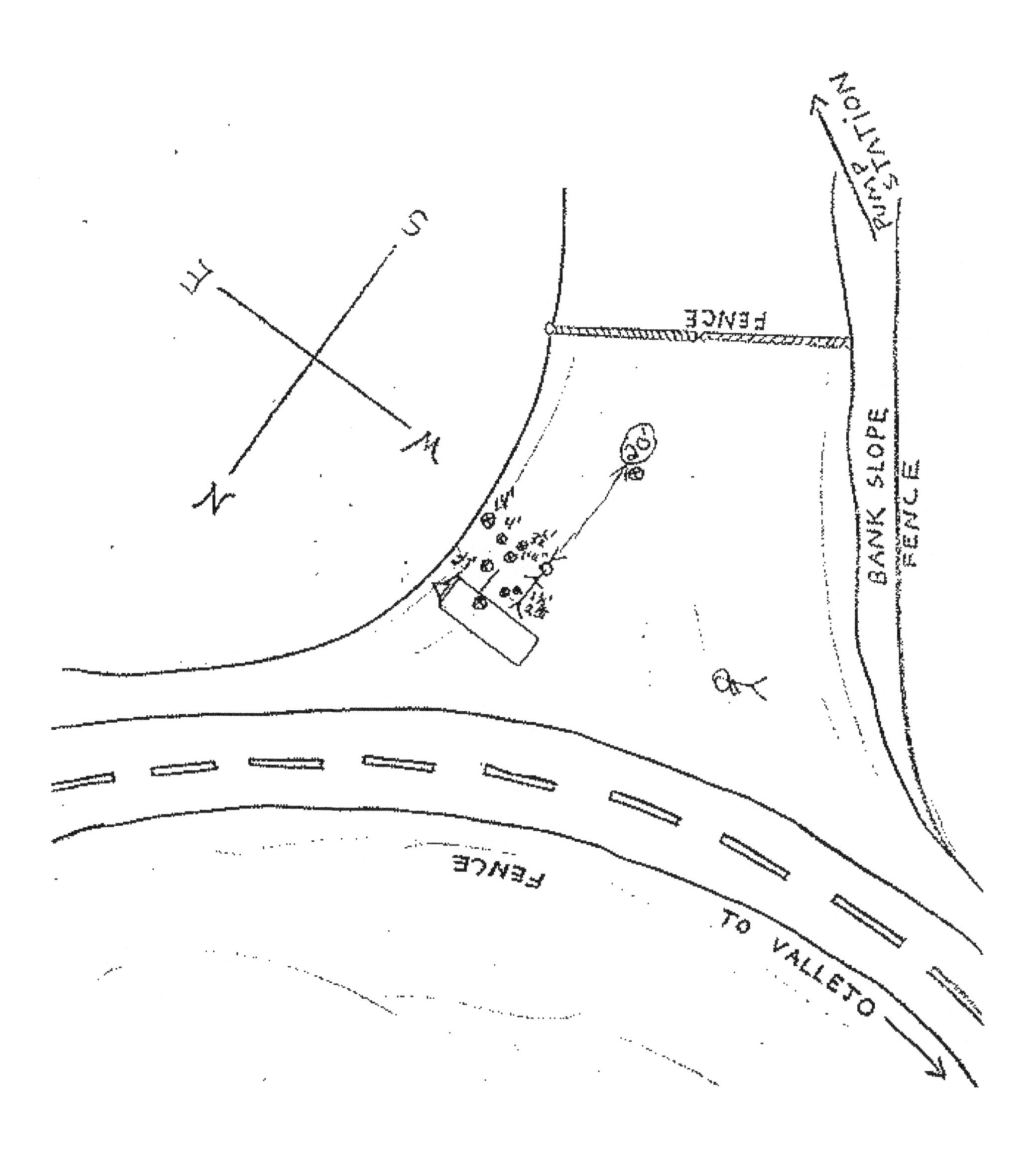

N
S
E
W
PUMP STATION
FENCE
BANK SLOPE
FENCE
FENCE
TO VALLEJO

OFFICE OF THE SHERIFF

COUNTY OF SOLANO

FAIRFIELD, CALIFORNIA

CRIME REPORT

Specific Offense	SOLANO COUNTY SHERIFF'S OFFICE, VALLEJO	Case Number
187 P.C.	*Reporting Department*	V-25564

[UNREADABLE] and time occurred; day of week	Location of occurrence	Division - [UNREADABLE]	Date and time reported to department
12/20/68 Between 11:14PM 11:20PM	Entrance to Lake Herman Rd.	Patrol	12/20/68 11:30PM
[UNREADABLE] SEE DETAILS BELOW	Residence address (business address if firm)	Residence phone	Business phone or address
[UNREADABLE] reporting offense DANIEL PITTA	Residence address Captain, Benicia P.D.	Residence phone	Business phone or address
WITNESS(ES), Names SEE WITNESS INDEX:	Residence address P.O. Box 477, Vallejo	Residence phone 644-1427	Business phone or address
STUDENT:	Residence address	Residence phone	Business phone or address
[UNREADABLE]	Type of premises or location where offense was committed Isolated County Rd .5 miles East of Vallejo, at entrance to Lake Herman Pumping Station		

CRIMES AGAINST PROPERTY	CRIMES AGAINST THE PERSON
[UNREADABLE] where entrance was [UNREADABLE]	Weapon – force or means used: J.C. HIGGINS, AUTO/PISTOL SEE LAB. REPORT ON IDENTIFICATION.
[UNREADABLE] location of property when [UNREADABLE]	Exact location of victim at time of offense STANDING ON RIGHT SIDE OF CAR
Instrument used (describe)	Victim's activity at time of offense INTERRUPTED NECKING
[UNREADABLE] to gain entrance	Exact words used by [UNREADABLE] UNKNOWN
[UNREADABLE] were occupants at time of offense?	

Apparent motive – Type of property taken or obtained

NO APPARENT MOTIVE, ROBBERY AND SEX RULED OUT.

[UNREADABLE] at suspect(s) – Actions or conversation

10-shots (2 in car, five un back of Female victim, 1-in male victim, 2-unaccounted

[UNREADABLE] used by suspect(s) – Year, [UNREADABLE], body type, color, license number and any other identifying marks

UNKNOWN, WITNESS OBSERVED DARK CAR, LACKING IN CHROME. NOT LARGE & NOT COMPACT.

ACT(S):

	Name	Address used	Hair	Eyes	Hgt.	Wgt.	Age	Identifications Numbers (if any)
1								
2	NONE							
3								

[UNREADABLE]

VICTIMS: #1 BETTY LOU JENSEN, WFJ, age 16, 123 Ridgewood Crt., Vallejo

#2 DAVID L. FARADAY, WMJ, age 17, 1930 Sereno Drive, Vallejo

SEE ATTACHED SHEETS:

CASE NUMBERS OF ANY OTHER OFFENSES CLEARED OR CONNECTED WITH THIS REPORT: USE ADDITIONAL SHEET IF NECESSARY

number and date 14 FFS 12/23/668	Signature of reporting officer Det/Sgt Lundblad-Butterbach	[UNREADABLE] or serial number	Date and time report written
[UNREADABLE]	Signature of supervisor [UNREADABLE] Det/Sgt Lundblad	[UNREADABLE] or serial number	Date and time report reviewed

SHERIFF'S OFFICE -	SOLANO COUNTY	Time	11:52PM	Date	12/20/68 V25564
Nature of Complaint:	MURDER			Location	Lake Herman Road
Complainant:	CAPTAIN PITTA			Address	Benicia P.D

Received by: Sgt. Cunningham ( ) Letter ( ) Desk ( ) Phone ( ) Teletype ( ) Radio

RO: DET/SGT. LUNBLAD 12/20/68 12:00 Midnight

VICTIMS: BETTY LOU JENSEN, WFJ, age 16
123 Ridgewood Court, Vallejo, Calif.

DAVID FARADAY, WMJ, age 17
1930 Sereno Drive, Vallejo, Calif.

11:30PM 12/20/68 The reporting officer was notified of a possible slaying on Lake Herman Road. Sheriff's Deputies, Coroner Dan Horan and the Benicia Police Department are standing by at the scene.

SEE CAPTAIN PITTA'S REPORT:

Upon my arrival, Horan and Capt. Pitta advised one of the victims, FARADAY, was enroute to the Vallejo General Hospital by Ambulance. The second victim BETTY LOU JENSEN had succumbed and was awaiting transfer to Colonial Chapels.

Lt. Little photographed the crime scene. Charts and measurements were recorded. .22 caliber shell casings were recovered at scene and their recovery positions were recorded on charts.

A search was made for a weapon and none was found, ruling out a possible murder and suicide. The ground was frozen solid under a reported 22 degree temperature. There were no visible fresh tire tracks leaving the scene.

12/21/68 1:04AM to Vallejo General Hospital, information was obtained that the victim FARADAY was DOA. 12/21/68 1:38AM- To Colonial Chapels. Information was obtained from coroner Dan Horan that the victim JENSEN had five (5) bullet holes on the right side of her back. Three (3) emerging from the front of her body. The entry holes were in a remarkable

SHERIFF'S OFFICE -	SOLANO COUNTY	Time	11:52PM	Date	12/20/68 V25564
Nature of Complaint:	MURDER			Location	Lake Herman Road
Complainant:	CAPTAIN PITTA			Address	Benicia P.D

Received by: Sgt. Cunningham ( ) Letter ( ) Desk ( ) Phone ( ) Teletype ( ) Radio

RO: DET/SGT. LUNBLAD PAGE 2

close pattern. FARADAY had one bullet hole thru his left ear and into the back of his head. The ear had a dark area around the hole that appeared to be a powder burn, indicating the shot was fired at close range.

The victim JENSEN was attired in black strap shoes that were blood stained. Blue/white padded bra, blood stained on the left side and straps. Full pantie-type hose. White cotton panties and pink panties. A purple dress with white collar and cuffs. The dress was thoroughly blood stained. There were five (5) holes in close pattern on the right side. There were two (2) holes on the front, one at the left breast area and the other on lower right side at the waist. When the mortician was removing the clothing from the body a .22 cal. pellet fell from the panties where it was apparently trapped after having passed through her body.

FARADAY was attired in black socks, low cut brown fruit boots, white cotton shorts, white cotton T-shirt, light blue, size 20, boys long sleeve shirt, brown corduroy trousers.

(Det/Sgt. Lundblad) ab

SOLANO COUNTY SHERIFF'S OFFICE

FAIRFIELD, CALIFORNIA

SUPPLEMENTAL INVESTIGATION REPORT

TYPE OF ORIGINAL REPORT	DATE ORIGINAL REPORT	CASE NUMBER
187 P.C. Murder	12/20/68	V-25564
VICTIM OR COMPLAINTANT	LOCATION ORIGINAL OCCURRENCE	DATE – TIME OR SUPPL.
CAPTAIN PITTA	Lake Herman Rd., entrance to Benicia Water Pumping Station	

ADDITIONAL DETAILS OF OFFENSE

EVIDENCE TO CII:

1 Damaged pellet removed from victim, DAVID FARADAY'S head during autopsy.

2 Two (2) pellets removed from victim, BETTY LOU JENSEN, during autopsy.

3 Pellet found in pants of victim BETTY LOU JENSEN, at Mortuary, during examination of the deceased. The pellet had entered the lower back, coursed through her body, emerging under the waist band elastic of her panties, were it was found.

4 Five (5) .22 casings found at scene by Coroner Dan Horan. Turned over to RO at the crime scene.

5 Four (4) .22 casings found at crime scene by Sgt. Silva of the Benicia Police Department. Turned over to RO at mortuary

6 Damaged pellet recovered in top of 1961 Rambler station wagon California license #DTL-962 (registered to JHAN FARADAY)

7 Damaged pellet recovered in 1961 Rambler. Pellet had entered right rear window, lodge in floor mat, left side of storage area.

8 Pellet recovered near victim BETTY LOU JENSEN, in blood splattered path on her attempted escape route. (Pellet entered her body in the back and emerged from the center of her stomach and dropped to the ground without penetrating the front of her dress)

9 Victims drees: Purple with white sleeves, five (5) bullet holes in back and one in front, soaked with blood.

(Det/Sgt Lundblad) ab

Cleared by Arrest ☐

Cleared Other ☐

Not Cleared ☐

Unfounded ☐

____
INVESTIGATING OFFICER

OFFENSE REPORT

OFFICE OF SHERIFF

County of Solano, California

OFFENSE 187 P.C. Murder CASE NO V25564

LOCATION Lake Herman Road, Entrance to Benicia Water Pumping Station

REPORTED BY CAPTAIN PITTA ADDRESS Benicia P.D. PHONE

RECEIVED BY Sgt. Cunningham DATE 12/20/68 TIME 11:52PM

( ) LETTER ( ) DESK ( ) PHONE ( ) TELETYPE ( ) RADIO

DESCRIPTION OF PROPERTY	
	Suspect No. 1
(1)	Sex Descent
(2)	Height Weight Age
(3)	Hair color Eye color
(4)	Marks/scars
(5)	
	Occupation
	Disguise or dress
	Arrested: Identification No.
TOTAL VALUE	(Yes or No)

RO: LUNDBLAD & BUTTERBACH 12/22/68 4:30PM

STATEMENT: WILLIAM [REDACTED], WMA 746 Avenue, Vallejo, CA (642-[REDACTED])

MR [REDACTED] saw an article in the paper requesting assistance and he phoned the office to report that he and his girl friend were in the Lake Herman area between 9:30 PM and 10:00 PM on 12/20/68. He stated he was driving his girl friends's sport car and he was testing it out and adjusting the motor. He was parked in the open area by the pump station and he observed a Blue car, possibly a Valient, coming down the road from Benicia towards Vallejo. They passed his location, stopped in the middle of the road and he saw the white lights of the reverse come on and the car started backing up towards them. MR [REDACTED] put the car in gear and took off at a high rate of speed and the car followed him at a high rate of speed. They did not attempt to gain on him but when they got to the turn off towards Benicia, [REDACTED] turned towards Benicia and the other car went straight ahead. The subject were both caucasians and there is no further identification on the car or the subjects.

APB	Date	Inv. Officer	Date

OFFENSE REPORT

OFFICE OF SHERIFF

County of Solano, California

OFFENSE 187 P.C. Murder CASE NO V25564

LOCATION Lake Herman Road, Entrance to Benicia Water Pumping Station

REPORTED BY CAPTAIN PITTA ADDRESS Benicia P.D. PHONE

RECEIVED BY Sgt. Cunningham DATE 12/20/68 TIME 11:52PM

( ) LETTER ( ) DESK ( ) PHONE ( ) TELETYPE ( ) RADIO

DESCRIPTION OF PROPERTY	
	Suspect No. 1
(1)	Sex Descent
(2)	Height Weight Age
(3)	Hair color Eye color
(4)	Marks/scars
(5)	
	Occupation
	Disguise or dress
	Arrested: Identification No.
TOTAL VALUE	(Yes or No)

RO: LUNDBLAD 12/21/68 5:15PM

STATEMENT: OFFICER WARNER,

Benicia Police Department

Officer WARNER phoned that he had received a phone call from a MRS PEGGIE [REDACTED] Husband's name, HOMER [REDACTED], residence at 3 West "L" Street, Benicia, CA (745 - [REDACTED])

MRS [REDACTED] is employed at Mr. Ed's drive-in restaurant, Benicia. Her husband HOMER is employed by the Frederickson Pipe Company, who have a contract to put the new sewer or water pipes in the Lake Herman area. She drives a 1967 gold Grand Prix, California license [REDACTED].

MRS [REDACTED] reports that at 11:00PM she was with her husband and he was checking the pipes and the equipment at the construction site and they arrived at the scene and they arrived near the scene at the pump station, went own to the bottom of the hill, turned into the Marshall Ranch to make a turn to go back towards Benicia. When they passed the area of the pumping station

APB	Date	Inv. Officer	Date

SOLANO COUNTY SHERIFF'S OFFICE

FAIRFIELD, CALIFORNIA

SUPPLEMENTAL INVESTIGATION REPORT

TYPE OF ORIGINAL REPORT	DATE ORIGINAL REPORT	CASE NUMBER
187 P.C. Murder	12/20/68	V-25564
VICTIM OR COMPLAINTANT	LOCATION ORIGINAL OCCURRENCE	DATE – TIME OR SUPPL.
CAPTAIN PITTA	Lake Herman	12/21/68 6:15 PM

ADDITIONAL DETAILS OF OFFENSE

OFFICER WARNER: PAGE 2

they observed the Rambler s/w and MRS [REDACTED] described the FARADAY car. At the time she saw the boy sitting in the driver's seat and the leaning against his shoulder. When the lights of their car flashed on the FARADAY car, the subject in the driver's seat put his hands on the wheel of the car and MRS. [REDACTED] had noticed this action. When the [REDACTED]'s returned a few minutes later, after having turned around, subjects in the Rambler were still sitting there in this position. The car was facing East towards the field at the left of the gate.

When they turned around into the Marshall Ranch, MRS [REDACTED] reports they saw a red pick-up truck with wooden board sides parked in the field about twenty-five feet in. At this time the car was facing put to the road. She stated there were two white male adults in the car, one of them was twenty-five to thirty years old, and had a stocking type hat or cap over his head, a three cell flashlight and a hunting jacket. MRS [REDACTED] reports that they did not pass any other car at the area and only the station wagon was parked at the Pumping Station entrance.

SEE ADDITIONAL REPORTS FROM MRS [REDACTED]

(Det/Sgt Lundblad) ab

Cleared by Arrest ☐

Cleared Other ☐

Not Cleared ☐

Unfounded ☐

INVESTIGATING OFFICER

SHERIFF'S OFFICE -	SOLANO COUNTY	Time	11:52PM	Date	12/20/68 V25564
Nature of Complaint:	187 P.C. MURDER			Location	Lake Herman Road
Complainant:	CAPTAIN PITTA			Address	Benicia P.D
Received by:	Sgt. Cunningham	( ) Letter	( ) Desk	( ) Phone	( ) Teletype ( ) Radio

RO: BUTTERBACH & LUNDBLAD 12/21/68 8:15AM

JAMES [REDACTED], 1735 [REDACTED] Drive, Vallejo, 644-[REDACTED]

MR [REDACTED] was driving home from work at Humble Oil, Benicia. MR [REDACTED] stated last night, Friday 12-20-68, at 11:20PM he drove by the location on Lake Herman Road. He states he saw two cars parked near the entrance to the pumping station. He stated the car parked nearest to the road was a 1955 or 1956 station wagon, boxy type, neutral color. The other was parked to the right and abreast of the Station Wagon. The cars were about ten feet apart. He stated he could not give a description of the make or color of the other car. MR [REDACTED] advised the RO's they might check with a MR [REDACTED] who lives at the apartments on the end of Springs Road. He stated MR [REDACTED] may have driven by the location last, as he ([REDACTED]) also works the graveyard shift at Humble Oil.

(Butterbach & Lundblad) ab

OFFENSE REPORT

OFFICE OF SHERIFF

County of Solano, California

OFFENSE 187 P.C. Murder CASE NO V25564

LOCATION Lake Herman Road, Entrance to Benicia Water Pumping Station

REPORTED BY CAPTAIN PITTA ADDRESS Benicia P.D. PHONE

RECEIVED BY Sgt. Cunningham DATE 12/20/68 TIME 11:52PM

( ) LETTER ( ) DESK ( ) PHONE ( ) TELETYPE ( ) RADIO

DESCRIPTION OF PROPERTY	Suspect No. 1
(1)	Sex Descent
(2)	Height Weight Age
(3)	Hair color Eye color
(4)	Marks/scars
(5)	
	Occupation
	Disguise or dress
	Arrested: Identification No.
TOTAL VALUE	(Yes or No)

RO: BUTTERBACH 12/21/68 8:33PM

TELEPHONE CONVERSATION: JAMES _______ 1735 _______ Drive

RO called [REDACTED] about the possibility of a MR [REDACTED] who is also employed at Humble Oil on the graveyard shift of his ([REDACTED]) driving pass the crime scene on the night of Friday 12/20/68. MR [REDACTED] stated he talked to [REDACTED] today and [REDACTED] said he did not drive to work by Lake Herman Road last night 12/20/68.

APB	Date	Inv. Officer	Date
		BUTTERBACH	

OFFENSE REPORT

OFFICE OF SHERIFF

County of Solano, California

OFFENSE	187 P.C. Murder			CASE NO	V25564
LOCATION	Lake Herman Road, Entrance to Benicia Water Pumping Station				
REPORTED BY	CAPTAIN PITTA	ADDRESS	Benicia P.D.	PHONE	
RECEIVED BY	Sgt. Cunningham	DATE	12/20/68	TIME	11:52PM

( ) LETTER ( ) DESK ( ) PHONE ( ) TELETYPE ( ) RADIO

DESCRIPTION OF PROPERTY	Suspect No. 1
(1)	Sex / Descent
(2)	Height / Weight / Age
(3)	Hair color / Eye color
(4)	Marks/scars
(5)	
	Occupation
	Disguise or dress
	Arrested: / Identification No.
TOTAL VALUE	(Yes or No)

RO: BUTTERBACH & LUNDBLAD 12/24/68 12:20PM

STATEMENT: JAMES A [REDACTED]

1735 [REDACTED] Drive

Vallejo, CA (644- [REDACTED])

MR [REDACTED] states as he went by the scene where the crime had occurred Friday night 12/20/68. He definitely saw two cars, a station wagon and another vehicle, parked approximately three or four feet to the right of the station wagon. He did not see anyone in the cars or around them. He stated as he traveled approximately one quarter of a mile beyond, he thought he heard a shot. He had his car radio on low.

MR [REDACTED] further stated that just before he approached the scene, a vehicle passed him going the opposite direction toward Vallejo. He could give no description of the vehicle. This occurred near the Borges Ranch. RO's asked MR [REDACTED] what time he left the house Friday 12/20/68. He stated it was 11:00PM. He checked the time on the cuckoo clock in the dining room. RO's had MR [REDACTED] phone for the time to test the accuracy of the clock.

APB	Date	Inv. Officer	Date

SOLANO COUNTY SHERIFF'S OFFICE

FAIRFIELD, CALIFORNIA

SUPPLEMENTAL INVESTIGATION REPORT

TYPE OF ORIGINAL REPORT	DATE ORIGINAL REPORT	CASE NUMBER
HOMICIDE	12/20/68	V-25564
VICTIM OR COMPLAINTANT	LOCATION ORIGINAL OCCURRENCE	DATE – TIME OR SUPPL.
CAPT. PITTA	Lake Herman Road	3/22/69 7:15PM

ADDITIONAL DETAILS OF OFFENSE

RO: BUTTERBACH

STATEMENT: PEGGY [REDACTED]

30 West [REDACTED] Street

Benicia, CA. 745- [REDACTED]

MRS [REDACTED] relates the following, re: case # V-25564 on 12/20/68. Sometime between 11:00PM and 11:20PM she and her husband HOMER and their children were returning from Sacramento, she states her husband is working for a construction company doing a job in the Lake Herman Area. HOMER wanted to check some pipe lines on Lake Herman Road she states as they were driving West on Lake Herman Road at the turn off to the Benicia Water Pumping Station, she observed a Rambler s/w parked with front and heading East, there were two Caucasian in the front seat male and female, when the lights from the [REDACTED] car came upon the station wagon, the male sat up in the seat. MRS [REDACTED] said it was a cold light and she noticed there was not any frost on the station wagon. She states her husband drove on to the bottom of the hill and turned into the road way on the right side, going into the Marshall Ranch. She states as the car got to the gate, she saw a tall WMA approximately 28 years dressed in dark clothing, standing by the gate on her husbands side of the car (the left side) approximately six feet from the car. He had a gun in his hand, it had a long barrel. A red pick up with white wooden sides was parked about 40 feet ahead of their car. She stated a WMA who appeared to be an old man got out of the truck and shined a flash light into their car. She states she told her husband there was a man

Cleared by Arrest ☐

Cleared Other ☐

Not Cleared ☐

INVESTIGATING OFFICER DATE

SOLANO COUNTY SHERIFF'S OFFICE

FAIRFIELD, CALIFORNIA

SUPPLEMENTAL INVESTIGATION REPORT

TYPE OF ORIGINAL REPORT	DATE ORIGINAL REPORT	CASE NUMBER
HOMICIDE	12/20/68	V-25564
VICTIM OR COMPLAINTANT	LOCATION ORIGINAL OCCURRENCE	DATE – TIME OR SUPPL.
CAPT. PITTA	Lake Herman Road	3/22/69 7:15PM

ADDITIONAL DETAILS OF OFFENSE

RO: BUTTERBACH

PEGGY [REDACTED]: PAGE 2

with a gun standing by the car, to get the hell out of there. She stated the man did not say anything or point the gun at the car, he just kept staring at her. They turned around and heading East on Lake Herman Road. She states the station wagon was still parked in the same spot. She states this was some time between 11:15PM and 11:18PM.

They drove slowly over the Old Lake Herman Road. She states she kept looking back and she did not see the lights from the pick up truck or any other lights on the road in back of them.

She states as they drove by the entrance to Humble Oil Company, she saw a long dark colored car. The guard was leaning over talking to the man who was driving the car. She states the car had a long speedometer indicator light that gave off a greenish glow.

RO asked MRS [REDACTED] if they had a gun in their car and if she pointed it at the man standing near the gate and if she said to him my gun is bigger than yours. MRS [REDACTED] stated they did have a gun with them that night, it was a .38 special with a small barrel and it was lying in the rear seat of the car. It was unloaded and MR [REDACTED] had the shells in his pocket. She states she did not point the gun at the man standing at the gate near their car, nor did she say anything to him.

Cleared by Arrest ☐

Cleared Other ☐

Not Cleared ☐

Butterbach

INVESTIGATING OFFICER

DATE

SOLANO COUNTY SHERIFF'S OFFICE

FAIRFIELD, CALIFORNIA

SUPPLEMENTAL INVESTIGATION REPORT

TYPE OF ORIGINAL REPORT	DATE ORIGINAL REPORT	CASE NUMBER
HOMICIDE	12/20/68	V-25564
VICTIM OR COMPLAINTANT	**LOCATION ORIGINAL OCCURRENCE**	**DATE – TIME OR SUPPL.**
CAPT. PITTA	Lake Herman Road	3/22/69 5:20PM

ADDITIONAL DETAILS OF OFFENSE

RO: BUTTERBACH

STATEMENT: HOMER [REDACTED], WMA

30 West Street

Benicia, CA. 745-

MR [REDACTED] states the following: RE 2/20/68 11:00PM – 11:20 PM

HE was going West on Lake Herman Road, he turned into the road going to the Marshall Ranch to turn around. He saw approximately 30 feet inside the road from the gate, a red pick up truck that had white wooden sides. A man was by the truck, he shined his flashlight into the [REDACTED] car. MR [REDACTED] wife, PEGGY who was sitting in the front seat on the passenger side, said there is a man with a gun lets get out of here. MR [REDACTED] states his wife did not say anything to the man with the gun. MR [REDACTED] states he had a .38 special on the rear seat of the car, it was unloaded. MR [REDACTED] had the shells in his pocket.

MR [REDACTED] showed RO the guns he had.

#1 .38 special 2" Smith & Wesson serial # 55246

#2 12 gauge automatic shot gun (Remington) serial # 248011

Cleared by Arrest ☐

Cleared Other ☐

Not Cleared ☐

Deputy Butterbach

INVESTIGATING OFFICER

DATE

OFFENSE REPORT

OFFICE OF SHERIFF

County of Solano, California

OFFENSE 187 P.C. Murder CASE NO V25564

LOCATION Lake Herman Road, Entrance to Benicia Water Pumping Station

REPORTED BY CAPTAIN PITTA ADDRESS Benicia P.D. PHONE

RECEIVED BY Sgt. Cunningham DATE 12/20/68 TIME 11:52PM

( ) LETTER ( ) DESK ( ) PHONE ( ) TELETYPE ( ) RADIO

DESCRIPTION OF PROPERTY	
	Suspect No. 1
(1)	Sex Descent
(2)	Height Weight Age
(3)	Hair color Eye color
(4)	Marks/scars
(5)	
	Occupation
	Disguise or dress
	Arrested: Identification No.
TOTAL VALUE	(Yes or No)

RO: DET/SGT LUNDBLAD 12/24/68 11:25AM

STATEMENT: STELLA MEDEIROS, WFA age 32

P.O. Box 477

Vallejo, CA (644-[REDACTED])

MRS MEDEIROS is the former STELLA BORGES. She lives on Lake Herman Road across from her parents home, two and seven-tenth's miles from the scene of the crime

MRS MEDEIROS relates that she came in from Oakland at approximately 10:50PM. Her mother called on the telephone and requested that she pick up her son, age 13, at the show. She states that she did not take her coat off, and glanced at the clock in the kitchen and she believes it was 11:10PM. She rode with her mother-in-law and her daughter and drove casually over the 2-7/10th miles, this time the distance being established by the officers, and she arrived at the area four or five minutes later. She estimates between 11:14 and 11:15 PM. Her clock is one minute fast as we had found during this interview. She states that no cars were going in either direction while she

APB	Date	Inv. Officer	Date

was on the road. When she arrived at the scene, headlights picked up the car and she observed a boy and he looked like he had fallen out of the open door. The girl was lying on her side facing the road. She had a purple dress on and looked well dressed. She saw only one car at the scene. It looked like a Rambler, grayish in color, it had a chrome rack on the top. This fits the description of the FARADAY Rambler. She states that she drove sixty-or seventy miles an hour enroute to Benicia to report the incident. When she saw the police car she honked her horn and blinked her lights to attract the attention of the police officers.

(Det/Sgt. Lundblad) ab

OFFENSE REPORT

OFFICE OF SHERIFF

County of Solano, California

OFFENSE	187 P.C. Murder			CASE NO	V25564
LOCATION	Lake Herman Road, Entrance to Benicia Water Pumping Station				
REPORTED BY	CAPTAIN PITTA	ADDRESS	Benicia P.D.	PHONE	
RECEIVED BY	Sgt. Cunningham	DATE	12/20/68	TIME	11:52PM

( ) LETTER ( ) DESK ( ) PHONE ( ) TELETYPE ( ) RADIO

DESCRIPTION OF PROPERTY	Suspect No. 1
(1)	Sex Descent
(2)	Height Weight Age
(3)	Hair color Eye color
(4)	Marks/scars
(5)	
	Occupation
	Disguise or dress
	Arrested: Identification No.
TOTAL VALUE	(Yes or No)

RO: LUNDBLAD & BUTTERBACH 12/21/68 9:22PM

STATEMENT: ROBERT [REDACTED], WMA age 27

1008 Avenue

Napa, CA

(Employee of PG&E, Vallejo 224-)

FRANK GASSER, WMA age 69

Gasser Ranch, Highway 21

North of Goodyear Station

[REDACTED] and GASSER have been identified by Deputy Villarreal as racoon hunters who were in the area of the Benicia Pumping Station and who have been identifying by MRS [REDACTED]. They had their 1959 pick-up truck, Red in color, with wood side-boards, parked inside the field of the Marshall Ranch.

In this interview it was learned that they were hunting in the area from 9:00PM to 11:00PM. 11:00PM was approximate, because [REDACTED] looked at his watch and he knew it was in the area of 11:00PM. It could have been five minutes to the hour or ten minutes to. It took them three or four minutes possibly five minutes to get back to their truck, walking up the road on the

APB	Date	Inv. Officer	Date

SOLANO COUNTY SHERIFF'S OFFICE

FAIRFIELD, CALIFORNIA

SUPPLEMENTAL INVESTIGATION REPORT

TYPE OF ORIGINAL REPORT	DATE ORIGINAL REPORT	CASE NUMBER
187 P.C. Murder	12/20/68	V-25564
VICTIM OR COMPLAINTANT	LOCATION ORIGINAL OCCURRENCE	DATE – TIME OR SUPPL.
CAPTAIN PITTA	Lake Herman Road	12/21/69 9:22PM

ADDITIONAL DETAILS OF OFFENSE

[UNREADABLE]

side of the creek. They are about to depart in their truck when a car pulled into the driveway, which was later identify as the car belonging to [REDACTED]. They claimed that they left the area a few minutes after MRS. [REDACTED] established the time 11:05 PM. So, that would put them at 11:05 PM when they left the scene.

They described the light colored 1960 Rambler S/W that was parked at the gate. It was parked Southwest of where we finally found the car. This discrepancy wasn't noted at first. This was a statement as to their activity during that night. They said that when they arrived there at 9:00PM a white 4-door hardtop, a '59 or '60 Impala, was parked there, and also, a truck coming out of the gate. This coincides with INFORMATION from BINGO [REDACTED] that when he came out of the gate he saw the same Impala and also saw the red pick-up truck go by.

SEE OTHER REPORT OF ROBERT [REDACTED]

(Det/Sgt Lundblad & Butterbach) ab

Cleared by Arrest ☐

Cleared Other ☐

Not Cleared ☐ INVESTIGATING OFFICER DATE

[UNREADABLE] ☐

OFFENSE REPORT

OFFICE OF SHERIFF

County of Solano, California

OFFENSE 187 P.C. Murder CASE NO V-25564

LOCATION Lake Herman Road, Entrance to Benicia Water Pumping Station

REPORTED BY CAPTAIN PITTA ADDRESS Benicia P.D. PHONE

RECEIVED BY Sgt. Cunningham DATE 12/20/68 TIME 11:52PM

( ) LETTER ( ) DESK ( ) PHONE ( ) TELETYPE ( ) RADIO

DESCRIPTION OF PROPERTY	Suspect No. 1
(1)	Sex Descent
(2)	Height Weight Age
(3)	Hair color Eye color
(4)	Marks/scars
(5)	
	Occupation
	Disguise or dress
	Arrested: Identification No.
TOTAL VALUE	(Yes or No)

RO: LUNDBLAD & BUTTERBACH 12/26/68 2:35PM

STATEMENT: ROBERT M. [REDACTED]

1008 Avenue

Napa, CA (DOB 5/14/[REDACTED])

SECOND INTERVIEW: Due to some discrepancies or misunderstandings in the first interview on 12/21/68.

MR [REDACTED] was asked to pin-point his activities closer on that day. He states that he went to the Gasser Ranch at approximately 6:00PM. Today sat around awhile and didn't leave until several hours later. They arrived in the area of the pump station around 9:00PM. They parked the car about 25 feet inside of the Marshall Ranch property off of the road. They walked the creek towards the pump station. They had the dogs loose and they treed either a cat or a racoon in the area of the Dotta Ranch. While they were there they saw some sort of activity up there, all the lights were on, but they were a little distance away and couldn't tell what the activity was. The dogs treed a racoon in an oak tree near the Pump Station. The racoon was shot with a

APB	Date	Inv. Officer	Date

SOLANO COUNTY SHERIFF'S OFFICE

FAIRFIELD, CALIFORNIA

SUPPLEMENTAL INVESTIGATION REPORT

TYPE OF ORIGINAL REPORT	DATE ORIGINAL REPORT	CASE NUMBER
187 P.C. Murder	12/20/68 11:52PM	V-25564
VICTIM OR COMPLAINTANT	LOCATION ORIGINAL OCCURRENCE	DATE – TIME OR SUPPL.
CAPTAIN PITTA	Lake Herman	12/26/68 2:35 PM

ADDITIONAL DETAILS OF OFFENSE

RE: [REDACTED] [REDACTED] Page 2 SECOND INTERVIEW

long barrel. .22 revolver. This revolver was obtained and has been eliminated by shell casings of the suspected weapon.

[REDACTED] remembers looking at his watch and be remember that it was in the area of 12:00PM, possibly five or ten minutes before and they headed back towards the car. He said it took then about 10 minutes to wall back to the truck. He was at the truck about a total of 5 minutes and a car came in, that has been identified as MRS [REDACTED]'S, it drove in, turned around and drove back in the opposite direction towards Benicia, again.

He states that approximately 5 minutes later they drove in his truck a '59 Chevrolet, red in color, with white wood sideboards, cattle guards, on the sides. They drove this truck back to the Gasser Ranch heading towards Benicia and they passed the car.

[REDACTED] insists that the Rambler was parked on the bank. That would be on the South side. He did not see any person in the car. He estimate he left the area between 11:00PM and 11:15PM. He remained at the Gasser's house about an hour and then left out through Highway #21, through the Jamison Canyon and headed home, arriving about 12:30AM.

He was asked if he had an rifle. He stated that he had a automatic rifle. The RO advised him of his constitutional rights at this time. Due to the fact that he was in the area and he did have a rifle which he claimed he

(Det/Sgt Lundblad & Butterbach) ab

Cleared by Arrest ☐

Cleared Other ☐

Not Cleared ☐

[UNREADABLE] ☐

INVESTIGATING OFFICER DATE

SOLANO COUNTY SHERIFF'S OFFICE

FAIRFIELD, CALIFORNIA

SUPPLEMENTAL INVESTIGATION REPORT

TYPE OF ORIGINAL REPORT	DATE ORIGINAL REPORT	CASE NUMBER
187 P.C. Murder	12/20/68 11:52PM	V-25564
VICTIM OR COMPLAINTANT	LOCATION ORIGINAL OCCURRENCE	DATE – TIME OR SUPPL.
CAPTAIN PITTA	Lake Herman	12/26/68 2:35PM

ADDITIONAL DETAILS OF OFFENSE

RO: LUNDBLAD

RE: [UNREADABLE] [REDACTED] page 3 Second Interview

didn't have with him that night. He was given a receipt for the rifle. The rifle was tested in the S/O by Rangemaster George [REDACTED]. On the basis of the findings of George Parks this rifle has been eliminated as a suspected weapon.

[REDACTED] states that MR GASSER does have an automatic rifle but that he doesn't have it at the house. He suggested that we call or see a gentleman by the name of HARLAN [REDACTED], who lives at 06 Hargus Avenue. It is possible that the gun is there, because GASSER does not leave his guns at the ranch because of recent thefts.

[REDACTED] car has California license # D-26024.

(Det/Sgt Lundblad & Butterbach) ab

Cleared by Arrest ☐

Cleared Other ☐

Not Cleared ☐ INVESTIGATING OFFICER DATE

[UNREADABLE] ☐

SHERIFF'S OFFICE -	SOLANO COUNTY	Time	11:52PM	Date	12/20/68 V25564
Nature of Complaint:	Murder			Location	Lake Herman Road
Complainant:	CAPTAIN PITTA			Address	Benicia P.D

Received by: Sgt. Cunningham ( ) Letter ( ) Desk ( ) Phone ( ) Teletype ( ) Radio

RO: DET/SGT LUNDBLAD & DEPUTY BUTTERBACH 12/21/68 8:00AM

RE: BINGO WESHER, WMA, Rancher, Old Borges Ranch by Humbel Oil Company, phone # 745-

MR WESHER arrived at the crime scene while the RO's were re-checking the area. He was questioned and relates that he tends sheep in the area East of the Benicia Pumping Station. Last night he was checking his sheep at approximately 10:00PM and he observed a White Chevrolet, Impala Sedan, parked by the South fence of the entrance to the pumping station. He also observed a Red Ford P/U with wood side boards in the area. (the pick-up was later identified as the one [REDACTED] and BOB [REDACTED] were riding in, (See MRS [REDACTED]'S report)

MR WESHER did not see the Nash Rambler.

(Det/Sgt Lundblad & Butterbach) ab

OFFENSE REPORT

OFFICE OF SHERIFF

County of Solano, California

OFFENSE 187 P.C. Murder CASE NO V-25564

LOCATION Lake Herman Road, Entrance to Benicia Water Pumping Station

REPORTED BY CAPTAIN PITTA ADDRESS Benicia P.D. PHONE

RECEIVED BY Sgt. Cunningham DATE 12/20/68 TIME 11:52PM

( ) LETTER ( ) DESK ( ) PHONE ( ) TELETYPE ( ) RADIO

DESCRIPTION OF PROPERTY	Suspect No. 1
(1)	Sex Descent
(2)	Height Weight Age
(3)	Hair color Eye color
(4)	Marks/scars
(5)	
	Occupation
	Disguise or dress
	Arrested: Identification No.
TOTAL VALUE	(Yes or No)

RO: DET/SGT LUNDBLAD 12/27/68 4:10PM

STATEMENT: MRS PEGGIE [REDACTED]

30 West [REDACTED] Street

Benicia, CA (745 - [REDACTED])

MR [REDACTED] was contacted on the telephone to establish a timing of her departure from Sacramento and her arrival in Vallejo. She states that she left Sacramento between 10:00PM and 10:15PM. Her husband was driving. He travels the speed limit or less. She estimates that she arrived in the Benicia area, off of Highway #21, at approximately 11:00PM. They drove the 3 or 4 miles at a slow rate of speed, while he checked the pipes and equipment along the side of the road. She described the location of the car as the front facing the fence, the rear section of the station wagon facing directly Went towards Vallejo.

MRS [REDACTED] was asked to check the clock in her car. It was found at this time to be 7 minutes fast. This would help to establish her arrival time closer to 11:00 o'clock than 11:15PM.

APB	Date	Inv. Officer	Date

OFFENSE REPORT

OFFICE OF SHERIFF

County of Solano, California

OFFENSE 187 P.C. Murder CASE NO V-25564

LOCATION Lake Herman Road, Entrance to Benicia Water Pumping Station

REPORTED BY CAPTAIN PITTA ADDRESS Benicia P.D. PHONE

RECEIVED BY Sgt. Cunningham DATE 12/20/68 TIME 11:52PM

( ) LETTER ( ) DESK ( ) PHONE ( ) TELETYPE ( ) RADIO

DESCRIPTION OF PROPERTY	
	Suspect No. 1
(1)	Sex Descent
(2)	Height Weight Age
(3)	Hair color Eye color
(4)	Marks/scars
(5)	
	Occupation
	Disguise or dress
	Arrested: Identification No.
TOTAL VALUE	(Yes or No)

RO: DET/SGT LUNDBLAD 12/23/68 11:55AM

STATEMENT: HELEN [REDACTED], age 18, WFJ
60 [REDACTED] Avenue
Vallejo, CA (642 - [REDACTED])

MISS [REDACTED] reports that she and her boy-friend, a sailor, were driving on Lake Herman Road. They passed the area of the Pumping Station, she recognized the Rambler and the victims, BETTY LOU JENSEN and DAVID FARADAY. Stated that when she went by about 10:15PM the car was facing in towards the gate and when she returned about 15 minutes later after having gone to the end of the road and then came back, the car was turned around and the front was facing the field, a little to the side.

There is some conflict in this statement and MISS [REDACTED] has consented to bring her boy-friend to the office to clarify the actual position of the car. The first time she stated when she called, that the car was backed in. Nothing this discrepancy, the RO contacted her by telephone on this date 12/25/68 at 12:00 noon.

APB	Date	Inv. Officer	Date

OFFENSE REPORT

OFFICE OF SHERIFF

County of Solano, California

OFFENSE	187 P.C. Murder			CASE NO	V-25564
LOCATION	Lake Herman Road, Entrance to Benicia Water Pumping Station				
REPORTED BY	CAPTAIN PITTA	ADDRESS	Benicia P.D.	PHONE	
RECEIVED BY	Sgt. Cunningham	DATE	12/20/68	TIME	11:52PM

( ) LETTER ( ) DESK ( ) PHONE ( ) TELETYPE ( ) RADIO

DESCRIPTION OF PROPERTY	Suspect No. 1
(1)	Sex Descent
(2)	Height Weight Age
(3)	Hair color Eye color
(4)	Marks/scars
(5)	
	Occupation
	Disguise or dress
	Arrested: Identification No.
TOTAL VALUE	(Yes or No)

RO: LUNDBLAD & BUTTERBACH 12/28/68 15:15AM

STATEMENT: RANGEMASTER GEORGE PARKS

At the above time and date Deputy Parks test fired three rifles and made comparisons of shell casings with the casings in evidence. On the basis of his findings the following guns are eliminated as suspected weapons.

#1 MARLIN automatic rifle

Property of ROBERT [REDACTED]

#2 REMINGTON automatic rifle, Model 550-1

Property of JAMEs [REDACTED]

#3 RUGER automatic rifle, SN 138577

Property of JAMES A. [REDACTED]

(Lundblad & Butterbach) ab

APB	Date	Inv. Officer	Date

SHERIFF'S OFFICE - SOLANO COUNTY Time 11:52PM Date 12/20/68 V25564

Nature of Complaint: Murder Location Lake Herman Road

Complainant: CAPTAIN PITTA Address Benicia P.D

Received by: Sgt. Cunningham ( ) Letter ( ) Desk ( ) Phone ( ) Teletype ( ) Radio

RO: DET/SGT LUNDBLAD & DEPUTY BUTTERBACH 12/21/68 9:05AM

RE: SHARON [REDACTED], WFJ, age 16 years, 926 Avenue, phone 642-

SHARON is a student at Hogan High School and was reported by MRS JENSEN to be one of her daughter's best friends.

She was contacted by the RO's and relates that BETTY LOU and DAVID come to her house at approximately 8:20PM on Friday. They remained there until 9:00PM. She stated she walked to the car with them. They did not state to her where they were going. SHARON attended a party at 254 Frisby Street from 10:30PM until 1:10AM. MRS [REDACTED] supplied the return home time. SHARON relates that BETTY LOU went with RICKY [REDACTED] from December 1st until December 14th, when she met DAVID at the Pythian Castle. RICKY and BETTY never went out but they talked together around the school grounds. To her knowledge he never drove a car or possessed a gun.

(Det/Sgt Lundblad & Butterbach) ab

OFFENSE REPORT

OFFICE OF SHERIFF

County of Solano, California

OFFENSE	187 P.C. Murder			CASE NO	V-25564
LOCATION	Lake Herman Road, Entrance to Benicia Water Pumping Station				
REPORTED BY	CAPTAIN PITTA	ADDRESS	Benicia P.D.	PHONE	
RECEIVED BY	Sgt. Cunningham	DATE	12/20/68	TIME	11:52PM

( ) LETTER ( ) DESK ( ) PHONE ( ) TELETYPE ( ) RADIO

DESCRIPTION OF PROPERTY	Suspect No. 1
(1)	Sex Descent
(2)	Height Weight Age
(3)	Hair color Eye color
(4)	Marks/scars
(5)	
	Occupation
	Disguise or dress
	Arrested: Identification No.
TOTAL VALUE	(Yes or No)

RO: LUNDBLAD & BUTTERBACH 12/22/68 5:20PM

[UNREADABLE] JOE [REDACTED], WMJ age 17 yrs, 112 Court, phone #643-

JOE [REDACTED] was interviewed at the FARADAY residence, 1930 Sereno Drive. He was a personal friend of DAVID. He states DAVID had no enemies to his knowledge. DAVID met BETTY LOU approximately a week ago at the Pythian Castel when they were decorating the hall for a social event.

On the fatal day Friday between 5:00PM and 6:00PM, DAVID and BETTY LOU and JOE were at DAVID [REDACTED] home at 450 Street. They did not say where they were going that evening.

When questioned about RICKY [REDACTED], JOE relates RICKY is a big talker, has no close friends, he is a bragger. He is alleged to have told a DANIEL [REDACTED] that he had his mothers car and was going out Friday night. [REDACTED] lives at 1044 Avenue)

(Lundblad & Butterbach) ab

APB	Date	Inv. Officer	Date

OFFENSE REPORT

OFFICE OF SHERIFF

County of Solano, California

OFFENSE 187 P.C. Murder CASE NO V-25564

LOCATION Lake Herman Road, Entrance to Benicia Water Pumping Station

REPORTED BY CAPTAIN PITTA ADDRESS Benicia P.D. PHONE

RECEIVED BY Sgt. Cunningham DATE 12/20/68 TIME 11:52PM

( ) LETTER ( ) DESK ( ) PHONE ( ) TELETYPE ( ) RADIO

DESCRIPTION OF PROPERTY	
	Suspect No. 1
(1)	Sex Descent
(2)	Height Weight Age
(3)	Hair color Eye color
(4)	Marks/scars
(5)	
	Occupation
	Disguise or dress
	Arrested: Identification No.
TOTAL VALUE	(Yes or No)

RO: DET/SGT LUNDBLAD & BUTTERBACH 12/22/68 9:30PM

RE: DANIEL [REDACTED], WMJ age 16 yrs, 1044 Avenue, phone 642-

[REDACTED] attends Hogan High School. He is acquainted with DAVID and BETTY and was at [REDACTED] house Friday between 5:00PM and 6:00PM, while they were there. He has observed DAVID pick up BETTY in the station wagon after school four or five times in the last two weeks.

[REDACTED] alleges that on Friday afternoon 12/20/68, he walked by RICKY [REDACTED]'S home and RICKY was washing his mother's maroon Grand Prix automobile at the curb. RICKY had the keys and the radio was playing. [REDACTED] alleges that RICKY said his mother was going out tonight and he had the car.

[REDACTED] has no knowledge of any fire are ever in the possession of [REDACTED]. He has never seen him driving an automobile. However, last summer he observed RICKY riding with SCOTT [REDACTED] in a '51 – '54 Green Ford pick-up.

(Det/Sgt. Lundblad & Butterbach) ab

APB	Date	Inv. Officer	Date

OFFENSE REPORT

OFFICE OF SHERIFF

County of Solano, California

OFFENSE 187 P.C. Murder CASE NO V-25564

LOCATION Lake Herman Road, Entrance to Benicia Water Pumping Station

REPORTED BY CAPTAIN PITTA ADDRESS Benicia P.D. PHONE

RECEIVED BY Sgt. Cunningham DATE 12/20/68 TIME 11:52PM

( ) LETTER ( ) DESK ( ) PHONE ( ) TELETYPE ( ) RADIO

DESCRIPTION OF PROPERTY	Suspect No. 1
(1)	Sex Descent
(2)	Height Weight Age
(3)	Hair color Eye color
(4)	Marks/scars
(5)	
	Occupation
	Disguise or dress
	Arrested: Identification No.
TOTAL VALUE	(Yes or No)

RO: DLUNDBLAD & BUTTERBACH 12/22/68 9:55PM

RE: DAN [REDACTED], WMJ

450 [REDACTED] Street

Vallejo, CA (642- [REDACTED])

[REDACTED] attends Hogan High School. He is acquainted with BETTY and DAVID and they were at his home playing records until 6:00PM, Friday night. They did not reveal their plans for the evening.

When questioned about RICKY [REDACTED], [REDACTED] stated he is a big mouth, one of those kind of guys. He, [REDACTED], does not like his and avoids him if possible. To his knowledge RICKY does not have a firearm.

[REDACTED] referred the RO's to a SCOTT [REDACTED], who previously lived at the [REDACTED] residence. [REDACTED] now lives in a big brown house at the end of Falcon Drive.

(Det/Sgt. Lundblad & Butterbach) ab

APB	Date	Inv. Officer	Date

OFFENSE REPORT

OFFICE OF SHERIFF

County of Solano, California

OFFENSE 187 P.C. Murder CASE NO V-25564

LOCATION Lake Herman Road, Entrance to Benicia Water Pumping Station

REPORTED BY CAPTAIN PITTA ADDRESS Benicia P.D. PHONE

RECEIVED BY Sgt. Cunningham DATE 12/20/68 TIME 11:52PM

( ) LETTER ( ) DESK ( ) PHONE ( ) TELETYPE ( ) RADIO

DESCRIPTION OF PROPERTY	Suspect No. 1
(1)	Sex Descent
(2)	Height Weight Age
(3)	Hair color Eye color
(4)	Marks/scars
(5)	
	Occupation
	Disguise or dress
	Arrested: Identification No.
TOTAL VALUE	(Yes or No)

RO: DLUNDBLAD & BUTTERBACH 12/24/68 1:15PM

STATEMENT: MRS [REDACTED]

926 [REDACTED] Avenue

Vallejo, CA (642- [REDACTED])

MRS [REDACTED] is the mother of SHARON [REDACTED], BETTY LOU'S friend. She relates that, in a conversation with her daughter, a subject identified as MARK [REDACTED] of 137 Way, had spoken of an incident that had happened at the Pancake House on Tennessee Street. The story went on to say that DAVID was going to turn in a subject for pushing grass (or Marijuana), and the man had threatened him. She also stated that BETTY LOU had mentioned to her daughter that she was going to San Francisco. This probably is not their intention because the time element involved will not allow them to get that far in back.

The above information will be checked out.

(Det/Sgt. Lundblad & Butterbach) ab

APB	Date	Inv. Officer	Date

OFFENSE REPORT

OFFICE OF SHERIFF

County of Solano, California

OFFENSE 187 P.C. Murder CASE NO V-25564

LOCATION Lake Herman Road, Entrance to Benicia Water Pumping Station

REPORTED BY CAPTAIN PITTA ADDRESS Benicia P.D. PHONE

RECEIVED BY Sgt. Cunningham DATE 12/20/68 TIME 11:52PM

( ) LETTER ( ) DESK ( ) PHONE ( ) TELETYPE ( ) RADIO

DESCRIPTION OF PROPERTY	
	Suspect No. 1
(1)	Sex Descent
(2)	Height Weight Age
(3)	Hair color Eye color
(4)	Marks/scars
(5)	
	Occupation
	Disguise or dress
	Arrested: Identification No.
TOTAL VALUE	(Yes or No)

RO: LUNDBLAD & BUTTERBACH 12/21/68 11:15AM

STATEMENT: RICKY ALLEN [REDACTED], WMJ 13 yrs, DOB 1/ /53

202 [REDACTED] Street,

Vallejo, CA (648- [REDACTED])

RICKY [REDACTED] was identified by BETTY LOU JENSEN'S parents as being a person who bugged BETTY LOU while she was attending school. In view of this fact he was advised of his constitutional rights. He stated that he understood his rights and wanted to help us. He stated that he went with BETTY LOU for two weeks and talked to her on the phone many times. The last time that he talked to her was on Thursday, about 4:30PM. He did not attend school that day and he had inquired of what was going on in school and he wanted to know what she was doing on the weekend. On Friday, December 20th, he left school and went over to DEBBY [REDACTED], 747 Avenue, Vallejo. He remained there from about 4:15 to about 5:00PM. His mother came by, picked him up in the car and brought him home. He had a TV dinner for supper and then he went to GallenKamp's store between 7:00 and 7:15 PM and returned

APB	Date	Inv. Officer	Date

STATEMENT: RICKY ALLEN [REDACTED], 12/21/68 11:15PM PAGE 2

back home.

His mother, his dad, his sister his brother-in-law and Mr. [REDACTED] and his son, were at the house. Mr. [REDACTED]. They watched Bob Hope in a TV show called "Global Affairs". This program lasted on the TV from about 9:00PM until 10:45PM. [REDACTED] left about 11:00PM.

His brother- LARRY [REDACTED] and his wife JANETTE talked until about 11:30PM and then they left. He further states that his father left about 10:55PM and there were only his sister, DIAN [REDACTED], his mother and himself in the house. He stated that he went to bed at 11:30PM and left the radio on. Stated he got up at 8:30AM this morning and was not aware of the shooting until his mother called the auto wreckers after being spoken to by the RO earlier this day.

RICKY further states that he received an allowance of $2 a week if he works in the yard and cleans up the laundry room. He is not allowed out at night after 9:00PM, especially on week nights. He does not go out on week-ends. His mother has a Maroon colored Grand Prix. He does not drive it.

States he was in trouble last summer for burglary, MR PATRICK [REDACTED] is his Probation Officer. RICKY further expressed a desire to help us in any way possible. He named a DARRYL [REDACTED] as a friend of his who lives on Cherrywood, address unknown.

(Lundblad & Butterbach) ab

SHERIFF'S OFFICE -	SOLANO COUNTY	Time	11:52PM	Date	12/20/68 V25564
Nature of Complaint:	Murder			Location	Lake Herman Rd.
Complainant:	CAPTAIN PITTA			Address	Benicia P.D

Received by: Sgt. Cunningham ( ) Letter ( ) Desk ( ) Phone ( ) Teletype ( ) Radio

RO: DET/SGT LUNDBLAD & DEPUTY BUTTERBACH 12/21/68 9:30AM

RE: MRS [REDACTED], 202 [REDACTED] Avenue, phone 648-[REDACTED]

MRS [REDACTED] is RICKY'S mother. The RO's contacted her at the above address. She states that RICKY is with his father at Sylvas Auto Wreckers on Napa Road. She stated that RICKY got out of school at 3:00PM, went to his sisters home until 4:00PM, returned home at 5:00PM, went to Gallenkamps to be fitted for a new pair of shoes that was to be a present from his brother-in-law. He returned home and remained home all evening.

They had guests, RICKY'S father, from whom she is separated, and his dads friend Mr. Othis [REDACTED] of 1121, who is a policeman at Mare Island, and RICKY'S sister and brother-in-law. It was his sisters birthday and they had coffee and cake. During the evening they watched TV. The program was GLOBAL AFFAIRS, it ran from 9:00PM until 11:00PM.

MR [REDACTED] left at approximately 10:55PM and Mr [REDACTED] left at the conclusion of the program at 11:00PM. MRS [REDACTED] stated Red Skelton was in the program (it was later learned that Bob Hope was the star) RICKY went to bed at 11:30PM

(Det/Sgt Lundblad & Butterbach) ab

OFFENSE REPORT

OFFICE OF SHERIFF

County of Solano, California

OFFENSE 187 P.C. Murder CASE NO V-25564

LOCATION Lake Herman Road, Entrance to Benicia Water Pumping Station

REPORTED BY CAPTAIN PITTA ADDRESS Benicia P.D. PHONE

RECEIVED BY Sgt. Cunningham DATE 12/20/68 TIME 11:52PM

( ) LETTER ( ) DESK ( ) PHONE ( ) TELETYPE ( ) RADIO

DESCRIPTION OF PROPERTY	Suspect No. 1
(1)	Sex Descent
(2)	Height Weight Age
(3)	Hair color Eye color
(4)	Marks/scars
(5)	
	Occupation
	Disguise or dress
	Arrested: Identification No.
TOTAL VALUE	(Yes or No)

RO: DET/SGT LUNDBLAD 12/26/68 11:33AM

RE: NOTES OR OTHER EVIDENCE IN LOCKER # 1003 HOGAN HIGH SCHOOL.

At the above time and date the RO contacted MRS [REDACTED] and her daughter SHARON [REDACTED]. SHARON had shared a locker at the above location with BETTY LOU JENSEN. The principal Mr Lee Y. Dean was present and all school property, after they were examined for possible evidence, were turned over to him. Notes and all personal papers that were not school property were retained for examination by the RO. SHARON further advised that BETTY LOU had a private locker in the gym class and any personal items might be there.

Mr Dean advised that he would make an examination of his locker possibly on Monday as he did not have a pass key for that area.

(Det/Sgt. Lundblad) ab

APB	Date	Inv. Officer	Date

SOLANO COUNTY SHERIFF'S OFFICE

FAIRFIELD, CALIFORNIA

SUPPLEMENTAL INVESTIGATION REPORT

TYPE OF ORIGINAL REPORT	DATE ORIGINAL REPORT	CASE NUMBER
187 P.C. Murder	12/20/68	V-25564
VICTIM OR COMPLAINTANT	LOCATION ORIGINAL OCCURRENCE	DATE – TIME OR SUPPL.
CAPTAIN PITTA	Lake Herman Road	12/26/68 [UNREADABLE]

ADDITIONAL DETAILS OF OFFENSE

RO: LUNDBLAD-BUTTERBACH

RE: [UNREADABLE]

Upon examining the papers and material obtained in the above locker. This RO's found an unsigned note that appears to be in the same hand writing as others articles that were signed by BETTY LOU JENSEN. The note read as follows:

QUOTE: DO YOU KNOW A KID NAMED RICHARD BURTON?
I WAS GOING WITH HIM, UNTIL TWO DAYS BEFORE
THE INSTALATION. HE STILL PHONES ME, AND IS
THREATENING ME TO KEEP AWAY FROM DAVE.
HE SAID IF HE'S EVER CLOSE ENOUGH TO DAVE, HE WOULD
PUNCH HIM ONE IN THE TEETH, I TOLD HIM TO LEAVE ME
ALONE, IF HE KNOWS WHAT GOOD HIM.

UNQUOTE: The note in the binder on the last page. It will be held for evidence.

1/3/69 3:08PM the principal, MR LEE DEAN, phoned to report the gym locker had been opened and it contained shoes, hair spray and a score card in Archery.

(DET/SGT LUNDBLAD & BUTTERBACH) ab

Cleared by Arrest ☐

Cleared Other ☐

Not Cleared ☐

[UNREADABLE] ☐

INVESTIGATING OFFICER DATE

SOLANO COUNTY SHERIFF'S OFFICE

FAIRFIELD, CALIFORNIA

SUPPLEMENTAL INVESTIGATION REPORT

TYPE OF ORIGINAL REPORT	DATE ORIGINAL REPORT	CASE NUMBER
187 P.C. Murder	12/20/68	V-25564
VICTIM OR COMPLAINTANT	LOCATION ORIGINAL OCCURRENCE	DATE – TIME OR SUPPL.
CAPTAIN PITTA	Lake Herman Road	12/26/68 [UNREADABLE]

ADDITIONAL DETAILS OF OFFENSE

RO: LUNDBLAD-BUTTERBACH

RE: [UNREADABLE]

1121 [REDACTED] Road

Vallejo, CA (643-[REDACTED])

The RO's contacted [REDACTED] at the above address. He [UNREADABLE]. RICKY'S father and is separated from MRS [REDACTED], but no divorce [UNREADABLE].

MR [REDACTED] relates that he went to his wifes house between 7: [UNREADABLE] and [UNREADABLE]:00PM on Friday 12/20/68 to celebrate jointly his birthday, which fells on 2/22/68 and his daughters on 12/20. When he arrived his two sons RICKY and HARRY and his daughter-in-law were already there. MR [REDACTED], and his son also named RICKY, arrived later.

He states that RICKY received a phone call around 8:30PM. There were no calls after that time and no one came to the house while he was there. During the evening they enjoyed cake and coffee and watched "A Global Affair" on television.

[REDACTED] states he did not like the program and he left before it was concluded, thinks the time was around 10:15 or 10:30PM. All of the above mentioned people were still at the house.

RICKY does not have a gun and to MR [REDACTED]'S knowledge there is none available to him. He is not allowed to drive a car, but he is capable of driving one. Upon the request of the RO MR [REDACTED] gave his consent to have RICKY take a Poly Graph examination. MR [REDACTED] was upset about a newspaper article, that appeared to refer to his son, even though no names were mentioned.

Cleared by Arrest ☐

Cleared Other ☐

Not Cleared ☐

[UNREADABLE] ☐

INVESTIGATING OFFICER DATE

SOLANO COUNTY SHERIFF'S OFFICE

FAIRFIELD, CALIFORNIA

SUPPLEMENTAL INVESTIGATION REPORT

TYPE OF ORIGINAL REPORT	DATE ORIGINAL REPORT	CASE NUMBER
187 P.C. Murder	12/20/68	V-25564
VICTIM OR COMPLAINTANT	LOCATION ORIGINAL OCCURRENCE	DATE – TIME OR SUPPL.
CAPTAIN PITTA	Lake Herman Road	12/29/68 4:30PM

ADDITIONAL DETAILS OF OFFENSE

RO: LUNDBLAD - BUTTERBACH

RE: [UNREADABLE] LEON [REDACTED]

1121 [REDACTED] Road

Phone #643-[REDACTED]

MR [REDACTED] is a police sergeant with the Mare Island Security force. He is separated from his wife and shares expenses for an apartment at the above address with DONALD [REDACTED]. He was identified as a guest at the [REDACTED]'S home on 12/20/68.

MR [REDACTED] states he had received a phone call from RICKY [REDACTED] and was invited to the home for coffee and cake. MR [REDACTED] had left a note in the kitchen also inviting him, but he did not see the note until he had received the phone call from RICKY.

Accompanying him was his son, also named RICKY. They arrived at the [REDACTED]'S DIANE and the son LARRY [REDACTED] and his wife JANNETTE. RICKY [REDACTED] was also there. They had coffee and cake for refreshments, and watched the movie Global Affaire starring Bob Hope, (channel #5 9:00PM to 10:45PM)

There were no phone calls to the house and there were no visitors. RICKY did not leave the room for over a few minutes during the time he was there. He left with his son five or ten minutes after the movie was over. MR [REDACTED] [UNREADABLE] had departed about a half hour earlier.

MRS [REDACTED], LARRY and JANNETTE, DIANE and RICKY were still at the

Cleared by Arrest ☐

Cleared Other ☐

Not Cleared ☐

[UNREADABLE] ☐

INVESTIGATING OFFICER DATE

SOLANO COUNTY SHERIFF'S OFFICE

FAIRFIELD, CALIFORNIA

SUPPLEMENTAL INVESTIGATION REPORT

TYPE OF ORIGINAL REPORT	DATE ORIGINAL REPORT	CASE NUMBER
187 P.C. Murder	12/20/68	V-25564
VICTIM OR COMPLAINTANT	LOCATION ORIGINAL OCCURRENCE	DATE – TIME OR SUPPL.
CAPTAIN PITTA	Lake Herman Road	12/29/68 4:30PM

ADDITIONAL DETAILS OF OFFENSE

RE: [REDACTED] Pg. 2

house. RICKY had been sitting on a chair and then moved to a couch.

MR [REDACTED] states to his knowledge there were no guns in the house. His departure time is estimated to be between 10:50PM and 10:55PM.

Cleared by Arrest ☐

Cleared Other ☐

Not Cleared ☐

[UNREADABLE] ☐

Det/Sgt. Lundblad - Butterbach

INVESTIGATING OFFICER

DATE

OFFENSE REPORT

OFFICE OF SHERIFF

County of Solano, California

OFFENSE	187 P.C. Murder			CASE NO	V-25564
LOCATION	Lake Herman Road, Entrance to Benicia Water Pumping Station				
REPORTED BY	CAPTAIN PITTA	ADDRESS	Benicia P.D.	PHONE	
RECEIVED BY	Sgt. Cunningham	DATE	12/20/68	TIME	11:52PM

( ) LETTER ( ) DESK ( ) PHONE ( ) TELETYPE ( ) RADIO

DESCRIPTION OF PROPERTY	Suspect No. 1
(1)	Sex Descent
(2)	Height Weight Age
(3)	Hair color Eye color
(4)	Marks/scars
(5)	
	Occupation
	Disguise or dress
	Arrested: Identification No.
TOTAL VALUE	(Yes or No)

RO: LUNDBLAD 12/21/68 9:30AM

RE: MRS MARY R. [REDACTED]

202 [REDACTED] Avenue

Vallejo, Calif.

MRS [REDACTED] is the mother of RICKY [REDACTED] who was identified by BETTY LOU'S parents as being a person who had been bugging BETTY LOU at school, (this information came via Dan Horan)

She states that RICKY did not go out last night. She accounts for his where abouts from 3:00PM when he got out of school, from there until 4:15PM he was at his sister's place, returning home at 5:00PM. They had dinner and at 7:15PM RICKY and his brother-in-law went to GallenKamps where the in-law purchased a pair of shoes for RICKY for Xmass. From there he returned home and they watched the movie on TV (Global Affair) from 9:00PM until 11:00PM. It was RICKY'S sisters birthday and coffee and cake was served.

Guests at the home at the time were RICKY'S father, from whom she is separated. A friend MR [REDACTED], THE sister and brother-in-law

APB	Date	Inv. Officer	Date

SOLANO COUNTY SHERIFF'S OFFICE

FAIRFIELD, CALIFORNIA

SUPPLEMENTAL INVESTIGATION REPORT

TYPE OF ORIGINAL REPORT	DATE ORIGINAL REPORT	CASE NUMBER
187 P.C. Murder	12/20/68 11:30PM	V-25564
VICTIM OR COMPLAINTANT	LOCATION ORIGINAL OCCURRENCE	DATE – TIME OR SUPPL.
CAPTAIN PITTA	Lake Herman Road	12/28/68 1:00PM

ADDITIONAL DETAILS OF OFFENSE

RO: DET/SGT LUNDBLAD

MARY [REDACTED],

Age 16, DOB [UNREADABLE]

At the above time and date RICKY [REDACTED] came to S/O accompanied by his mother and father. He was again advised of his constitutional rights. He knowledge that he understood his rights and expressed a desire to help.

In a previous interview, [REDACTED] stated that no went to RICKY [REDACTED]'S house at 747 Avenue after school on Friday 12/20/68. When affronted with a statement made by DANIEL [REDACTED] that RICKY stated it could have been but he washed the car several times a week and it must have been Wednesday or Thursday that the car was washed. He denied making a statement that he was going to get the car that night. RICKY admits having taken the car on a previous time and was found out by his mother.

He denies having seen DAVID FARADAY at school on Friday. Stated he never made any threats to DAVID FARADAY to his face. He might have told BETTY LOU that he was going to tell her parents that she smoked and this only because he did not approve of it.

At this time the RO showed the English note book with the threatening note, allegedly written by BETTY LOU JENSEN. RICKY acknowledge that it was her handwriting. He was surprised that she had written it. He was not upset and passed it off that he could have made a remark during a telephone conversation with her.

Cleared by Arrest ☐

Cleared Other ☐

Not Cleared ☐

[UNREADABLE] ☐

INVESTIGATING OFFICER　　DATE

SOLANO COUNTY SHERIFF'S OFFICE

FAIRFIELD, CALIFORNIA

SUPPLEMENTAL INVESTIGATION REPORT

TYPE OF ORIGINAL REPORT	DATE ORIGINAL REPORT	CASE NUMBER
187 P.C. Murder	12/20/68 11:30PM	V-25564
VICTIM OR COMPLAINTANT	LOCATION ORIGINAL OCCURRENCE	DATE – TIME OR SUPPL.
CAPTAIN PITTA	Lake Herman Road	12/28/68 1:00PM

ADDITIONAL DETAILS OF OFFENSE

RO: RICKY [REDACTED] PAGE 2

The subject of a polygraph examination came up and RICKY [REDACTED] about the results if a person was nervous. He was advised that the operator would explain the procedure.

At this time the RO asked [REDACTED] if he would consent to asking the examination and he stated he would. His parents acknowledge their consent also. The RO informed them that arrangements would be made and they would be notified.

12/29/68 11:00AM

MR [REDACTED] called on the telephone and he stated that RICKY has decided not to take the polygraph examination. He stated RICKY is too nervous plus he and his family know that RICKY is innocent and that he was at home at that time.

Cleared by Arrest ☐

Cleared Other ☐

Not Cleared ☐

[UNREADABLE] ☐

DET/SGT LUNDBLAD

INVESTIGATING OFFICER DATE

SHERIFF'S OFFICE -	SOLANO COUNTY	Time	11:52PM	Date	12/20/68 V25564
Nature of Complaint:	Murder			Location	Lake Herman Rd.
Complainant:	CAPTAIN PITTA			Address	Benicia P.D

Received by: Sgt. Cunningham ( ) Letter ( ) Desk ( ) Phone ( ) Teletype ( ) Radio

RO: DET/SGT LUNDBLAD 12/21/68 4:39PM

STATEMENT: DIAN C. [REDACTED], 766 Street, phone #643-[REDACTED]

DIAN states she rode home from school about four times with DAVE and BETTY LOU. BETTY LOU and RICK are good friends.

DAVE told her that RICK saw him in the halls at school on Friday 12/20/68, he didn't say what time it was. She stated RICK [REDACTED] does not drive a car as far as she knows. She stated she never heard of anyone being bothered.

DIAN stated BETTY LOU had been going with RICK [REDACTED] 2 weeks before the 14th of this month when BETTY LOU had met DAVID FARADAY, DIAN stated BETTY LOU had been going with BOB [REDACTED] a short time before she started going with RICK. DIAN stated BETTYLOU never went out with RICK [REDACTED], except to walk in the halls with RICK at school. DIAN stated BETTY LOU had been ignoring RICK [REDACTED] the last two weeks. She said talk to ALICE [REDACTED], 1481 Avenue, phone # 642-

(Det/Sgt Lundblad & Butterbach) ab

SHERIFF'S OFFICE -	SOLANO COUNTY	Time	11:52PM	Date	12/20/68 V25564
Nature of Complaint:	187 P.C. MURDER			Location	Lake Herman Road
Complainant:	CAPTAIN PITTA			Address	Benicia P.D

Received by: Sgt. Cunningham ( ) Letter ( ) Desk ( ) Phone ( ) Teletype ( ) Radio

RO: DEPUTY VEHRS 12/21/68 4:57AM

COMPLAINT: MR VINCENT JENSEN, 123 Ridgewood Ct., Vallejo

The above called to report that on receiving information on daughter's death, they had called home from Mare Island, their daughter MELODIE JOB, who resides at the above location. She told her father that her younger sister, who was shot, had confided in her the evening before 12/20/68 that a RICHARD [REDACTED] had threatened her.

RO advised Sgt. Lundblad would contact in AM.

(Vehrs)ab

OFFENSE REPORT

OFFICE OF SHERIFF

County of Solano, California

OFFENSE 187 P.C. Murder CASE NO V-25564

LOCATION Lake Herman Road, Entrance to Benicia Water Pumping Station

REPORTED BY CAPTAIN PITTA ADDRESS Benicia P.D. PHONE

RECEIVED BY Sgt. Cunningham DATE 12/20/68 TIME 11:52PM

( ) LETTER ( ) DESK ( ) PHONE ( ) TELETYPE ( ) RADIO

DESCRIPTION OF PROPERTY	
	Suspect No. 1
(1)	Sex Descent
(2)	Height Weight Age
(3)	Hair color Eye color
(4)	Marks/scars
(5)	
	Occupation
	Disguise or dress
	Arrested: Identification No.
TOTAL VALUE	(Yes or No)

RO: LUNDBLAD & BUTTERBACH12/21/68 3:37PM

STATEMENT: MELODY JOBE, WFA age 24,

Sister of BETTY LOU JENSEN

123 Ridgewood Court, Vallejo, Ca

MELODY was questioned in regards to any threats that her sister may have received prior to the time of her death. She stated that her sister had not dated and that they had a discussion prior to his fatal day and she advised BETTY LOU to bring DAVID home to meet her parents. While they were enroute out to A.G.E. about 6:00PM on the 20th, the fatal day, BETTY LOU confided to her that she was afraid of RICKY [REDACTED] because RICKY had threatened to tell her parents that she smoked and that she was having dates. Said that he was going to beat DAVE up. Said something about using brass knucks.

Acting on her advice, BETTY LOU brought DAVID home to her parents at 8:00PM on the 20th. There he met her parents and they left with their permission to go to Hogan High School and then to a party afterwards. They were to be home sometime around 11:00PM.

APB	Date	Inv. Officer	Date

STATEMENT: MELODY JOBE 12/21/68 3:37PM

MELODY also states that on Friday, in the afternoon, DAVID came over to Hogan and he had words with [REDACTED]. It seems that while they were talking Mr. Grove came upon the scene unaware that anything was in progress. There was no physical conflict. DAVE, realizing that he was in a school where he should not be, left without any further discussion.

MELODY also stated that her sister use to say, "close the blinds, [REDACTED] is spying on me." In other words, she did not want to be in house with him peeking around outside. At the same time, MRS JENSEN, BETTY LOU'S mother was there and stated that upon several occasions she found the gate open leading to the side of the house. They, at that time, suspected that [REDACTED] might have been prowling around the house. No one ever saw him but it was suspicioned that he might have.

(Lundblad & Butterbach) ab

OFFENSE REPORT

OFFICE OF SHERIFF

County of Solano, California

OFFENSE	187 P.C. Murder	CASE NO	V-25564
LOCATION	Lake Herman Road, Entrance to Benicia Water Pumping Station		

REPORTED BY	CAPTAIN PITTA	ADDRESS	Benicia P.D.	PHONE	
RECEIVED BY	Sgt. Cunningham	DATE	12/20/68	TIME	11:52PM

( ) LETTER ( ) DESK ( ) PHONE ( ) TELETYPE ( ) RADIO

DESCRIPTION OF PROPERTY	Suspect No. 1
(1)	Sex Descent
(2)	Height Weight Age
(3)	Hair color Eye color
(4)	Marks/scars
(5)	
	Occupation
	Disguise or dress
	Arrested: Identification No.
TOTAL VALUE	(Yes or No)

RO: LUNDBLAD & BUTTERBACH12/21/68 3:45PM

At the above time and date the reporting officers contacted MR & MRS JENSEN at their home, 123 Ridgewood Court, Vallejo, Ca. The phone number is 644-2049. MRS JENSEN stated that it was BETTY LOU'S first date. They had met DAVID FARADAY at their home approximately 8:00PM on 12/20/68. They were going to a concert at Hogan and then to a party. They did not know the address the party was supposed to have been held. They were to be home at 11:00PM.

MRS JENSEN gave the reporting officer a list of phone numbers that BETTY had in a small book. MRS JENSEN also stated that BETTY LOU wanted the curtains closed that [REDACTED] was spying. She stated that [REDACTED] called the house anytime after 3:00 PM pretty near every fifteen minutes. Sometimes BETTY talked to him and sometimes she cut him off. This happened many times.

To MRS JENSEN'S knowledge, BETTY LOU never had any other boy friend. MRS JENSEN referred the RO to BETTY LOU'S two best friends:

APB	Date	Inv. Officer	Date

RO: LUNDBLAD & BUTTERBACH 12/21/68 3:45PM PAGE 2

#1 SHARON [REDACTED] (642-[REDACTED])
926 [REDACTED]
Vallejo, Ca.

#2 DIAN [REDACTED] (643-[REDACTED])
766 [REDACTED] Drive
Vallejo, Ca.

(Lundblad & Butterbach) ab

OFFENSE REPORT

OFFICE OF SHERIFF

County of Solano, California

OFFENSE 187 P.C. Murder CASE NO V-25564

LOCATION Lake Herman Road, Entrance to Benicia Water Pumping Station

REPORTED BY CAPTAIN PITTA ADDRESS Benicia P.D. PHONE

RECEIVED BY Sgt. Cunningham DATE 12/20/68 TIME 11:52PM

( ) LETTER ( ) DESK ( ) PHONE ( ) TELETYPE ( ) RADIO

DESCRIPTION OF PROPERTY	Suspect No. 1
(1)	Sex Descent
(2)	Height Weight Age
(3)	Hair color Eye color
(4)	Marks/scars
(5)	
	Occupation
	Disguise or dress
	Arrested: Identification No.
TOTAL VALUE	(Yes or No)

RO: BUTTERBACH 12/21/68 8:51PM

Officer G. MEYRING (#298 Vallejo P.D.) came into the S/O. He stated to RO that a STAN [REDACTED], 14 yrs, 406 [REDACTED] Street 644-[REDACTED], told him today that he ([REDACTED]) and a friend of his, a student from Solano College, were going towards Blue Rock Springs on Columbus Parkway and a Olds, 2-door H.T. 88 (Don) blue in color and a 63 Chevrolet, Impala, Blue, with two persons in it turned of Lake Herman Road on to Columbus Parkway heading in the direction of Blue Rock Springs, this was at approximately 10:30PM Friday 12/20/1968

APB	Date	Inv. Officer	Date
		BUTTERBACH	

OFFENSE REPORT

OFFICE OF SHERIFF

County of Solano, California

OFFENSE 187 P.C. Murder CASE NO V-25564

LOCATION Lake Herman Road, Entrance to Benicia Water Pumping Station

REPORTED BY CAPTAIN PITTA ADDRESS Benicia P.D. PHONE

RECEIVED BY Sgt. Cunningham DATE 12/20/68 TIME 11:52PM

( ) LETTER ( ) DESK ( ) PHONE ( ) TELETYPE ( ) RADIO

DESCRIPTION OF PROPERTY	Suspect No. 1
(1)	Sex Descent
(2)	Height Weight Age
(3)	Hair color Eye color
(4)	Marks/scars
(5)	
	Occupation
	Disguise or dress
	Arrested: Identification No.
TOTAL VALUE	(Yes or No)

RO: BUTTERBACH & LUNDBLAD 12/22/68 4:54PM

STATEMENT: MRS JEAN L. FARADAY, Mother of deceased, 1930 Sereno Drive

MRS FARADAY stated she did not know BETTLOU that she and DAVID had only been going together for a short time, she had never met BETTYLOU. She stated she did not know of any enemies DAVID may have had. She stated that on Friday night at 7:10PM DAVID drove his sister Debbie to a meeting of the Rainbow girls at the Pybian Castle on Sonoma Blvd., and DAVID came back home at 7:20PM and left again at 7:30PM. She had given him a dollar and fifty five cents all in change (quarters and dimes)

RO talked to Debbie Faraday, WFJ 16 years, sister of DAVID. She relates the following DAVID told her on the afternoon of Friday 12/20/68 that he was going out to Lake Herman Road that night because a bunch of the kids were going out there that night. She stated she knew who some of the kids were, but she could not contact them by phone now, but she would get in touch with them and let RO know later.

APB	Date	Inv. Officer	Date

BUTTERBACH - LUNDBLAD 12/22/68

OFFENSE REPORT

OFFICE OF SHERIFF

County of Solano, California

OFFENSE 187 P.C. Murder CASE NO V-25564

LOCATION Lake Herman Road, Entrance to Benicia Water Pumping Station

REPORTED BY CAPTAIN PITTA ADDRESS Benicia P.D. PHONE

RECEIVED BY Sgt. Cunningham DATE 12/20/68 TIME 11:52PM

( ) LETTER ( ) DESK ( ) PHONE ( ) TELETYPE ( ) RADIO

DESCRIPTION OF PROPERTY	Suspect No. 1
(1)	Sex Descent
(2)	Height Weight Age
(3)	Hair color Eye color
(4)	Marks/scars
(5)	
	Occupation
	Disguise or dress
	Arrested: Identification No.
TOTAL VALUE	(Yes or No)

RO: LUNDBLAD & BUTTERBACH 12/27/68 11:00AM

STATEMENT: LARRY [REDACTED], age 20

1616 [REDACTED] Street

Napa, CA

and wife,

LINDA [REDACTED], age 18

1616 [REDACTED] Street

Napa, CA (no phone)

[REDACTED] is employed at Standard Oil Company at 800 West Imola Avenue in Napa, CA, on the graveyard shift, 12:00 midnight until 8:00AM.

MRS [REDACTED] reports that at 2:00 this AM, a subject known to her as PETE, who formerly lived in an apartment complex near then, came to the house and when she went to the door she let him in because they (both husband & wife) knew him. He said, "what would you do if I raped you?" She stated that she would pound on the wall and the man next door would call the police. He asked her if she was happy. She said she was and he said, "happy people piss me off" He said that he has been fighting with his wife and has been going to Vallejo. Also, he stated he was going back to Redding because all the people are

APB	Date	Inv. Officer	Date
		BUTTERBACH - LUNDBLAD	12/22/68

SOLANO COUNTY SHERIFF'S OFFICE

FAIRFIELD, CALIFORNIA

SUPPLEMENTAL INVESTIGATION REPORT

TYPE OF ORIGINAL REPORT	DATE ORIGINAL REPORT	CASE NUMBER
187 P.C. Murder	12/20/68	V-25564
VICTIM OR COMPLAINTANT	LOCATION ORIGINAL OCCURRENCE	DATE – TIME OR SUPPL.
CAPTAIN PITTA	Lake Herman	12/27/68 [UNREADABLE]

ADDITIONAL DETAILS OF OFFENSE

RE: [UNREADABLE]   Page 2

stabbing him in the back and twisting the knife after it was in. He remained in the apartment about 45 minutes. After [UNREADABLE] around outside, but that she did not look out [UNREADABLE] she it was.

[REDACTED] supplied information that this fellow [UNREADABLE], [UNREADABLE] not remember the last name, drove a '52 Chevrolet coupe, blue in color. He also has a '55 Buick that is cream and maroon. He owns a rifle and a pistol, calibers unknown. He carries a fishing knife in his pocket.

[REDACTED] stated that the fellow had come to the station at 1:45AM and walked to him there, and fifteen minutes later showed up at his home at 1616 [REDACTED] (according to his wife). [REDACTED] further states that this PETE is about 28 yrs old, 5'11", jet black hair, acne pits on the face. He is a helper at Kaiser Steel and is working the day shift.

Deputy Butterbach was detailed to Kaiser Steel with [REDACTED] to try to identify the car in the parking lot or gain any information from Kaiser Steel as to the identify of this subject "PETE". SEE DEPUTY BUTTERBACH'S REPORT

(Lundblad & Butterbach) ab

Cleared by Arrest ☐

Cleared Other ☐

Not Cleared ☐ ______________________ INVESTIGATING OFFICER DATE

[UNREADABLE] ☐

OFFENSE REPORT

OFFICE OF SHERIFF

County of Solano, California

OFFENSE 187 P.C. Murder CASE NO V-25564

LOCATION Lake Herman Road, Entrance to Benicia Water Pumping Station

REPORTED BY CAPTAIN PITTA ADDRESS Benicia P.D. PHONE

RECEIVED BY Sgt. Cunningham DATE 12/20/68 TIME 11:52PM

( ) LETTER ( ) DESK ( ) PHONE ( ) TELETYPE ( ) RADIO

DESCRIPTION OF PROPERTY	Suspect No. 1
(1)	Sex Descent
(2)	Height Weight Age
(3)	Hair color Eye color
(4)	Marks/scars
(5)	
	Occupation
	Disguise or dress
	Arrested: Identification No.
TOTAL VALUE	(Yes or No)

RO: DET/SGT LUNDBLAD 12/27/68 1:30PM

STATEMENT: MRS JEAN [REDACTED]

132 San [REDACTED] Court,

Vallejo, CA (644-[REDACTED])

MRS [REDACTED] was hesitant to make a statement. She related however, that her children, ages 18, 16, 14 and another boy who lives at the house, age 17, had made a statement that they knew who did it. It was possibly just a speculated guess. MRS [REDACTED] said that the boys had named GARY [REDACTED].

They had no further information on this and the information possibly passed between the children in their conversations about the incident. MRS [REDACTED] could give no concrete proof of anything along this line.

(Det/Sgt. Lundblad) ab

APB	Date	Inv. Officer	Date

OFFENSE REPORT

OFFICE OF SHERIFF

County of Solano, California

OFFENSE 187 P.C. Murder CASE NO V-25564

LOCATION Lake Herman Road, Entrance to Benicia Water Pumping Station

REPORTED BY CAPTAIN PITTA ADDRESS Benicia P.D. PHONE

RECEIVED BY Sgt. Cunningham DATE 12/20/68 TIME 11:52PM

( ) LETTER ( ) DESK ( ) PHONE ( ) TELETYPE ( ) RADIO

DESCRIPTION OF PROPERTY	Suspect No. 1
(1)	Sex Descent
(2)	Height Weight Age
(3)	Hair color Eye color
(4)	Marks/scars
(5)	
	Occupation
	Disguise or dress
	Arrested: Identification No.
TOTAL VALUE	(Yes or No)

RO: DET/SGT LUNDBLAD 12/27/68 4:45PM

STATEMENT: MR [REDACTED]

437 [REDACTED] Street

Vallejo, CA (643- [REDACTED])

MR [REDACTED] is a gunsmith at Al's Sport Shop who was contacted by the RO and information was requested regarding certain types of self-loading revolvers or pistols. MR [REDACTED] suggested on the basis of the evidence that we have here, could be the type of Ruger, self-loader, that has a tube magazine and carries from twelve (12) to fifteen (15) rounds, depending whether or not they are long rifle longs or shorts. MR [REDACTED] offered any assistance possible in trying to identify the suspect weapon.

(Det/Sgt. Lundblad) ab

APB	Date	Inv. Officer	Date

OFFENSE REPORT

OFFICE OF SHERIFF

County of Solano, California

OFFENSE	187 P.C. Murder			CASE NO	V-25564
LOCATION	Lake Herman Road, Entrance to Benicia Water Pumping Station				
REPORTED BY	CAPTAIN PITTA	ADDRESS	Benicia P.D.	PHONE	
RECEIVED BY	Sgt. Cunningham	DATE	12/20/68	TIME	11:52PM

( ) LETTER ( ) DESK ( ) PHONE ( ) TELETYPE ( ) RADIO

DESCRIPTION OF PROPERTY	
	Suspect No. 1
(1)	Sex Descent
(2)	Height Weight Age
(3)	Hair color Eye color
(4)	Marks/scars
(5)	
	Occupation
	Disguise or dress
	Arrested: Identification No.
TOTAL VALUE	(Yes or No)

RO: BUTTERBACH 12/29/68 4:10PM

TELEPHONE CONVERSATIONS RECEIVED BY RO LISTED BELOW:

12/23/68 10:15AM LOUIS D. [REDACTED], 741 [REDACTED] Street,
Vallejo, CA 643-[REDACTED]

LOUIS [REDACTED] called and stated his wife had a girlfriend who had been going around with a Latin type man. She, the girlfriend, split up with this' man and went back with her old boyfriend. The old boyfriend drives a Nash station wagon fitting the description of the FARADAY vehicle. MR [REDACTED] states that his wife told him that her girlfriend said this man, the Latin type, is very jealous and he could be capable of doing such a thing by mistaken identity

12/23/68 9:46AM

Received a call from Captain Byrd, Vallejo P.D., he was calling regarding a report received by the Vallejo P.D., 1:30AM 12/23/68. Report of complainant, ROBERT [REDACTED], 533 [REDACTED]. See Vallejo Police report in file.

12/23/68 10:38AM

APB	Date	Inv. Officer	Date

SOLANO COUNTY SHERIFF'S OFFICE

FAIRFIELD, CALIFORNIA

SUPPLEMENTAL INVESTIGATION REPORT

TYPE OF ORIGINAL REPORT	DATE ORIGINAL REPORT	CASE NUMBER
187 P.C. Murder	12/20/68	V-25564
VICTIM OR COMPLAINTANT	LOCATION ORIGINAL OCCURRENCE	DATE – TIME OR SUPPL.
CAPTAIN PITTA	Lake Herman Road	

ADDITIONAL DETAILS OF OFFENSE

RO: DET/SGT LUNDBLAD 745-

Officer Warner, Benicia

RE: Mrs PEGGY [REDACTED] Benicia P.D

MRS STELLA MADEIROS	P.O. BOX [UNREADABLE]	644-
JAMES A. [REDACTED]	1235 [REDACTED] Drive	644-
HELEN AXE	60 [REDACTED] Avenue	642-
ROBERT [REDACTED]	1088 [REDACTED] Avenue, Napa	224-
FRANK GASSER	Gasser Ranch, [UNREADABLE]. 621	
[UNREADABLE] [REDACTED]	926 [REDACTED] Avenue	642-
DAN [REDACTED]	450 [REDACTED] Street	642-
DANIEL [REDACTED]	1044 [REDACTED] Avenue	642-
JOE [REDACTED]	112 [REDACTED] Court	643-
MRS JEAN FARADAY	1930 Sereno Drive	
WILLIAM [REDACTED]	746 [REDACTED] Avenue	642-
OFFICER MEYRING	Vallejo P.D.	
MRS JENSEN	123 Ridgewood Court	

MELODY JOBE	123 Ridgewood Court	
RICKY ALLEN [REDACTED]	202 [REDACTED]	648-
MRS MARY [REDACTED]	202 [REDACTED]	648-

Cleared by Arrest ☐

Cleared Other ☐

Not Cleared ☐

[UNREADABLE] ☐

INVESTIGATING OFFICER

DATE

SOLANO COUNTY SHERIFF'S OFFICE

FAIRFIELD, CALIFORNIA

SUPPLEMENTAL INVESTIGATION REPORT

TYPE OF ORIGINAL REPORT	DATE ORIGINAL REPORT	CASE NUMBER
187 P.C. Murder	12/20/68	V-25564
VICTIM OR COMPLAINTANT	LOCATION ORIGINAL OCCURRENCE	DATE – TIME OR SUPPL.
CAPTAIN PITTA	Lake Herman Road	

ADDITIONAL DETAILS OF OFFENSE

[UNREADABLE]:

[UNREADABLE]	[UNREADABLE]	
[UNREADABLE]	[UNREADABLE]	
[UNREADABLE]	[UNREADABLE] Street, Napa	No Phone
[UNREADABLE]	[UNREADABLE], Benicia	
MRS JEAN [REDACTED]	[UNREADABLE] [REDACTED] Court	644-
MR [REDACTED]	Al's Sport Shop	643-
GEORGE [REDACTED]	Sheriff's Office	
DONALD [REDACTED]	1121 [REDACTED] Road	
LOUIS [REDACTED]	741 [REDACTED] Street	643-
MARK [REDACTED]	137 [REDACTED] Way	642-
WAYNE T. [REDACTED]	837 [REDACTED] Road	644-
SHARON [REDACTED]	926 [REDACTED] Avenue	642-
DIAN [REDACTED]	965 [REDACTED] Street	643-
BINGO WESKER	Old Borges Ranch	745-
MRS [REDACTED]	150 [REDACTED] Avenue	643-
A.G. [REDACTED]	114 [REDACTED] Street, Napa	224-

Cleared by Arrest ☐

Cleared Other ☐

Not Cleared ☐

[UNREADABLE] ☐

INVESTIGATING OFFICER   DATE

Darlene Elizabeth Ferrin and Michael Renault Mageau

Killed: Ferrin, July 5, 1969 (Saturday)

Wounded: Mageau, July 5, 1969 (Saturday)

~~~~~~

Case number: 243146

Time of attack: Approximately 12:10 a.m.

Place of attack: The parking lot of secluded Blue Rock Springs Park on the eastern outskirts of Vallejo, Calif.

Method of attack: Darlene Ferrin, age 22, was shot five times. Mike Mageau, age 19, was shot four times. The weapon was a 9mm semi-automatic pistol. There was no indication of robbery or sexual molestation. There were no witnesses.

See more at:

https://zodiackiller.com/zodiac-killer-victims-darlene-ferrin-and-mike-mageau/

Here is the extensive, 75-page Vallejo Police Department report pertaining to the murder of Darlene Ferrin and wounding of Mike Mageau –
~~~~~~

CRIME REPORT

Specific Offense	VALLEJO POLICE DEPARTMENT	Case Number 243 146

Date and time occurred; day of week	Location of occurrence	Division - [n/a]	Officer
7-5-69 12:10AM SAT	BLUE ROCK SPRINGS	2	LYNCH-RUST
[victim's name (firm if business)	**Residence address (business address if firm)**	**Residence phone**	**Business phone or address**
DARLENE FERRIN	1300 VIRGINIA ST.		642-8989
Person reporting offense	**Residence address**	**Residence phone**	**Business phone or address**
DEBRA [REDACTED] ROGER [REDACTED]	1909 [REDACTED] ST 1055 [REDACTED] ST	642-[REDACTED] 642-[REDACTED]	
Person who discovered crime	**Residence address**	**Residence phone**	**Business phone or address**
JERRY [REDACTED]	938 [REDACTED]	644-[REDACTED]	
WITNESSES: Name	**Residence address**	**Residence phone**	**Business phone or address**
NONE			

Victim's occupation race sex age	Type of premises or location where offense was committed
WAITRESS W F 22	MACADAM PAVED PARKING LOT

CRIMES AGAINST PROPERTY	CRIMES AGAINST THE PERSON
Point where entrance was made:	Weapon – Force or means used: 9MM LUGER
Exact location of property when [UNREADABLE]	Exact location of victim at time of offense SITTING IN AUTOMOBILE
Method used to gain] entrance	Victim's activity at time of offense TALKING – LISTENING TO RADIO
Instrument used (Describe)	Exact words used by suspect NONE
There were occupants at time of offense?	

Apparent motive – Type of property taken

JEALOUSY - REVENGE

Modus Operendi at suspect(s) – Actions or conversation

WALKED UP TO CAR SAID NOTHING BEGAN FIRING GUN

Vehicle used by suspect(s) – Year, mark, body type, color, license number and any other identifying marks	Where [UNREADABLE]
CORVAIR – MUSTANG MEDIUM LIGHT BROWN	

SUSPECT(S):

	Name	[UNREADABLE]	Eyes	Hgt.	Wt.	Age	Description of Area
No. 1							
No. 2							
No. 3							

Value of Property stolen. [UNREADABLE], Serial [UNREADABLE], Identifying marks.

SEE DETAILS.

CASE NUMBERS OF ANY OTHER OFFENSES CONNECTED WITH THIS REPORT: USE ADDITIONAL SHEET [UNREADABLE] IF NECESSARY

number and date	Signature of reporting officer	[UNREADABLE] number	Date and time report reviewed
[UNREADABLE]	Signature of supervisor [UNREADABLE]	[UNREADABLE] number	Date and time report written

PD FORM No. [UNREADABLE]

VALLEJO POLICE DEPARTMENT

EVIDENCE/PROPERTY RECORD

243 146

CRIME

CLASSIFICATION DARLENE FERRIN DATE 1300 VIRGINIA ST

PRINCIPAL'S

NAME SGT J. LYNCH ADDRESS #152

EVIDENCE SUBMITTED BY

(Name & Badge No.)

ITEM #	DESCRIPTION OF PROPERTY	SPECIFIC LOCATION WHERE FOUND
OP	BLACK DRESS	CORONER DAN
AE	1 PAIR BLUE SHOES	HORAN AT TWIN
RR	1 WHITE PANTIES	CHAPELS
LR	1 WHITE BRASSIERE	" " "
EI	SLUG REMOVED FROM	RECEIVED FROM
NN	RIGHT END RIB	DR SHIRAI AT
E	SLUG REMOVED FROM	TWIN CHAPELS
	LEFT 7-8 RIB	" " "
	RECEIVED FROM DR. JANTZEN	
	AT KAISEN HOSPITAL SLUG	
	REMOVED FROM LEFT THIGH	
	DR MICHAEL MAGEAU	

CHAIN OF CUSTODY

DATE	STORED	SIGNATURE	DATE	STORED	SIGNATURE

LIST EXAMINATION REQUEST ON REVERSSE SIDE

VPD FORM #22 12/66

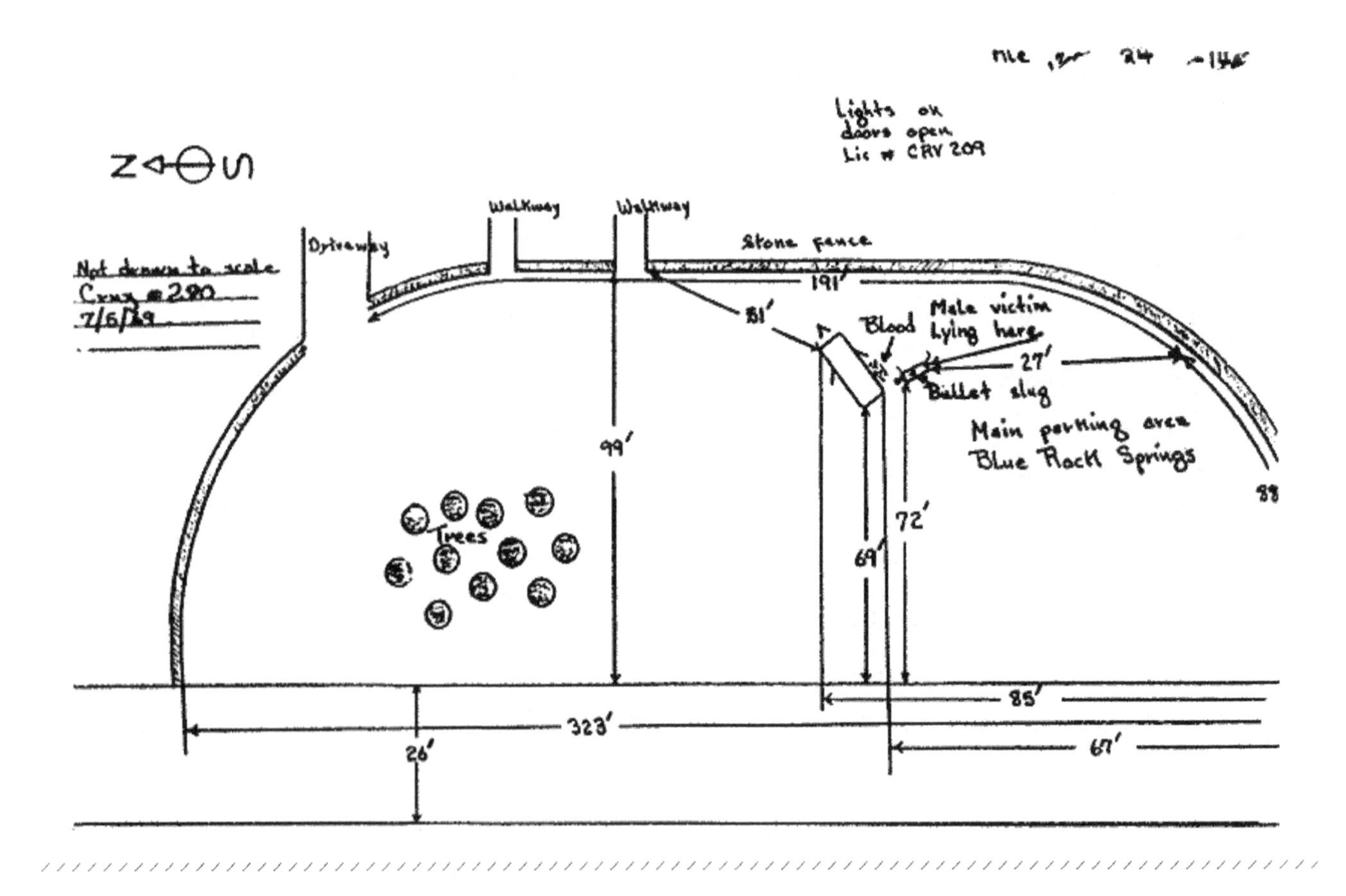

SUPPLEMENT

Vallejo Police Department

CRIME CLASSIFICATION ______________________ CASE NO. 243 146

7/5/69 – 12:10am

Writer received a call from female citizen stating that two (2) juveniles were being shot at at the Blue Rock Springs parking lot. This information was passed on to the Radio Operator on duty. (F. Shook)

7/5/69 – 12:40am

Writer received call from male subject who did not identify himself. Substance of statement was as follows:

"I want to report a double murder. If you will go (1) one mile east on Columbus Parkway to the public park you will find the kids in a brown car. They were shot with a 9 MM luger. I also killed those kids last year. Goodbye."

7/8/69

At the request of Captain Bird writer asked to elaborate on telephone call from subject mentioned above.

Writer could distinguish no trace of accent in voice. Subject seemed to be reading or had rehearsed what he was saying. Subject spoke in an even, consistant voice (rather soft but forceful). When writer attempted to get information from subject his voice became louder covering what writer was trying to say. Subject did not stop talking until his statement was complete. Subject's voice was nature. The only real change in the voice was when he said "goodbye." Subjects voice deepened and became <u>taunting</u>. During the course of subjects statement writer connected subject with desk officer, but the subject completed his statement and hung up before desk officer picked up call.

NANCY L. SLOVER

SUPPLEMENT

Vallejo Police Department

CRIME CLASSIFICATION ______________________ CASE NO. 243 146

5:15am 7-5-69 Off. Hoffman

Approx. 12:10am 7-5-69 writer copied a radio message from KMA 818 regarding two teenagers being shot at in the area of Blue Rock Springs. R.O. had just checked this area approx. 15 min. prior to this transmission, and found the parking lot of Blue Rock Springs clear of people or motor vehicles.

Proceeding to the above area, driving V.P.D. unit 130, and following unit 119. Observed unit 119 make a U-turn on Columbus Parkway just south of the Blue Rock Springs Golf Course. At this time the Police Unit stopped a late model Grey Cad. that was proceeding towards Vallejo on Columbus Parkway. As the driver got out of this Cad. he was recognized by writer as Andy [REDACTED] Jr. WMA 19yrs. residing at 22 [REDACTED] Ct. Vlo.

R.O. then proceeded to Blue Rock Springs parking lot, thus being the first Police vehicle to arrive at this location. It was observed being parked in the southern portion of the parking lot, east of Columbus Parkway. The vehicle described in the Police broadcast as a Brown Corvair, belonging to the victims of the shooting.

The first subject observed by this writer was a WMA laying on his back on the ground, at the right rear of the car. This subject was later I.D. as MICHAEL RENAULT NAGEAU WMA 19yrs. DOB 10-29-49 residing at 864 Beechwood, Vlo. This person advised he had been shot but could afford no further info. to this Off. at this time. It was evident this subject in severe pain and suffering from multiple gunshot wounds. Blood was running freely from his mouth, with another wound visible in his lower left leg.

The second subject observed by R.O. was a WFA in a sitting position behind the steering wheel of the afore mentioned auto. She was sitting with her head resting on the inside of the left door, at the window level. The observation of this girl was made from the open window of the right door. It was noted that her body bore three bullet holes, viewing it from this position. There were two gunshot wounds in her upper right arm, and one bullet entry visible in her right side a few inches below the arm pit. R.O. at this point went to the left side of the auto and viewed this girl thru the open left door widow. Writer did not observe another bullet wound from this position. But did view a substantial amount of blood splattered about the car. This subject was later I.D. as Darlene ELIZABETH FERRIN WFA 22yra. DOB 3-17-47 residing at 930 Montery, Vlo.

At this point Sgt. Conway arrived at the scene and was informed by R.O. that in fact this was a shooting. Also requested of Sgt. Conway by writer, was to proceed back the area where Police unit 119 was. And in fact detain Andy [REDACTED] Jr. for further investigation as to the responsibility of his crime.

Off. D. Clark arrived at the scene next and he plus R.O. attempted to render aid to victims until the ambulance arrived.

SUPPLEMENT

Vallejo Police Department

CRIME CLASSIFICATION Murder CASE NO. 243 146

5:15am 7-5-69 Off. Hoffman

Prior to the arrival of the ambulance, R.O. searched the area of the parking lot in which the victims vehicle was standing. This search discovered what happened to be seven (7) empty shell casings. These casings believed to have been ejected from an automatic pistol. The seven (7) empty shells were found a few feet away from the victims auto on the right side. All of these shell cases have been tagged into evidence under this case number.

Solano ambulance arrived and transported the victims to Kaiser Hosp. Writter rode with the victims enroute to the hosp. Neither of these subjects spoke while in the ambulance.

Approx. 12:38am 7-5-69

Arrived Kaiser Hosp. subject DARLENE FERRIN was attended by Dr. Borden] and pronounced Dead On Arrival. Her body was transferred to Twin Chapel at 2:45am 7-5-69.

Subject MICHAEL MAGEAU was attended by Dr. Jantzen for multiple gunshot wounds and transferred to I.C.U in critical condition. This subject was wearing an assortment of clothing consisting of three (3) pairs of trousers, one (1) T-shirt, three (3) sweaters and one long sleeved button shirt. These items of clothing were received by R.O. and placed into evidence under this case number.

During the time MEGEAU was being treated for his wounds he remained conscious. He was in severe pain and couldn't tell a continuing story. Through different questions, he gave the following story in segments.

"A white man drove up in a car, got out, walked up to car, ~~STRIKETHROUGH~~ shined flashlite inside and started shooting. Man was older than me, window was down. After stop shooting I got out of car, I tried to get the people to come over but they drove off. After finally ten minutes the Policeman came."

At the time this subject was taken to I.C.U. this Off. left Kaiser returning to V.P.D. (Hoffman)

9pm 7-5-69

STATS

7-8-69 Copy to D.A. Office..bt

7-8-69 Vehicle impounded at AAA. (Waricher)

SUPPLEMENT

Vallejo Police Department

CRIME CLASSIFICATION

CASE NO. 243 146

7-5-69 6AM - report written

7-5-69 12:10AM – Rovd call via KMA 818 that someone had been shot at in the vicinity of Blue Rock Springs & that the couple would be waiting there. Operator gave detail to Off's Meyring & Lindemann in unit 119. RO also responded from the East side of town & upon arriving on Columbus Parkway in vicinity of golf course, observed detailed officers on a car stop. Off. Meyring advised they stopped the veh because it was in the area & that they were making P.I. reports. RO then proceeded to the parking lot on the W side of street at the park & noted that Off. Hoffman was at the scene & a wht male subj. lying on the ground to the rt rear of a 1963 brn Chev. Corvair, 2dr, CRV 209. This subj, with blood all over his face & later identified as Michael R. Megeau, WM, 19 of 864 Beechwood. Prior to getting out of the unit Off. Hoffman requested I return to car stop of Off. Mayring & Lindemann & have then gold the subj's they had stopped. RO proceeded back to carstop & instructed Officers to arrest the two subj's. a WM & WF for investigation of felony, & make a search of their veh. RO then returned to OFF. Hoffman.

On initial arrival, RO requested by radio an ambulance & an investigator at the scene & upon returning to Off. Hoffman RO went to assistance of subj. on ground, as Off. Hoffman was with a subj that was sitting on left front seat behind wheel that was also injured. This subj. later identified as Darlene E. Ferrin, WF, 19, of 864 Beechwood. On preliminary examination of Mageau, it was apparent that he had been shot a number of times, he had blood all over his face & blood coming from his mouth as well as his left leg with blood, RO felt it was necessary to question subj. inspight of the fact the subj. was in great pain. Subj. Was coherent & RO asked him, "do you know who shot you?" & he replied "no". RO then asked Mageau to give me some type of description & he replied that he can't. RO then asked a series of question & was told by Mageau that the resp. was a wht male, young, & heavy set by himself & that he was in a brown veh. RO then asked if the resp. said anything & Megeau replied, "no, he just started shooting & kept shooting. Questioning continued until arrival of ambulance at which time both veh. Was placed in ambulance & removed from the scene. By this time Sgt's Rust, Lunch & Odiorne had arrived at the scene & RO gave then the information obtained from the victim & gave a description over the air to all units. It was at this time it was determined that Sgt's Lynch & Rust would be the investigating officers & the investigation was then turned over to them.

RO then left the scene upon being advised by radio that the possible resp. had called the station from a pay phone at the corner of Toulumne & Springs Rd. RO proceeded to that location to cover the detailed unit 122, Off's Agenbroad & Peach. Upon arriving at the that location it was determined resp. was that location & the detailed off's were instructed to stand by until an I.D. technician could get there to check the prints. (Conway)

CRIME CLASSIFICATION Murder CASE NO. 243 146

7-6-69 3:00 PM

Location: Intensive Care Unit, Kaiser Hospital

RO went to location and contacted shooting victim, Michael Mageau. Was advised by Dr. Scott that RO could talk to him for a short time, however he was under medication at this time and would possibly be going to sleep shortly. RO contacted Michael who still was in very bad condition and was very strained to talk as he had had a wound in his mouth. RO asked him if he could as best as possible relate the facts as he knew them as to the occurrences of Friday night when he and D. FERRIN were shot. Michael states that he would do his best to give a statement and gave it as following.

States that at approximately 4:00 p.m. Friday afternoon, that D. Ferrin called him up, and in their conversation stated they agreed that they would go to a movie in San Francisco that night and she would be at the house at approximately 7:39 p.m. Michael states he next heard from her at approximately 8:00 p.m. when she again called and stated that she had to go with her sister, Christine, to the Miss Firecracker contest, that she would call him as soon as she could, as soon as she was clear from this. Michael states that he stayed home and at approx. 10:30 he received another call from Dea stating she would be over shortly.

He stated that Dea came over at approximately 11:30 or shortly thereafter and picked him up in her car. They were both hungry as they had not had supper and were going to go get something to eat. Stated that she was driving her vehicle, the Corvair they were found in. Stated they drove west on Springs Road and as they were driving down Springs Road to go get something to eat, Dea state to him that she wanted to talk to him about something. Michael stated that approximately at the location of Mr. Ed's on Springs Road they turned around and headed east at his suggestion to go to Blue Rock Springs Park where they could talk. They went directly out to this location, pulled the car in the parking lot where it was found by the police. Dea turned the lights and the motor off and had the radio playing. States they were there just a very short time, a few minutes, and three cars pulled in to the parking lot where they were. They were apparently young kids, and they heard some laughing and carrying on and a few firecrackers were set off, then the three vehicles left within a short time. This was just a very short space of time, a few minutes. Shortly after his and about five minutes before the shooting occurred, Michael states a vehicle pulled into the lot, coming from the direction of Springs Road and Vallejo. The driver turned the lights off on the car and pulled around to the left or east side of their car, approximately six or eight feet away and sat there for a minute. Michael states he asked Dea if she knew who it was and she stated, "Oh, never mind."

Michael stated at this time he is always kidding Dea about knowing so many people and does not know whether she meant this as she knew the fellow or not. Michael states as best as he can recall, he could not see the car too clearly, however the shape of the car looked similar to the car that Dea owns, a Corvair. He could not see the color or anything as it was very dark out there.

Ed Rust

States as far as he could tell this car had one male subject in it. The car then drove off and headed in the direction of Vallejo & Springs Road at a fairly fast rate of speed. He stated approximately five minutes later, the vehicle pulled up, coming from the direction of Vallejo & Springs Road. This vehicle pulled up approximately ten feet behind and to the right side of Dea's car, which would be the side that Michael was sitting. The vehicle's lights were left on and the subject got out and walked toward the car. He had a large high-powered flashlight, the kind you carry with a handle. This subject walked up to the car and Michael stated that both he and Dea believed that it was a policeman and that he wanted to check their I.D. or something.

Stated subject stepped up to Michael's side of the car, which is the right side, shining the flashlight on them. Subject did not say anything to them, nor did they say anything to him. Michael stated he started to reach for his wallet as he felt it was a policeman who wanted to see his I.D. States as he did so, he heard a muffled sound and felt a pain in his back and his neck area. He states he heard some more muffled sounds, sounding like a gun with a silencer on it, and felt pains in his body, his back and around his neck. States he tried to climb over the back seat to get away from the shooting and subject kept shooting him again and again. States finally the subject quit shooting him and apparently turned the gun on Dea and started shooting her again and again.

States subject then turned around and started to walk back to his vehicle which still had the headlights on. Michael stated he could not tell if he meant to yell at the subject or if he just yelled from pain, but he let out some type of yell. At this time, the subject apparently hearing him, came back to the car and shot Michael two more times, once in the back and once in the left leg. States the subject then turned the gun on Dea and shot her twice more. Michael states that all the shots that he heard were muffled, sounding similar to a gun with the silencer on. It was not loud. States the subject then turned around and casually walked back to his vehicle and got in.

Michael at this time stated that he had to reach outside the car door to open it as the handle inside was broken. Stated he reached outside and opened the car door and fell outside on the ground. As he fell out onto the ground the vehicle the subject was in backed up in a turning movement and then took off toward Springs Road in Vallejo at a very high rate of speed. Michael states as the vehicle drove off he only saw the rear portion of it, this rear part appearing to be a vehicle similar to or the same type as Dea's car, a Corvair. Also a very similar color, possibly a little bit lighter brown. It had a California license, however he could not tell what the numbers were. Stated the subject continued on Blue Rock Springs Road at a very high rate of speed towards Springs Road in Vallejo.

Michael states that in what seemed to be eight to ten minutes after this a car came by with three young hippy types in it. He can recall two boys and one girl. States he waved and yelled to the occupants of this vehicle to come over and help him. Stated they came close to him

Ed Rust

and he asked them to get a doctor quick. Stated the girl told him to lie still and they would get a doctor. States approximately five to ten minutes later the police arrived in a vehicle that was not a black and white police car, and other policemen arrived, and he was then taken to the hospital.

RO asked Michael if he could give a description of the responsible subject, and he stated as best as he could recall the description is as follows. Subject appeared to be short, possibly 5'8", was real heavy set, beefy build. Stated subject was not blubbery fat, but real beefy, possibly 195 to 200, or maybe even larger. Stated he had short curly hair, light brown, almost blond. He was wearing a short-sleeved shirt, blue in color. Cannot remember if it was light or dark blue. States he just saw subject's face from the profile, side view, and does not recall seeing a front view. States there was nothing unusual about his face, other than it appeared to be large. Michael stated the subject did not have a mustache, nor was he wearing glasses or anything. He could not recall anything unusual except that he had a large face. Michael reemphasized that he really did not get a good look at subject other than his profile. Also, it was dark out and it was hard to see the subject.

Michael states that he could possibly recognize responsible if he had a profile view, as this is the best view he had of the subject. Stated subject was a white male, approximately 26-30 years. Was unable to judge real well what his age was. States he feels sure the subject wanted to make sure that they were dead. This due to the fact that he returned and shot each one of them twice again after the first shooting.

When questioned about Dea's vehicle having the headlights on when the police arrived, Michael was unable to explain fully, however states he recalls something about possibly flashing the lights on and off to attract attention of passing vehicles. States he cannot remember if he did this or possibly Dead did it. States while still in the car he called to Dea, does not recall what he said, but recalls the only thing that she was able to do was make a small moaning sound. She was unable to say anything.

RO questioned Michael as to a possible motive, if he had had any argument or trouble, etc. with anyone recently, or if there was any reason at all that anyone would want to harm him. He stated he could not recall anything at all, having any arguments or anything to give anyone reason to do anything like this. Also stated that Darlene did not say anything about any trouble that she has had. States they have always been very truthful with each other and confided very closely in each other's problems and he is sure if she had known about someone after her or had a hate for her enough to do something like this, she would have said something about it. Stated as far as he knows, the only type of trouble that Dea has had was sometimes her friends got mad at her. There were sometimes petty jealousies between her and her friends.

Ed Ruest

Sometimes some possibly boyfriends, not exactly dating type boyfriends, but friends, just acquaintances, would become jealous over just petty incidents.

The interview of Michael MAGEAU was terminated by RO at this time as he was becoming very tired due to the medication and also his condition due to the gunshot wounds.

RO wishes to emphasize that throughout the entire interview with Michael it was a very strained situation for him as he had been given a sedative type of medication to relax him and put him to sleep and he was straining to keep himself awake in order to give the information to RO. RO advised him to rest at this time and when he woke up if he felt better and if he felt he possibly could give more information to have the nurse call RO at the police department. (Rust) tm

Ed Rust

SUPPLEMENT

Vallejo Police Department

CRIME CLASSIFICATION ______________________________ CASE NO. 243 146

4:30am 7-5-69 Sgt. RUST

RO checked files for names of victims, nothing pertinent to investigation at this time. Found one report on Michael MAGEAU where he had been arrested for petty theft at the Purity Store on Springs Rd. on 9-6-68, was booked for 484 PC, misd. Michael had given the alias William James JANSSEN, then his real ID discovered, address given at this time was 1214 Oakwood, Apt 12. 5x8 #214 080. Nothing in files on alias.

9am Robert MAGEAU, WM-43, 864 Beechwood, father of victim Michael, to VPD. RO and Sgt. [UNREADABLE] interviewed him after informing him of the incident. Robert could give no reason for shooting. Stated Darlene called the house quite often and had called several times on Friday asking for Michael. Unknown if she ever got hold of him until whenever it was they got together before shooting. Robert stated he had stayed the night at Kentwig Motel and has no idea how Michael and Darlene got together. Robert stated he is divorced and his wife lives in Los Angeles, also his son Steve, Michael's identical twin, has been living with the mother in L.A. for about 4-5 weeks. Robert will contact them and notify of the shooting. Robert very upset at this time and stated he was going to the hospital. Will contact the VPD later and will try to obtain any info that may help.

9:30am ID tech. John SPARKS checking vic FERRIN veh which is in the VPD basement garage, for fingerprints and other evidence. Will also develop all photos taken up to this point ASAP. (Rust)

EDR T

SUPPLEMENT

Vallejo Police Department

CRIME CLASSIFICATION ______________________ CASE NO. 243 146

7-5-69 12:10 AM Citizen-Female reports two Juveniles being shot at the Blue Rock Springs Parking Lot. Stated that they were in a brown Corvair.

A call received at 12:40 AM by unknown citizen. "I want to report a double murder. If you will go 1 mile east on Columbus Parkway to the public park you will find the kids in a brown car. They were shot with a 9 mil. Luger. I also killed those kids last year. Good-Bye (NS)

At 12:47 am Mrs JOHNSON PT&T operator called. The above call was traced to a coin operated telephone at Joe's Union, Tuolumne and Springs Road. The call was traced by Betty MAIN who se supervisor would not allow her to give a statement at this time. (ns).

12:35 AM With Sgt RUST went to the parking lot in front of Blue Rock Springs and observed a 1963 brown Corvair parked in the south east area of the lot. This Corvair had the head and tail lights on. The left blinker light was blinking front and rear. The ignition was in the on position, the transmission was in first gear, and the hand brake had not been set. The radio was playing. The door on the right side open.

In the front seat of the Corvair slumped over the steering wheel was a WFA wearing a while and blue flowered slack dress. She bleeding profusely and appeared to be badly injured. At the time the ambulance attendants arrived and removed her from the vehicle.

On the pavement at the rear of the Corvair lying at right angles to the car was a WMA. He bleeding profusely and was being assisted by Sgt CONWAY. His body was outlined with crayon and he was put in the ambulance and taken to Kaiser Hospital. Officer HOFFMAN went with the ambulance to assist the attendants.

Officers CRUZ and GUERRA detailed to make a sketch of the entire scene.

Fire Captain O'GARA and fireman WILLIAMS arrived with a fire unit with floodlights to illuminate the area in the search for physical evidence.

The WFA was identified as Darlene Elizabeth FERRIN 1300 Virginia St. Blonde, green, 5' 4", 128, dob 3-17-47. The WMA was identified as Michael Renault MAGEAU dob 10-29-49, black hair, green eyes, 6' 0", 170.

The entire area was searched but nothing of any significance found. The car was removed after being photographed to the VPD garage. It appeared that all the shots were fired from the right side of the vehicle.

Went to Kaiser Hospital and contacted Dr GORDY. He states that

SUPPLEMENT

Vallejo Police Department

CRIME CLASSIFICATION ______________________________ CASE NO. 243 146

Darlene FERRIN deceased and her body had been taken to Twin Chapels. Michael MAGEAU is in the intensive care unit. Not available for questioning Officer HOFFMAN received the clothing that had been worn by Michael. They brought to the station and put in evidence locker.

3:30 AM With ID Technician John SPARKS went to Twin Chapels and numerous photos taken of the body of Darlene FERRIN.

Received from Coroner Dan HORAN the clothing that had been worn by Darlene FERRIN 1 pair blue shoes, 1 blue and white flowered slack dress, 1 pair white pants and 1 white brassiere. These items tagged and put in ID evidence locker.

6:55 AM With Sgt RUST went to the parking lot at Blue Rock Springs. It daylight at this time. Searched the lot for physical evidence negative.

While at this location Linda Doris Del BUONO WFA 21 years 449 Cedar St phone 648-0806 arrived with her husband Steven, Linda the sister of Darlene FERRIN.

Linda states that her parents are Mr and Mrs Leo SUENNEN 130 Jordan St phone 643-1980. Darlene worked as a waitress at Terry's Magazine and Highway 40.

Linda states that a bartender who formerly worked part time at Kentwig "GEORGE" tried to date Darlene many times. States that Darlene didn't particularly like "George" but was friendly towards him but wouldn't date him. Linda states George had a pink pickup and a brown car that she believes was a Corvair. Describes George as a very neat dresser, short, stocky, dark hair. Linda states that George visited Darlene frequently, was very emotional, and would get up all tight when Darlene didn't pay too much attention to him

Linda states that some of Darlenes closest friends are:

Bobby a blonde who works at Terrys.

Lee who used to bring Darlene presents from Tia Juana.

Sue Deans cousin.

7-5-69 6:25 PM Went to Twin Chapels and contacted Dr SHARAI, pathologist, and Jim O'BRIEN, mortician. Dr SHARAI had removed to copper jacketed slugs from the body of Darlene. #1 was removed from the right second rib. This was marked by Dr SHARAI with two bars on the rim. #2 was removed from between the seventh and eight rib left and was marked with 4 bars on the rim. Darlenes body had multiple and massive injuries. See Autopsy report for complete details. The two slugs were brought to the station, labeled for identification and put in the evidence locker.

SUPPLEMENT

Vallejo Police Department

CRIME CLASSIFICATION ______________________ CASE NO. 243 146

7-5-69 7:55 PM George R. BRYANT WMA 22 years, employed at the Selby SMELTER, came to the station. George states that his father is the caretaker at Blue Rock Springs and he lives in the house that is located approximately 800 feet from the parking lot at Blue Rock Springs.

George states that at approximately 11:30 PM on the 4th his father went to bed and all the lights were turned out in the house. George couldn't sleep so he reversed the pillow on his bed and laid on his stomach and looked out the window. He could hear laughing and a few firecrackers being shot off but he couldn't see anybody, George states that approximately midnight he heard what appeared to be a gunshot. This was much louder than any of the firecrackers. A short time later he heard what appeared to be another gunshot. After another short pause he heard rapid fire of what appeared to be gunshots. He then heard a car take off at super speed and it burned rubber and was squealing its tires as it sped along the road. George not sure of its direction of travel. George states that he didn't check as it was the Fourth of July and he thought it was just someone celebrating.

8:25 PM Call received from Dr JANTZEN, Kaiser Hospital, who states that he and Dr BLACK had just finished operating on Michael MAGEAU. He states that they removed one slug from the left thigh of Michael. He has the slug in his possession and would like to personally turn it over to the VPD. Went to Kaiser Hospital and received from Dr JANTZEN the slug which was marked by Dr BLACK. Slug was in a glass bottle in some type of solution. Slug brought to the VPD. Bottle labeled and put in ID property room evidence locker.

Checked at the Union Station Springs Road and Tuolumne St and they closed at 8:25 PM 7-4-69.

11;15 PM With Sgt RUST went to 130 Jordan St and contacted Mr and Mrs Leo SUENNEN. They the parents of Darlene FERRIN. They state that to their knowledge Darlene had no known enemies. State that at times Darlene appeared to be afraid of Michael MAGEAU.

He had told Darlene that he was wanted by the FBI in New York City. He later told Darlene that he was just kidding her and had used this statement as a ruse to get acquainted with her.

7-6-69 12:02 AM Went to 864 Beechwood and contacted Carmen MAGEAU. Carmen the mother of Michael MAGEAU. She states that she is divorced from Robert MAGEAU and is presently living in southern California. When she heard that Michael had been shot she came to Vallejo on 7-5-69 and brought her two other children with her. Steven who is Michaels twin brother and a younger son. Mrs MAGEAU states that to her knowledge Michael has no known enemies and could shed no light on who might possibly have shot him. (Lynch-Rust).

John P. Lynch

At this time Steven and his brother returned to 864 Beechwood St. Steven states that he doesn't get along well with his father and approximately 3 weeks ago went to Southern California to live with his mother. Steven states that he knows Darlene and gets along well with her. Doesn't know of any enemies that Darlene or Michael might have. Steven states that he gets along well with his brother Michael and if any thing was wrong he is sure that his brother would have told him.

On Officers return to the station Steven phoned and stated that several months ago Darlene told him and his brother that "George had broken into her apartment and told her that he was going to rape her". Darlene stated that she had talked him out of it. Steven states that neither he nor his brother had taken her seriously and didn't think any more about it.

7-6-69 7:45 PM Judith Anita [REDACTED] WFA 25 years 139A [REDACTED] Court came to the station. She states that she is formerly a close friend of Darlenes when they worked together at Terrys on Highway 40. Approx. 4 months ago she went to the movies with Darlene and when they returned they stopped by the restaurant where Dean worked. Darlene asked Dean to take them to the Coronado Inn and Dean refused and they got into a family argument. Judith states that she didn't want to become involved and since then she sees Darlene infrequently. Judith states that she is now working at Terrys on Benicia Road. Judith states that she knows of no enemies that Darlene might have. States that a Bobby Ramos is a close friend of Darlenes and she may have some information. Judith states that she does not know anyone named George who may have been a friend of Darlene.

8:05 PM Robert W. MAGEAU WMA 43 years 864 Beechwood phone 643- [REDACTED] came to the station. Robert states that he did not know Darlene but she phoned Michael every day and sometimes several times a day. He stated that his ex-wife Carmen had met Darlene and approved of her. He could add nothing to assist in the investigation. States that the man that works for him Ralph [REDACTED] can be contacted at 644- [REDACTED].

(Lynch-Rust).

SUPPLEMENT

Vallejo Police Department

CRIME CLASSIFICATION ______________________ CASE NO. 243 146

7-5-69 7:10am (report written)

7-5-69 12:10am – Writer on patrol received report of shots being fired at a brown vehicle in the area of Blue Rock Springs and that the complainant [REDACTED] was waiting for officers. Upon writers arrival at the scene officer Hoffman was bending over a WMA who was lying on the ground at the right rear of a 1963 Corvair Calif Lic #CRV 209, the WMA, later identified as Michael Renault MAGEAU WMA 19 yrs d.o.b., 10-29-49, was bleeding from the mouth and had a large quantity of blood on his face and chest. As Officer Hoffman was assisting this subject writer went to the drivers side of the corvair where there was a WFA slumped over the steering wheel and appeared to have at least three bullet holes through her left arm and side, the WFA, (Later identified as Darlene Elizabeth FERRIN WFA 22yrs d.o.b., 3-17-47) was trying to say something which sounded like either "I" or "MY" to writer, these were the only words that the victim said. Writer felt the victims pulse which was very weak, at this time the victim passed out. At this time Sgt. Conway returned to scene and bent down over subject MAGEAU who was attempting to say something. Subject MAGEAU stated in response to Sgt. Conways questions that the resp was a WM young, and heavy set, MAGEAU further stated that the resp was by himself and in a brown vehicle.

Writer then returned to the vehicle to check on subject FERRIN, who was still unconscious. Writer again checked her pulse and it was very weak and her breathing was very shallow. At this time Solano ambulance arrived and writer assisted in getting her out of the corvair and into the Ambulance. After subject FERRIN was placed in the Ambulance writer then assisted in placing subject MAGEAU in the Ambulance where both victims were taken to Kaiser Hosp.

After both victims were taken to Kaiser Hosp., writer checked the area for any spent bullets, upon checking the corvair writer observed what appeared a bullet hole in the left door panel, also the victims purse (FERRIN) was on the left rear floor of the vehicle. After it was learned that Sgt. Rust and Officer Hoffman had located several spent bullets at the scene writer was requested by Sgt. Lynch to call for a tow truck and have the victims vehicle taken to the V.P.D.

A short time later A.A.A tow arrived and writer had the vehicle taken to the V.P.D., and had same placed downstairs where it was to be checked later this date for prints by I.D.

When writer first arrived at the scene the corvair which contained subject FERRIN had the head lights on, the ignition was in the on position, the radio was playing and the vehicle appeared to be in low gear. (Doug Clark) 7-5-69 8:00am)

Officers report receiving a call from KMA 818 at 12:10am, 7/5/69, of two persons shot at in the Blue Rocks Springs area. Upon arrival at Blue Springs golf course club house, RO observed a veh, traveling south on Columbus Park Way at approx. 20 mph. As RO made a U-turn at same location, veh. stopped and backed up to parking area, westside of roadway. Ad officers approached veh, 1963 Cad., 4dr ht., Blk/grey, Lic. CXB 890, a white male sub. emerged from behind the wheel and approached officers. RO asked sub. for ID. Same ID as ANDREW Y. [REDACTED] JR., 19 yrs, DOB 2/4/50, 22 [REDACTED] Ct.

As sub was removing his ID, same stated "Is this about that guy laying down back there".

RO was then contacted by Sgt. Conway, enroute to scene, and advised by RO that the victims were apparently in the parking lot area, of Blue Rocks Springs.

RO was then contacted a few min. later by Sgt Conway at location of car stop to place a hold on subjects for investigation of a felony. Sgt. Conway also instructed RO to search veh. Same searched veh. for possible weapon with neg. results.

Also in veh with [REDACTED] was a WF ID as BETTY [REDACTED], 19 yrs, DOB 1/25/50, 721 [REDACTED] St.

Both subjects were then taken to VPD after being placed under arrest for investigation of a felony, and turned over to Sgt. Odiorne.

Subject [REDACTED] veh was impounded and taken to VPD by Bobs tow service.

Officer Meyring

SUPPLEMENT

Vallejo Police Department

CRIME CLASSIFICATION ______________________ CASE NO. 243 146

Responded to scene at Blue Rock Springs, and observed scene as described in earlier reports.

Proceeded to the Kaiser Hosp. emergency ward, and was informed that the female subject, Darlene FERRIN had expired from the wounds received. That Michael MAGEAU was being treated at this time and could not be interviewed. Off. HOFFMAN at scene and had accompanied the subjects to the Hosp. in the ambulance. He detailed to stand by at the Hosp. and to interview MAGEAU if at all possible.

Proceeded to the Union Service Station at Springs Rd. and Tuolumne St. and directed ID Technicion WARICHER to the phone booth at that locale and requested that he dust same for prints.

Arrived at Sta. at 1:15 AM and began interviews with poss, witness'

Interviewed the following.

Debra [REDACTED] WFA 19 Yrs. 1909 [REDACTED] St. Ph. 642- [REDACTED]

Roger [REDACTED] WMJ 17 Yrs. 938 [REDACTED] Ave. PH. 642- [REDACTED]

Jerry [REDACTED] WMJ 17 Yrs. 938 [REDACTED] Dr. Ph. 644- [REDACTED]

Above related the story regarding their finding the victims at scene. All made written statements regarding same. Statements attached. At. approx. 2:35 AM victim FERRIN'S husband Dean to station with one Bill LEE. LEE stated that he is FERRIN'S employer and that they had just receive information from police Offs. that Mrs. FERRIN had been shot.

FERRIN informed that his wife was deceased and he became very distraught. Both FERRIN and LEE related the following.

Stated that Darlene and her sister Christina SUENNEN WFJ 15 Yrs. Had been at Mr. FERRIN's place of employment "Ceasers" in the 300 Blk of Tenn. st. at approx. 10:30 PM and at this time Darlene left, stating that she was going to take Christina home, then go home herself to 1300 Virginia st. Take her baby-sitter home, and return home herself.

Stated that at Approx 11:30 PM LEE called Darlene to ask her if she would try to find a Fire-works booth open, and to purchase some as they were going to have a party at 1300

Virg. St. after they closed "Ceasers", and had decided to have some fire-works at that time. She stated that she would try to find one and hung up. Stated that this was the last any of them had heard from her.

Stated that after they arrived at 1300 Virg. and waiting for Darlene that there was two phone calls where there was no answer on the other end.

Mr. FERRIN could shed no further light on who may have been the responsible. Stated that he would certainly call, upon receiving any further information.

Approx. 3:15 AM Interviewed Christina SUENNEN as to above, and she collaborated above story, but stated that she and her sister had gone from "Ceasers" to Terry's on Magazine St. before going home. Stated that at no time did Darlene speak to anyone other that some of the girls she works with at Terry's. Could add nothing to above. Stated that she did know victim MAGEAU through Darlene, but knew nothing about him. (Odiorne)

CRIME CLASSIFICATION Murder CASE NO. 243 146

7-5-69, 2 AM. RO was detailed by LT. Allbritton to the scene of the 187 at Blue Rock Springs parking lot to take photographs, search crime scene and dust for finger prints. Took photographs of the victims car, both interior and exterior shots taken. Did not dust for prints as it was decided to bring the vehicle to the VPD garage and have same done there. Search area for any evidence with negative results. Waited for tow truck and followed same to VPD. Took 9 pictures of Auto.

7—69, 3:45 AM. Was detailed along with Sgt Lynch to Twin Chapels to take photographs of victim Darlene E. Ferrin. At Twin Chapels took six pictures of Darlene E. Ferrin.

7-5-69, 4:45 AM Was about to print victims vehicle when LT Allbritton stated RO could do this when returning to work at 8 AM. (SPARKS)

7-5-69, 8 AM. Dusted victims vehicle in the VPD Garage. Lifted two partial prints from the door handle on [REDACTED] right side of vehicle. These tagged and placed in evidence. Also removed two slugs from vehicle. One from the left hand door. And one from the back of the front seat on drivers side. These tagged and placed in evidence locker. (SPARKS)

SUPPLEMENT

Vallejo Police Department

CRIME CLASSIFICATION ______________________ CASE NO. 243 146

7-6-69 6:45pm Sgt. RUST Rm 16 VPD

RO rec info from William [REDACTED], Dean FERRIN'S employer, as to the ID of the two girls who babysat for Darlene FERRIN, Friday, 7-4-69. Using this info RO contacted the parents of the two girls and request they bring them to the VPD. This was done and at 6:45pm in Rm16 RO interviewed the following: Pamela Key [REDACTED], WF-15, 12-10-53, 247 [REDACTED], 644-[REDACTED], and Janet Lynn [REDACTED], WF-14, 8-13-54, 406 [REDACTED], 644-[REDACTED], both accompanied by their fathers. They stated the following:

Pamela was doing the actual babysitting and this was the first time she had sat for Darlene, altho she had known Darlene slightly prior to this. Janet was just going along to keep Pamela company. Stated that at 7pm Mr. SUENNEN, Darlene's father, picked up both of them and had Darlene's sister, Christine, with him also. They were taken to Darlene's home at 1300 Virginia where they were met by Darlene. Darlene and Christine were going to the festivities downtown and Darlene said she would be back by 10pm, and left about 7:45pm. Darlene also told them she was going to go to S.F. when she got back, didn't say who with or why. While Darlene was gone a phone call was rec and a female asked to have Darlene come to the Terry's Rest. when she worked, this message relayed to Darlene when she called the house at about 9pm.

The girls stated that Darlene didn't return until about 11:30pm or shortly before that. Darlene then told them that she had changed her mind about going to S.F. and was going to have a small party when her husband got home. Darlene then spent a few minutes cleaning up the house and then she said she was going to go out and buy some fireworks and other things for the party and that she would be back by 12:30am. Darlene left the house around 11:40pm and they didn't see her again.

About 1:30am Darlene's husband and some friends came home and they told her husband what she has said and he didn't seem worried, said she's always late. Husband then took the two girls home, this shortly before 2am, and apparently was going right back home... Both girls stated they were not close to Darlene and could offer no other info. (Rust)

SUPPLEMENT

Vallejo Police Department

CRIME CLASSIFICATION ______________________ CASE NO. 243 146

7-7-69 Contacted Joseph [REDACTED] 238 [REDACTED] Ave. Vlo. 643- [REDACTED] at Kaiser Steel at Napa via Land Line and he stated that there had been a George [REDACTED] working at that location up until the 13th of June, at which time he had been laid off. Stated that he was a painter while he was working. Stated that [REDACTED] had given an address of 2118 Monroe st. Yountville Calif.

Contacted the Napa Co. S.O. and requested that an Off. from their Dept. meet with writer and Off. Blair and assist them in locating above address. Proceeded to the Napa Co. S.O. where we were met by Sgt. MUNK of that Dept. From there proceeded to Yountville where the above address was located. Parked in the front of this location was a 1964 Maroon Pont. Lic. MGW681. This registered to George [REDACTED] of Benicia Calif. This information obtained by Napa S.O. radio. While near the above address observed one WMA come from the front door of above location and walk to the side of the above Veh. and then return to the house. This subject appeared to be of the same description as George [REDACTED]. Requested Sgt. MUNK to attempt to follow up on this by contacting neighbors in an attempt to obtain more info. on subject, re. cars, friends, etc. He stated that he would do this and requested that we call him at 8:00 PM tomorrow.

(Odiorne-Blair)

SUPPLEMENT

Vallejo Police Department

CRIME CLASSIFICATION ______________________ CASE NO. 243 146

7-7-69 11:00 AM Note received from Capt BIRD stating "Mrs Peggy [REDACTED], phone 746- [REDACTED] has information regarding a Bob that matches the description of the responsible in the Blue Rock Park case. She knows the subject. Mrs Your lives in a pink house on the frontage road. One mile north of Lake Herman Road between Benicia and Cordelia".

7-7-69 3:35 PM Mr Arthur J. FERRIN and Mrs Mildred FERRIN 930 [REDACTED] St phone 644- [REDACTED] came to the station and report that shortly after 11:30 AM on 7-5-69 their telephone rang and the party on the other end of the line said nothing but they could hear deep breathing and they are sure that some one was there.

Questioned Mr and Mrs FERRIN but they could add nothing to assist in the investigation.

4:15 PM Went to 1300 Virginia St and contacted Arthur Dean FERRIN phone 643- [REDACTED]. Questioned Dean regarding "George" and he states that he only met George once. States that he formerly owned a 1951 Ford ½ ton pickup faded red in color. He decided to sell this truck and his wife mentioned it to George and he purchased the truck. When George came to the house to purchase the truck his wife introduced him to George. Describes George as 5' 8", stocky build, dark complex. Mexican appearance. Was employed as a bartender but lost his job. Dean states that Darlene worked varied shifts and he has been employed on the night shift a Caesars Palace. Dean states that on occasions George has given his wife rides to work but he has no reason to suspect that his wife was involved with George.

Officer HUSTED phoned to report that he has checked at Kentwig Lodge and GEORGE identified as George [REDACTED]. He only worked there one day and when he left he gave his address as 20 Sandy Beach Road. Stated that he could be contacted there if his services were needed.

7-7-69 TT sent to CII requesting all information on George W. [REDACTED].

7-8-69 11:40 AM Stephen Craig MAGEAU 19 years dob 10-29-49 present address 832 South Palos Verde, mothers address 2117 Grenedier Drive both Los Angeles, Calif. Presently staying at 864 Beechwood Vallejo.

Stephen states that he did not know George personally but had many conversations with Michael and Darlene concerning George. George was constantly bothering Darlene and had followed her many times. She was deathly afraid of him but was friendly towards him in an effort to keep him at a distance. On one occasion he walked into her apartment at 560 Wallace Street and told her that he was either going to rape her or get into bed with her one way or another. Darlene had told Michael about this incident and then Michael told Stephen. Darlene also told Michael that she had talked George out of causing any trouble and after some time he left the apartment. Stephen lived in Los Angeles from February to the 1st of June. He returned to Vallejo and stayed approximately 3 weeks and then returned to Los Angeles. States that he is not too familiar with what has happened lately.

Darlene often went to Blue Rock Springs with boyfriends at night. It was common knowledge amongst her friends that this was her favorite place.

4 PM Went to the Elks Club and contacted Myra [REDACTED], Office manager. She states that George W. [REDACTED] worked there on several occasions. These were special functions when extra bartenders were needed. He was never steadily employed. On his job application form when he applied for work he listed C. S. [REDACTED] SR. father, phone 237- [REDACTED]. Clayton Richard [REDACTED], Pinole and Wilbur [REDACTED] 23rd St Richmond Bar Manager. Mrs [REDACTED] describes George as 5' 8", average build, dark hair, well groomed.

TT received from CII reflects "No Record" on subject [REDACTED]. (Lynch)

SUPPLEMENT

Vallejo Police Department

CRIME CLASSIFICATION ______________________ CASE NO. 243 146

7-8-69 1:25pm Rm 28 Sgt. RUST

At VPD RO re-interviewed Jerry [REDACTED], WM-17, and Roger [REDACTED], WM-17, the two youths who, along with Debra [REDACTED], found the victims, MAGEAU and FERRIN, at Blue Rock Springs Park. Jerry and Roger gave the following statement: They, along with Debbie and in Debbie's vehicle (Rambler brown in color) had been downtown to see the festivities for the 4th of July. After this was over, at about 11pm. They decided to look for this girl that Roger knows. They drove around town and did not see her and decided to go to Blue Rock Park to look for her. They went out the freeway to Columbus Parkway and came in to the Park the back way. While they were driving in toward the Park neither boy recalls seeing any vehicle coming out, none parked along the road, nor did they pass any vehicle.

When they came to the park area it was dark and they looked for any vehicles. The only one they saw was the victims brown Corvair, same was parked in location as found by the police. They stated that when first observed the Corvair did not have any lites on. Debbie stopped the car in the road and they were trying to decide to go check the vehicle to see if Roger's girl was in it when the lite same on. They thought the occupants were going to leave and then thought they heard someone scream. Debbie backed up her car and turned to shine her high beams onto the car and then they saw a male subject on the ground beside the passenger side of the Corvair, door was open. The male was rolling around on the ground and screaming. Debbie then pulled her car up behind the Corvair and Jerry jumped out and ran up to the male and asked "are you all right?" and the male said "I'm shot and the girl's shot, get a doc." Jerry said "All right we'll get one", and the male said "hurry". Roger had jumped out of the car also and heard this talk. Neither of them looked in the Corvair and didn't see the girl. Then Jerry wanted to stay there while Debra and Roger went to get a doctor, but they insisted he come with them. They got back in the car and all three drove toward Springs R. in Vallejo and the only vehicle they saw on the drive in was a vehicle's tail lites on the Lake Herman Road turnoff. The vehicle was too far off to tell what kind it was or if it was going fast. All they could tell was that it was headed away from them. They then proceeded into Vallejo and went to 938 Castlewood, Jerry's home and called police to report what they had seen.

They all three waited there a short while and then went to Debbie's brother-in-law, Rob [REDACTED], house, he being a policeman. They were afraid the police would think it was just a hoax. [REDACTED] then called the police again and they found the police had located the car. They then went to the VPD and talked to Sgt. ODIORNE.

Both boys guess the time they were at the park as real close to midnite, possibly a little before midnite. They state the male victim did not say anything about responsible or his vehicle, only conservation was as they stared above. No other vehicles were seen other than the victim's and the one seen going away from them on Lake Herman Road. Both will call PD if any other info is obtained or if they remember anything else. (Rust)

SUPPLEMENT

Vallejo Police Department

CRIME CLASSIFICATION ______________________ CASE NO. 243 146

7-9-69-12:20am

RO interviewed a Odell R. [REDACTED] NMA of 905 [REDACTED] Street. Ph. 642-[REDACTED]. States that on the fourth of July, this the morning of between 10:30am & 11:30am he and his two year old son went for a ride in his HC with the top off. States that he was on Magizine St. and had stopped at a stop sign close to Terrys parking lot. States there were quite a few cars and that he was at the stop sign for a couple of minutes. States he observed a white girl standing by a 1963 Brn. Covair 2 dr. sport kind. States that the vehicle was parked into the parking slot at Terrys parking lot and what drew his attention to the girl was that she had on a white uniform. States that the girl had blndist redist hair.

Further states that a van was parked length ways behind the car the girl was at. Van appeared to be a faded gray in color and approx two to three years old. Mr. [REDACTED] does not know the make of the van, but is sure that it isn't a Chev. or Volkswagen. States the windshield of the van was slanted and that a white man was standing across from the girl next to the rear of the covair. Covair had the motor hood up and it appeared that the girl was looking at the motor or showing the man the motor.

Mr. [REDACTED] describes the WMA as approx 30 yrs. old, close to six feet tall with a heavy upper body build. Was wearing a drk. Jacket similar to what a beer driver wears (This Mr. [REDACTED] wording,) also subject had on gray pants. Mr. [REDACTED] also states that the white mans hair was a champane white color on the sides and combed straight back with darker streaks running thru the light hair on the sides. It appeared to Mr. [REDACTED] that the girl was showing the WN subject the motor and at this time Mr. [REDACTED] left the area and went home. (Barber)

W. Barber

SUPPLEMENT

Vallejo Police Department

CRIME CLASSIFICATION ______________________ CASE NO. 243 146

7-9-69 8:30pm Sgt. RUST & LYNCH

RO's contacted at Terry's Rest., Mag. St., a waitress named Phyllis [REDACTED], WF-30, 620 [REDACTED] St., 644- [REDACTED]. She stated she knows a subject who fits desc of resp and also drives a vehicle similar to the one desc in the newspaper. Subj name is Steve [REDACTED], 1305 [REDACTED] Dr. Stated he is 5-8, heavyset, lite brn hair and she thinks he told her once that he had bought a 9mm pistol. Phyllis stated that he sometimes acts very strange and his mother has mental problem history. Phyllis stated she didn't know Darlene FERRIN as a close friend and could give no other info as to who resp. might be. (Rust – Lynch) rst

7-13-69 9pm Rm 28 VPD Steve [REDACTED], WM-24, 7-19-44, 1305 [REDACTED] Dr., called by RO and came to station. Steve was advised of the info we had rec and gave the following statement: Steve stated he and his cousin, Gary [REDACTED] of [REDACTED] Ave., Oakland, 533- [REDACTED], and two of Gary's friends left for Antelope Creek, this near Payne's Creek and about 200 miles north of Vallejo, left Thursday nite about midnite, July 3rd and stayed there until early Sunday morning when they returned. Steve stated the only guns he owns are a Ruger .22 magnum pistol and a 30-30 rifle. Has never owned a 9mm rifle or pistol. Does not know either victim. Steve stated he owns a 65 Ford Falcon 2dr, MMK 543, blue, but drove on trip in his pickup. No one used his vehicle while he was gone. (Rust – Lynch)

7-9-69 5:20pm

Rec info from Off. and Mrs. [REDACTED] that a neighbor of their's had told them that a Mrs. [REDACTED] of 415 Los [REDACTED] Dr. told her the following story: Mrs. [REDACTED] said that her daughter Terry and her husband, Donald Lance [REDACTED], had been up to visit her over the weekend of the 4th. They live in a motel in Santa Maria. Donald and Terry were supposed to have been contacted by a subject who told them he was involved in some shootings and wanted to go back to Santa Maria with them. Donald would not have anything to do with it. Subject was unnamed by Mrs. [REDACTED].

RO and Sgt. LYNCH went to 415 Los [REDACTED] Dr. and contacted Mrs. [REDACTED] and advised her of the story given to RO. Mrs. [REDACTED] stated that her Daughter, Terry and her son-in-law, Don [REDACTED] had been up to visit and had arrived early Saturday morning, this July 5th. Stated that while they were up here that Terry and Donald told her that they had been contacted by a WM who told them he had been involved in the shooting of two people and wanted a ride to Santa Maria. Donald stated he would not have anything to do with the subj. Mrs. [REDACTED] stated that Donald had told her the subj's name but she had forgotten it. Donald said the guy was short, heavyset, owns a brown car and supposed to use dope. Mrs. [REDACTED] stated Donald and Terry returned to Santa Maria Sunday and are staying at the Caravan Motel. Mrs. [REDACTED] stated another of her daughters heard this and will contact her for more info. (Rust – Lynch)

SUPPLEMENT

Vallejo Police Department

CRIME CLASSIFICATION ______________________ CASE NO. 243 146

7-11-69

At approx. 12:30 AM talked to William H. [REDACTED] of [REDACTED] St. George St. [REDACTED], Sa. 415-687- [REDACTED] owner of the Mat Pad on Sacto. St. [REDACTED] stated he had some information reguarding the murder at Blue Rock Springs. RO with Sgt. Barber contacted Mr. [REDACTED] at the Kat Pad who stated one of his waitresses had talked to a man by the name of [REDACTED]. who told her that a subject by the name of George had told him he killed the two people at Blue Rock Spgs. and that he came in every evening before going to work at Mare Island and after he got off work and had a beer and that he should be in about 1:00 AM. Off. while waiting for [REDACTED] to showtalked to Mr. [REDACTED] who also knew George. Said he used to own the Krazy Kat at 663 San Pablo Ave. in Albany. Said George started coming into his place about Feb. of 68 and that he went out with George a few times to other bars in Albany and had a few drinks but he never knew his last name. Said George was always telling him some goof ball story about being rich but didn't drive a good car because he didn't want to show off in front of his friends. Said he lost contact when he sold his place of business. At this time [REDACTED] brought in a Linda [REDACTED] WFA 25 of 438 [REDACTED] St. 644- [REDACTED] his manager of the Kat Pad who said that this George started coming in the Kat Pad around Feb. of 69 and started brothering her like grabbing her legs when she was dancing on the bar and one night he followed her out grabbed her and threw her on the hood of his car. At this time she grabbed his hair and hit him with her fist and he turned her loose and she told him to leave her alone and quit brothering her. Said she thought he was driving a 54 or 55 chev. white of green or white over blue.

About this time the subject [REDACTED] came in and Off. had Mr. [REDACTED] bring him back to the office. Subject gave his name as Walter W. [REDACTED] of 601 [REDACTED] Ave WMA 57 phone 643- [REDACTED]. [REDACTED] stated he was a personal friend of the murdered girl's family and that he did not know this subject George and all the information he had he received from the family.

[REDACTED] also said that George used to be a steady customer of the Viking Bar in Albany. Both [REDACTED] and Linda [REDACTED] described George as per description we already have on George [REDACTED] (Blair-Barber)

SUPPLEMENT

Vallejo Police Department

CRIME CLASSIFICATION ______________________ CASE NO. 243 146

7-11-69 8 PM With Sgt RUST went to Yountville and contacted George William [REDACTED] WMA 29 years dob 1-14-46. Resides 2180 [REDACTED] St PO Box 2218 Yountville. This contact made at 8:35 PM. George is employed as a bookkeeper and Officer Manager by Harold [REDACTED] in St. Helena. He was born in Manila in the Philippine Islands. George wears glasses when reading. George described as 150, 5' 9", olive complexion, black hair, medium build slightly overweight. Brown eyes. Is married wifes name is Judith.

George was employed in the following bars in Vallejo on a part time basis. Elks, Casa De Vallejo, Kentwig, and the Fireside.

George has owned a 1956 Chevrolet blue over white, a 1951 pink Ford pickup which he purchased from Dean FERRIN and a 1964 Maroon Pontiac Bonneville in the past year. States that he has not owned a corvair and to the best of his recollection has never borrowed Darlenes.

George was employed at the Pastime Club in Benicia from January until March. He quit there March 9 and went to work for Kaiser Steel where he received 12 weeks training as a boilermaker. At the end of the training period he was laid off.

George states that he became acquainted with Darlene around the first of the year and called her Deedee. Stated that he used to tease her at Terrys and sometimes she would become angry with him. It was his practice to go to Terry's for breakfast after the bars closed at 2 AM He would then usually give her a ride home at the conclusion of her shift. Many times she would call him and ask him to give her a ride to work. He visited her at her home when she lived at the rear of the Pizza Restaurant. Doesn't know the street but it was just off the frontage road on the west side of High 40. He has never visited her home at 1300 Virginia St.

George states that he only met Darlenes husband once and that was when he bought the pickup. Denies ever threatening Darlene but does state that many times he did tease her and make her angry. States that Darlene was a very capable waitress and had many friends. States that he knew many of them by sight but doesn't know any of them by name.

George states that the last time he saw Darlene was approximately 1 ½ months ago when he stopped at Terrys with his wife to have something to eat. States that he kidded with her a little bit at that time but Darlene was kind of quiet.

George doesn't doesn't know any of Darlenes close friends but states that she usually went to the Coronado Inn when she went out. She usually went with girlfriends. (Lynch – Rust).

John P. Lynch

SUPPLEMENT

Vallejo Police Department

CRIME CLASSIFICATION ______________________________ CASE NO. 243 146

George states that he is not a citizen of the United States and he doesn't own a gun. States that he has never been to Blue Rock Springs with Darlene.

George manages a girls softball team in Yountville. On July 4th he played a game with the a team sponsored by the Napa Police Department in Napa. This game started at approximately 10:30 AM. When the game was over he returned home and took a nap. He then went to the Fair in Calistoga. Returned home at approximately 7 PM. He and his wife then went to the Fireworks Display at the Veterans Home and returned home at approximately 11PM. States that he did not leave the house after that.

George states that all during the time that he was seeing Darlene he was single and was not seriously involved with her as he knew that she was married.

(Lynch – Rust)

John P. Lynch

12:30AM 7-21-69 Received phone call from Dep. Sheriff Ben VILLARREAL who stated that he had just arrested 2 subjects and that one of them had concealed on his person a 9mm automatic.

12:40AM Sheriff's Office Vallejo. VILLARREAL states that when these two subjects were arrested, #1- Donald Warren [REDACTED], WMA, 24 yrs., 227B [REDACTED] st., was carrying at 9mm P38 automatic pistol, serial #5170, fully loaded, one bullet in the chamber.

12:45AM Questioned subject #2- James Phillip [REDACTED], WMA, 19 yrs., 526 [REDACTED] st., [REDACTED] was inst. as to his const. rights, states he understands his rights and will answer questions.

[REDACTED] states that he and [REDACTED] were only looking for a friend named "Willie", who failed to answer their knocking on his door, and were arrested as they left their house. Denies knowing that [REDACTED] had the gun. Does admit hearing the statement by [REDACTED], after the officers found the gun, that he would be booked for murder.

1:10AM While [REDACTED] was being booked and completely searched, a pistol was found inside his undershorts, this was a .32 revolver, 2" bbl., Iver Johnson, serial #B-9650.

1:15AM Donald Warren [REDACTED], WMA, was inst. as to his const. rights., states he understands his rights and will answer questions. Admits having this P38 in his possession, states he was going to have a fight with "some guy" and that this guy had a shotgun.

States he borrowed this gun from an ex-con in S.F., Sunday, 7-20-69, refuses to name this subject.

[REDACTED] denies any knowledge of this murder, states he went to San Jose July 4th and did not return until July 5th.. [REDACTED] to be booked by S.O..

ATTENTION I.D. A member of the Sheriff's Office will pick up a copy of this report, our evidence and take same to CII, along with the P38 for comparison tests. (Allbritoon-Lammon)

7-23-69 Bullets and empty cases mailed to CII for analysis.

7-23-69 [UNREADABLE]

(Waricher)

REQUESTING AGENCY NO.	STATE OF CALIFORNIA	C.I.I. Case Number
243146	DEPARTMENT OF JUSTICE	37-F-4910

BUREAU OF CRIMINAL IDENTIFICATION AND INVESTIGATION

P. O. Box 1859, Sacramento 95809

To: Jack E. Stiltz
Chief of Police
Vallejo, California 94590
Attn: Capt. Bird

Copies To:

Following is a report concerning physical evidence examinations requested by your office. In any future correspondence regarding this case please use the C.I.I case number appearing at the top of this report. If court testimony is required, please notify the Bureau at least two weeks in advance whenever possible.

A. L. Coffey

A.L. COFFEY

Chief of Bureau

PHYSICAL EVIDENCE EXAMINATION REPORT

TYPE OF CASE		REQUESTING AGENCY
187 PC		VALLEJO POLICE DEPARTMENT
SUBJECT		
[REDACTED]: Donald Warren/[REDACTED]: James Phillip		FERRIN: Darlene (V)
EXHIBITS RECEIVED FROM	DATE	TIME
E. HALSTEAD #149	7-22-69	11:15 AM
REFERENCES		
CII EVIDENCE LOCKER #12		

The following exhibit was removed from CII Evidence Locker #12 by the undersigned on July 24, 1969 at 1:30 PM:

9. a) P38 auto pistol.
   b) Clip.

On July 24, 1969 at 11:30 AM the following items of additional evidence were received by Registered Mail #41991 from Capt. Bird of the Vallejo Police Department:

1. Seven empty cases – 9mm.
2. Lead object and jacket
3. a) Bullet 9mm.
   b) Bullet 9mm.
4. Bullet, 9mm.
5. Bullet, 9mm.
6. Bullet, 9mm.
7. a) Bullet 9mm.
   b) Bullet 9mm.
8. Two empty cases, 9mm.

Date of Report: Examinations by: Continued -

Title:

[UNREADABLE] [UNREADABLE] [UNREADABLE]

CRIME CLASSIFICATION Murder CASE NO. 243 146

8-1-69 Anonymous letter received by Times Herald Paper. See

5-8 245 834. (jmc)

STATS

INDEXED

8-7-69 12:45 PM Detailed by Captain BIRD to go to the Stockton PD and contact Lt James RILEY. He has received information from a resident of Stockton that a David A BAGANO [REDACTED] who formerly lived with them in Stockton has an emotional problem and when upset drew cryptograms.

1:20 PM At the Fairfield Probation Office contacts Supervising Probation Officer Paul DENNAN. He states that David has been in various foster homes since his mother died. His father is Santos [REDACTED] of P.O. Box [REDACTED] Vacaville. Phone 448- [REDACTED].

Paul states that they have been looking for David in regards to a check for $20.00 that was issued by David bounced. This was in Vacaville. David is now 18 dob 5-21-51 and is no longer under the custody of the Probation Office. Had an address of 1017 [REDACTED] St in Vacaville but they have been unable to locate him at that address. No warrant has been issued and the case is being handled by Officer MALLORY of the Vacaville PD their case 69-13 2450.

Paul states that David formerly lived in Benicia. Appeared to be mild mannered, stable, no custody trouble, and had no girlfriend trouble. Has a Honda.

3:10 PM At the Stockton PD contacted Lt James RILEY. He reports that a Mr and Mrs JAMES L. [REDACTED] 1107 [REDACTED] Road Stockton phone 478- [REDACTED] formerly had custody of David A. [REDACTED]. While living with Mr and Mrs [REDACTED] David wrote cryptograms. He presented a copy of these cryptograms and a copy of David [REDACTED] handwriting.

4:10 PM Went to 1107 [REDACTED] Road and contacted Mr and Mrs James L. [REDACTED]. They state that David [REDACTED] was a foster child in their home from May of 1968 until February 1969.

Mrs [REDACTED] states that shortly before Christmas David was in Vallejo to attend the funeral of his brother who had been killed in Vietnam. Believes that he was in the Vallejo area at the time of the murders on Lake Herman Road, December 20, 1968. At that time David was given a gun that was the property of his brothers. David pointed out a gun that is in a gun rack in the [REDACTED] home as being similar to the gun that was his brothers property. This is a .33 Cal rifle but Mrs [REDACTED] has never seen the gun that David has.

Mrs [REDACTED] describes David as being a youth who couldn't discuss his problems with anyone. When belligerent, angry or upset he would sit and stare. Would write messages in code. Was very dependent, violent in nature. When he returned from the Vallejo area after his brothers funeral and the murders David regressed badly and seemed to be going down hill. He ran around with a group that mixed in narcotics but to Mrs [REDACTED] knowledge David did not get involved in narcotics.

John V. Lynch

SUPPLEMENT

Vallejo Police Department

CRIME CLASSIFICATION Murder CASE NO. 243 146

When David returned to Stockton he stated several times that he knew the girl that had been murdered on Lake Herman Road had spoken to her and that she was very pleasant to talk to. Mrs [REDACTED] gave RO a photo of David.

8-8-69 Mrs [REDACTED] phoned to report that she had received a letter from David and that he is presently in the army and is stationed at Fort Lewis Washington. States that his address is David [REDACTED] Pvt RA 189-35-809 Co E Bn 4 BDE 2 P1Pn 3 Fort Lewis Washington 98433.

6:35 PM Received a phone call from George MURPHY, SF Chronicle who stated that he had received a letter from Donald HARDEN 54 [REDACTED] St Salinas, California. In the letter Donald had broken the code and sent his work sheets to the Chronicle. Probation Office notified.

Went to San Francisco and received from George MURPHY the work sheets and the message contained in the cryptograms. The message is as follows

I LIKE KILLING PEOPLE BECAUSE IT IS SO MUCH FUN IT IS MORE FUN THAN KILLING WILD CAME IN THE FOREST BECAUSE MAN IS THE MOST HONGERTUE ANIMAL OF ALL TO KILL SOMETHING ERYETHEYO A THRILLING EXPERIENCE IT IS EVEN BETTER THAN GETTING YOUR ROCKS OFF WITH A GIRL THE BEST PART OF IT I ATHAE WHEN I DIE I WILL BE REBORN IN PARADICE AND ALL THE I HAVE KILLED WILL BECOME MY SLAVES I WILL NOT GIVE YOU MY NAME BECAUSE YOU WILL TRS TO SLOI DOWN OR ATOP MY COLLECTING OF SLAVES FOR MY AFTERLIVE EEEE RIET EMETH HPITI

Called Mr and Mrs HARDEN and they states that this is an accurate deciphering of the cryptogram. The message checks out against itself in all respects.

8-10-69 1:40 PM Call received from a Robert H. [REDACTED] 345 [REDACTED] St San Francisco who stated he decoded the remaining portion of the cipher as follows: THE TIP I'M ROBERT E EEEE. COON fells that the four E's may stand for a name such as FORESE or FOURIEs. (Bawart).

8-10-69 1:55 PM Call received from a Fred [REDACTED] Stanford Research Center Menlo Park who 0states the conscept that persons killed with be the killers slaves in the life here-after originates in South East Asia and particularly in Mindanao in the Southern Philippines. [REDACTED] feels that possibly the responsible will either be of South East Asian extraction or have knowledge of the area. (Bawart).

8-11-69 Letter received from Mrs. J. L. [REDACTED] 1107 [REDACTED] Road Stockton, Calif. Mrs [REDACTED] enclosed a letter that she had received from David [REDACTED] also enclosed a photo of David in Armey uniform.

An anonymous letter, post marked San Francisco, received. This letter contained a card which enclosed a "key" which writer hoped will be beneficial in connection with the cipher letter writer. The "key" is the solution to the cryptograms that appeared in the papers. The "key" also contained a set of alternatives to some of the symbols and letters that appeared in the cryptogram. Copy of this "key" will be sent to Donald HARDEN for possible decoding of unscrambled letters in the original cryptograms. Letter went to the FBI for fingerprints.

8-12-69 Called Lt FLANDERS, Atherton PD, and he states that one of the local residents had unscrambled the 18 letters that do not seem to conform to the rest of the cryptogram. Translated these letters say "ROBERT EMET THE HIPPI". Lt Flanders states that he had the working sheets of the translator and he will forward them to the VPD.

8-12-69 Anonymous phone call received y the desk which stated that a John [REDACTED] WMA very big 47-49 years may be a suspect in this case. [REDACTED] writes messages about killing, religion and poems etc. This man loves to hunt and has been a patient at Napa State Hospital. A Captain THOMPSON of the Alameda PD may have some information about [REDACTED].

Called Cap THOMPSON 514 422 1220 and he states that he knew [REDACTED] but has had no contact with him since 1960. He has been arrested several times in Alameda. States that [REDACTED] was 31 years in 1959. CII # 498 069 FBI 358 161 A. States that [REDACTED] at one time used the name John M. STUHLSATZ.

Search of VPD Files reflect no record on John [REDACTED] or John M. STUHLSATZ.

Received from Captain BIRD a letter from Dr. D. C. B. MARSH the

John P. Lipck

President of the American Cryptograph Association. Dr MARSH also enclosed a list of the Association members in the bay area.

8-12-69 Anonymous letter received post marked Palo Alto enclosing a newspaper clipping from the San Francisco Examiner & Chronicle suggesting that the last 18 letters were a telephone number 1 digit missing. Checked VPD Directory and no such number listed. 6 3 2 1 2 4.

6:10 PM Mrs PEGGY [REDACTED] 833 [REDACTED] St phoned to report that she had read about the cryptograms in the newspaper and observed the way the letter with the cryptograms was signed. States that her ex-husband John Francis [REDACTED] signed some of the letters that he wrote with a circle and cross hairs.

Went to 833 York St and received from Mrs [REDACTED] a copy of an accident report that [REDACTED] had printed. Also received a partial photograph of him. Describes him as WMA 24 5' 11", 135, brown hair, brown eyes, ruddy complexion. States that at the present time he is a hippy in San Francisco. Has been arrested in San Mateo County for Grand Theft and Armed Robbery. Doesn't know his present address.

8-13-69 Letter received from Mrs Jean B. [REDACTED] 6 [REDACTED] Ave #7C San Francisco, Calif. 94122. Mrs [REDACTED] had deciphered the last 18 letters in the cryptogram. "Before I meet them I pity them". SEE letter for method used. (Lynch).

8-18-69 10AM

Letter received by Captain Bird from a subject whose signature appears to be Vaughn BAL- unable to ascertain last two letters in last name. Copy of letter attached in which subject thinks he has broken code in recent cryptograms mailed to bay area papers concerning recent murders in this area. He is of the opinion that signature on code letter is ETTORE [REDACTED]. Stated a subject by this names resides at [REDACTED] Street, Benicia.

10:30AM

Contacted Captain Pitta, Benicia P.D. [REDACTED] family well known to him personally. Father, Ettore, is retired from Mare Island and is approximately 70 years of age. Two boys in family, elder son named Dennis and approximately 30. Is married and known as a good citizen as is all the family. Younger son is named David who is 20-21. David served in US Army and has been discharged for approximately one year. Drives a blue GTO, about a 67 model. Physical description WMA, 5-8, 160, brn, & brn. No record on either boy.

11:30AM

Contacted Pamela Grant, 117 Jordan St., sister of murdered Farrin girl. Pamela was asked if she knew anyone her sister associated with named [REDACTED]. She stated she was baby sitting at her sister's apt. a few months prior to the murder when she received a phone call from a male who asked to speak to her sister. He was told that sister was not at home and stated it was very important that Charleen meet him as soon as possible. Left his name for sister to contact him and Mrs. Grant stated she thought he gave the name of Dave [REDACTED]. (It appears to RO that power of suggestion might possibly have influenced Mrs. Grant to unintentionally connect [REDACTED]'s name with this sometime prior phone call). Mrs. Grant informed her sister of call and sister said she did not want to have anything to do with subject and to just forget it. Mrs. Grant suggested that RO also contact her younger sister Christina Suenner, 130 Jordan for possible information she might have on murdered sister's friends.

12:00 Noon

Contacted Christina, WFJ 16, at her home. She stated she did not recognize name but that a WMA had come to her sister's apt. while she was baby sitting who drove a blue GTO, late model. This person approx. 30, 5-8, 165-170, dark brown hair, casual dress. This man asked to see her sister and when told she was not home left the area. Did not recall name, if in fact name given.

Capt. Bird advised signature on letter received from him is Vaughn [REDACTED]

(Mulanax)

8-23-69 Lt George LITTLE, Benicia PD, phoned to report that a WM came into the Benicia PD and put a handwritten note on the counter and left. Lt LITTLE states that the WM gave the name Perry [REDACTED] and then walked out. Appeared to be very agitated and upset. With Sgt RUST went to the Benicia PD and received the handwritten note. Copy attached. No valid reason in the note to support the allegations of Perry [REDACTED] in connecting the person mentioned with the murder of Darlene FERRIN. States that the mans name is "Rocky."

Lt LITTLE states that Benicia PD files reflect no mention of Perry [REDACTED]. Describes him as 6' 1", 16-18 years, blonde hair, blue eyes, wearing a blue levi jacket.

Lt LITTLE states that he knows a man as described by Perry [REDACTED]. This is Rocky [REDACTED] and is employed as a cook on a tug boat in Benicia. (Lynch-Rust).

Search of VPD files relects no record or mention of Perry [REDACTED].

Copy of letter to Sgt Les LUNDBLAD SO.

8-26-69 9:30 AM Captain TOWNSEND and Sgt ROBERTSON Napa PD ame to the station. They had with them 17 5 x 8 paper that contained quite a few handwriting similarities as those in the letters that were written to the San Francisco Examiner, San Francisco Chronicle and the Vallejo Times Herald. The handwriting samples on the 5 x 8 cards were written by a Glenn Wyland [REDACTED] while he was an inmate of Napa State Hospital.

The anonymous letter that had been written to the Benicia PD, two samples of James A. [REDACTED] signature, an accident report that had been filled out by John F. [REDACTED] III, a letter written by David A. [REDACTED] sent to CII to be compared with the letters that were written to the newspapers. (Lynch).

8-29-69 Report received from Agt. BARRUS FBI re the letter that was received by the Times Herald Editor and referred to the FBI for a lab check. This the letter that started "This is ZODIAC". Report indicates a latent print was found on Page2 and another on Page 3 of the letter, and will be retained for comparison with any suspects prints that we may obtain. The report also indicates the paper used is sold by Woolworth Stores. (Bird) mds

SUPPLEMENT

Vallejo Police Department

CRIME CLASSIFICATION ______________________ CASE NO. 243 146

9/1/69 11:00pm

RO was contacted at the Station by subject ID as GORDON ARTHUR [REDACTED] JR, WM, 21 yrs, DOB 5/15/48, 4639 [REDACTED] St. Fremont, assigned to the Navel Sub-school in New London Connecticut, and is on leave at this time for approx one week. Subject is the person aforementioned in this report of being a friend of DARLENE FERRIN. GORDON gave RO the following statement:

Stated that he was on leave from the Navy after being released from the Naval Schools Command Nuclear Power School in Idaho Falls, Idaho. Came to Fremont where his parents lived and then came up to Vallejo and decided to stop by TERRY's restaurant to see DARLENE FERRIN and was informed by the waitress that she had been killed and that the police would like to talk to him. This is when he came to the station. GORDON stated that he first met DEE at TERRY's on Magazine St in Dec, 1968, while she was working. Stated she was very friendly. About one month after they met, he stated that they walked up and down the beach and talked some, she being very friendly towards them. GORDON stated that after this they went out on a few dates, and that he would sometimes pick her up after work and take her out for awhile and then would drive her home. GORDON stated that he was going to be transferred to the Idaho Falls Nuclear Power School in Feb, and that around the end of January or the first part of Feb he had picked up DEE at work at approx 1am at TERRY's and they went out to Blue Rock Springs for a short tie and that he brought her home around 1:30-2:00am. States that she insisted on him coming into the house and meeting her husband. This would be the apt on Lincoln Road West, by JACKS Hangout. GORDON stated that she wanted him to meet her husband and that he finally went in and was introduced to her husband who was very friendly towards him. Stated that he was in the house painting at the time. GORDON stated he then left shortly after this.

He stated the next time he saw DEE was either one of two days before he left for IDAHO falls, and he went and picked DEE up after she had gotten off work at her house. Stated she had gotten off early, and that her husband knew that she was going out with GORDON. Stated they went to some dance place in San Francisco or Oakland and that he brought her home around 1am. She had left her baby at her mothers house, and also GORDON stated that he went in and met her parents that night. GORDON stated that DEE had told him that she wanted to leave her husband and go with him to Idaho Falls, but that GORDON talked her out of it for the better of her baby, as the baby had a good home at this time and he could not afford it. GORDON stated that after he got to Idaho Falls he received two or three letters, from DEE, and in one of the letters she stated that she wanted him to call her. Stated that he did call her and over the phone she said that she thought she was pregnant. GORDON stated that he told her he would come and see her in May when he was on leave from the Navy. Stated that he received one more letter from her, and it said she had been in the hospital for a short time but did not state the reason. GORDON thought that possibly she had been pregnant and went and got abortion somewhere. GORDON stated at this time that he decided not to have anything to do with DEE and not to see her again. In May

When he got off leave he did not even come to Vallejo, and went home to his home in Fremont and did not come up to see DEE at all or did not contact her. GORDON stated that when he got off leave he returned to IDAHO Falls and did not see her or did not hear from her again. Stated he has not seen her since February when he left, and has only talked to her once or twice on the phone, and only wrote one or two letters to her. GORDON stated that he felt that their relationship was more serious on her part than on his, and he did not consider it a lasting thing. GORDON also stated that he did not at any time send her any money, nor sent any type of correspondence, or ask her to come back to Idaho Falls with him. GORDON could no further info, advised RO that he would be at his parents home in Fremont until the end of the week and then was going to drive back to New London Connecticut. Stated that he would contact the Police Department in Vallejo if he was able to come up with anymore info at all. Interview terminated at this time and GORDON left.

(Sgt. Rust/oh)

SUPPLEMENT

Vallejo Police Department

CRIME CLASSIFICATION ______________________ CASE NO. 243 146

9-9-69 12:55 PM Anonymous letter received "Badly rusted beat up Corvair getting a bright green paint job at 909 [REDACTED]. Owner about 25, 5' 9" over 200 lbs brownish thinning hair sloppy fat, strange acting. Lives with parents. Calif BTU 179."

1:03 PM With Sgt KRAMER observed this car parked in the Mobile Station at the corner of Georgia and Monterey Sts. BTU 179. Car has maroon top lt grn hood and dark green panels. Car is a 1963 Corvair 2 door.

Checked the registration of the car and it reflects that Patrick [REDACTED] 909 [REDACTED] St. Went to that address and contacted Patrick Dennis [REDACTED] WMA 23 years dob 3-19-46. Is employed as a stevedore at Port Chicago.

Patrick states that on 7-4-69 he went to the fireworks display at the waterfront and from there he went home. States that he parked his car in front of the house at approximately 11:30 PM and did not leave after that time. Patricks mother Dolores was present and verified Patrick's statement. Patrick doesn't own a gun and he did not know Darlene FERRIN. Patrick stated that the car can be started without a key but he is sure that no one else used the car as it was in the same place in the morning as it was the night before. This car apparently has a bd oil leak as the street in front of the house showed oil on the pavement as though the car was leaking oil. (Lynch-Kramer).

3:55 PM With Sgt RUST went to 607 Falcon Ave and contacted Bobbie RAYMOS WFA 27 years dob 10-4-41. Is employed as a waitress at Terrys. Bobbie states that Marlene had a friend who was in the Navy or was stationed at the Maritime Academy. States that this man was a WMA approximately 21 years and was sent to Idaho for some training or to go to school. Describes him as 5' 1'", husky, curly hair. Before he left he made arrangements with Marlene that as soon as he could save enough money he was going to send her enough money so she could join him. States that Marlene did receive letters from him but doesn't know if he sent her any money. States that this mans name was "Robbie" "Rowdy" or "Gordon". Doesn't know what kind of a car he owned. Marlene did go to San Francisco with him.

Bobby states that the last time she saw George was approximately 11 months ago. States that he came in one night with a girl. Sometime previous to that he had been in almost every night. States that he drove Marlene to work many times.

The only other close friend that Marlene had was a Richard who drove a white Cougar. Describes him as 6' 0" slender.

Bobbie states that a Phyllis [REDACTED], waitress at Terrys, may have some information. (Lynch-Rust).

John P. Lynch

9-29-69 9AM

RO detailed by Captain BIRD to contact Mr. Warren [REDACTED], Principal Springtown Junior High.

At this location met with Mr. [REDACTED] and Vice-Principal Wes [REDACTED]. Both subjects expressed concern that responsible in this case might very possibly be a former student named CHRISTOPHER DAVID [REDACTED]. [REDACTED] described as WMA DOB 4-25-51, 5-10 – 6 ft. 180-185, bushy blonde hair. During the period [REDACTED] attended Springtown J.H. he exhibited numerous acts of behavior that led both Mr. [REDACTED] and Mr. [REDACTED] to believe that he could be capable of this crime. Stated [REDACTED] had an I.Q. well above average but that his attitude towards other students appeared anti social. He had no contact with the opposite sex and appeared to be a person dominated by his mother's influence. His mother died with in the past year. [REDACTED] now lives with his father and younger brother at 455 [REDACTED] Drive. The father has not re-married and is employed as a salesman pharmaceutical firm.

Mr. [REDACTED] related on one occasion [REDACTED] lost a cap off his tooth during gym class. He became so upset that he started to bang his head against the side of a building. Teachers had to physically restrain him from doing serious injury to himself. From the explanation he finally gave Mr. [REDACTED], [REDACTED] seemed to fear what his mother would do because he had lost the cap off his tooth.

On another occasion [REDACTED] was alleged to have attacked a much smaller Negro juvenile who promptly punched him in the face, thus ending the fight. [REDACTED]'s attitude was sullen and withdrawn after this fracas.

His entire two years at the school were marked by anti social acts. Numerous incidents in which teachers had unpleasant contacts with both parents because of trouble [REDACTED] had encountered at school.

After graduation from Springtown Barry [REDACTED] Hogan Sr. High.

10:30 AM

RO drove by 455 [REDACTED] Drive. Two vehicles parked in front at this time. One was a gold colored late model Ford 4 dr. se., license XAP 275. This vehicle parked in driveway. In front of residence was a blue 4 dr. sedan, Ford, fairly late model, -license MGW 447. (Note: Page #6 this report states Deputy Villareal, Solano CO. S.O. observed a blue 1967 Ford sedan parked in lot near where murder vehicle (victim's) found. Time given as shortly prior to midnight 7-4-69.) License information requested from DMV on both above mentioned vehicles.

11:15AM

With Sgt. Thacker contact Vice-Principal Joe [REDACTED] at Hogan Sr. High. Mr. [REDACTED] was aware that [REDACTED] was considered a possible suspect through conversations he had had with [REDACTED] and [REDACTED].

He was asked if [REDACTED] had done anything during his attendance at Hogan which would cause him to think he could be capable of committing a crime of violence. Mr. [REDACTED] stated he was a loner, did not mix well with other students and was unpopular with others at school. While at Hogan [REDACTED] did not present any particular problem but again school authorities had trouble with his parents. Mr. [REDACTED] stated [REDACTED] had an I.Q. of approximately 175.

Obtained pictures of following students who graduated from Hogan last year. Pictures pasted on cardboard, RO blocked off names. Pictures in following series:
#1 Richard [REDACTED]
#2 Chris [REDACTED]
#3 Tom [REDACTED]
#4 Edd [REDACTED]
#5 Mike [REDACTED]

Also obtained a sample of [REDACTED]'s handwriting from personal jacket.

9-29-69 1:30 PM

Attempted to contact Michael Mageau at 864 Beechwood Ph. 643-3939. Writer was informed by his father that Michael had moved to 1813 Weymouth Avenue, Apt. "A" San Pedro, California 90732. Elder Mageau requested that this information be kept confidential.

With permission of Captain Bird letter sent to Mageau at this address with pictures of above mentioned subjects enclosed, requesting him to attempt identification. Return of pictures requested. Pictures had names removed and numbered in above sequence.

(Mulanax)

[UNREADABLE]

10-1-69 9:30 AM Information received that a Tommy SOUTHERN, WMA, DOB 1-13-44, 73", 210 lbs., brown hair, blue eyes, living at 1117 Sutter St. could be the responsible in this case.

Tommy and his wife, [REDACTED], were married approximately three years ago, and last July they had marital troubles and [REDACTED] became mentally disturbed and had to be committed to Napa State Hospital on 6-4-69 by the VPD, see 5x8 #240919.

[REDACTED] has allegedly stated that her husband was sexually impotent and that Tommy used an imitation penis to have sexual activity with [REDACTED], and that he drugged her and also used a salve to prolong the activity, [REDACTED] also related that he, Tommy, used physical violence on her while in the act of love making.

The informant has been in [REDACTED]'s apartment which was located at the southwest corner of Tuolumne & Redwood Sts. and while there observed many sexually oriented books and pictures of naked women in the apartment bedroom. Also observed was a false penis attached to a waist belt in the bedroom. Also observed in the living room were many books pertaining to Astrology.

In conversations with [REDACTED], the informant stated that [REDACTED] stated that her husband believed in reincarnation and that "she would be his slave in the hereafter," and that "he believed that only those that are strong would survive."

[REDACTED] is now allegedly mentally disturbed and the doctor at Napa State Hospital stated he doubted she could ever return to normal.

Tommy reportedly drives a 1968 Plymouth, Lic. VLZ 911, black vinyl over bronze, and also drives a blue Honda motorcycle.

Info developed through Mare Island PD Investigation Division, Bill [REDACTED], that SOUTHERN works the swing shift at Mare Island in Shop 56 as a pipefitter, and that he is off on weekends.

The informant stated she was informed by [REDACTED] that her husband, Tommy, had a hand gun. Also that Tommy had turned the gas stove on in the apartment and left his wife in the apartment asleep. Stated she found [REDACTED] in the apartment with the burners on and not lit.

Tommy SOUTHERN reportedly wears black leather desert boots with a buckle instead of laces. (Refer to the Berryessa murder).

SOUTHERN wears sunglasses, but is not known to wear prescription glasses.

Interview terminated at 11:00 a.m. (Nilsson)

3:30 PM Employment forms with handwriting & printing of Southern obtained from M.I. Invest. & to be checked by FBI against the writing that appears on the cryptograms. Photo of Southern also obtained.

10-1-69 5:00 PM SOUTHERN's habits were checked by interviewing neighbors at 1119 & 1117A Sutter. Both families stated that Southern works the swing shift and has only occasional visitors. No female visitors seen at Southern's home. Both families stated that to their knowledge Southern was not home on the weekend of Sept. 27 & 28. Sothern is known to be gone from his residence quite often on the weekends.

RO & Sgt. Mulanax observed the suspect in a garage on the north side of Capitol St. at Marin working on his blue motorcycle. The suspect apparently rents the garage to store his motorcycle.

The suspect apparently did not report for work this date. Mare Island Invest. will follow up & forward work record of suspect as soon as possible.

TT sent to FBI Headquarters, Wash. D.C. Attn. Latent Print Dept. as follows: Please compare latents obtained from FBI Latent Case A-10042 against prints of Thomas L. Southern, WMA, DOB 1-13-44, San Antonio, Texas. Physical desc. 73", 210 lbs., brown, blue, Served USN prior to 1967. Since that date civilian employee Mare Island Naval Shipyard. Please reply by TT. Refer our case 243146. Also request copy of Jack E. Stiltz, COP VLO /Det. Sgt. Mulanax/tm"

Reply to above rec'd:
1 FBD 10-2-69 1:00 AM
Re ur radiogram 10-1-69, your case 243146, latest fingerprints this case not identical fingerprints Thomas Leonard Southern, born 1-13-44, Navy Service 5987707, who may be identical suspect named ur rad. No palm prints here for Southern. Hoover Director FBI Wash. D.C."

10-2-69 12:00 PM

RO contacted the Mayor of Daisy, Arkansas, and he will contact Mr. & Mrs. Ashley and have them phone RO.

Copy of Southern's leave application and job application forms along with the three cryptogram letters sent to the FBI Lab this date for handwriting analysis.

A copy of Southern's leave and sick leave record for 1968 & 1969 from Mare Island attached.

TT sent to CII requesting record on SOUTHERN. (Nilsson)tm

Vlo

227 CII 10-2-69 Crim

[UNREADABLE] Vlo Ref Det Sgt. Nilsson

[UNREADABLE] 1 Vlo 10-2-69 Find no record our files on Thomas L. Southern as given.

CII WANTED PERSONS [UNREADABLE] JONES 1343 PDT (mds)

SUPPLEMENT

Vallejo Police Department

CRIME CLASSIFICATION Murder CASE NO. 243 146

10/3/69 – 9:40 pm

The following subjects came to the station to give information regarding a suspect in the 187.

Subjects were: Mary R. [REDACTED], WFA, 40 yrs., of 141 [REDACTED]., Benicia, ph. 745-3648 and Freddie [REDACTED], WMA, 33 yrs., of [REDACTED] St., Benicia, 745-3077.

The above state that they were in the Redwood Inn at approx. 10:00pm approx. 10 months ago when this subject came in and sat down on the steel beside them and started talking. Subject indicated that he had gotten back from Viet Nam 5-6 months ago, that they had taught him how to kill and that he was an expert shot and, also, that he had been in the Psycho Ward since he had been back, however, at this time he was a Postman. Apparently his first name was Jimmy. They did not know if he was working in Vallejo or Napa.

Stated that this subject bought 4-5 rounds of drinks for the whole bar until the bartender refused to accept anymore money from him. He just kept rambling on about various things, not making any sense about anything.

Mrs. [REDACTED] stated that she got up and went to the Rest Room and that when she came out of the Rest Room this subject was standing with his hands on the doorframes of the door when she came out the door automatically closed and pushed her toward him. Stated that he put his hand over her mouth and one hand to her throat and told her not to make any sound or he would kill her, however, he stated he would rather kill both of them at the same time. At this time, she stated, an unknown subject came near where they were standing and that subject known as Jimmy dropped his hand from her mouth and throat and told her that if she made a sound he would kill her instantly. When she went back to sit down with Freddie, the subject advised her not to tell him anything about it or her would kill them both right then. She stated she went back to her seat by Freddie and Freddie wanted to know what was wrong as she had been crying. She stated that she could not tell him at that time but that she would tell him later. At this time they both got up and left and went to their car and got away from the area as fast as they could.

Freddie stated that they had almost forgotten all about the incident until he saw the composite drawing in the paper of the suspect and this refreshed his memory of this subject at the Redwood Inn. Stated this subject was in his twenties, about 6-1, 180 lbs to 190 lbs, brown eyes and brown hair. Stated that a song was playing on the jukebox which he stated he could not stand as he wanted to do mean things when he heard this song. (blair-ns)

10-7-69 Information received from Sgt BAWART that a Pat [REDACTED] has a tattoo on his forearm of crosshairs and a circle. [REDACTED] described as 6' 2" heavy build, rides a motorcycle and live in Benicia. States that he frequents Mr Ed's on Redwood, St.

Called Sgt Pierre BIDOU, Benicia PD, and he states that subject is David Patrick [REDACTED] WMA 21 years DOB 1-9-48. Weighs 240, Brown hair, brown eyes, heavy build, 6' 6". Possibly has a home made tattoo on his right forearm. Went to the Benicia PD and received a mug shot of [REDACTED]. His parents reside at 63 [REDACTED] Benicia. Is well known to Benicia PD Officers and has been arrested on a Marijuana violation.

4:05 PM Phone call placed to Hal [REDACTED] 689- [REDACTED] Concord, Security Officer Sears Roebuck. He states that one of the employees at Sears saw the composite of the murderer at Lake Berryessa on TV. This composite strongly resembles a person that he went to school with in San Francisco. The employee has a yearbook with a photo and a sample of handwriting of this person.

Went to Sears Roebuck in Concord and received a yearbook dated 1959 George Washington High School. In this yearbook is a photo of Stephen [REDACTED] who resembles the composite. Also there is a lengthy note to the owner of the yearbook Dave [REDACTED]. (Lynch).

John P. Lynch

10-7-69 Letter received post marked San Mateo signed "A good Citizen". The letter states that the writer has a strong feeling of ESP. While having these feelings the writer writes with a pencil. On this occasion while thinking of the code letters the pencil wrote "Go to 56 Beach Street, I get the name Jerry, perhaps he knows people or his name is [REDACTED]".

City Directory lists no Jerry [REDACTED]. Beach Street starts in the 1100 Block. Beechwood Street starts in the 700 Block. (Lynch)

Letter received post marked Vallejo containing a composite of the possible responsible in the Lake Berryessa murder. Written on the composite was "Looks like Mitch [REDACTED] of Napa-works at Mare Island X51 soft spoken under 6' on the chubby side about 190 likes to hunt".

Called Bill AMICK, Chief of Detectives MI, and he states that this is Mitchell L. [REDACTED] WMA 33 years dob 9-25-36 resides 1481 [REDACTED] phone 226- [REDACTED] Napa, Calif. Works on the swing shift at Mare Island.

TT sent to CII requesting mug shots and rap sheets on Stephen [REDACTED] and David [REDACTED]. (Lynch).

Phoned Capt TOWNSEND, Napa SO, and he given the information concerning [REDACTED]. (Lynch)

John P. Lynch

CRIME CLASSIFICATION ____________________ CASE NO. 243 146

10-6-69 Information received from Richard [REDACTED], Springstown B of A, that the flyer on James M. [REDACTED] FBI 359 729 F resembles the composite of the subject wanted in the killings at Lake Berryessa. May also be the subject wanted for the murder at Blue Rock Springs.

Obtained FBI Flyer I. O. 4316 concerning James Michael [REDACTED] Jr. He wanted by the FBI for "Interstate Flight-Murder" also wanted by the Boston Massachusetts Police Department for Murder 2 counts. Victims were shot.

Called local FBI 644-7797 and they will check and ascertain all information on [REDACTED].

FBI Agent Gaven KAMMER phoned and stated that they have no information in their local files. He will check central files and notify VPD as soon as he receives information. (Lynch).

Phoned Mrs Iris [REDACTED] 752 [REDACTED] Drive phone 644- [REDACTED] and requested to talk to Russell [REDACTED]. She states that Russell is presently employed at the Springmaid Textile Company in Seattle, Washington. States that the last time Russell was in Vallejo was at Christmas time and he was here for three days. Exact days unknown. (Lynch).

4:05 PM Went to Elmer Cave School and contacted Arthur Lee ALLEN WMA 35 years dob 12-18-33. Resides 32 Fresno St., is single lives with his parents. Arthur 6'1", 241, heavy build and is bald. On 9-26-69 Arthur went skin diving on salt point ranch, stayed overnight and returned to Vallejo on 9-27-69. This at approximately 2 to 4:30 PM. Is a student at Vallejo Jr College and works part time as a custodian at Elmer Cave School.

Arthur states that on 9-27-69 after he returned from skin diving he stayed at home the remainder of the day. Unable to recall whether or not his parents were home on that day. (Lynch).

5:50 PM Anonymous phone call received that a Gary [REDACTED] 109 [REDACTED] resembles subject who may be responsible for the Berryessa slaying. Called 643-[REDACTED] and spoke to Paul [REDACTED]. He states that no Gary lives at that address. Requested Paul to come to the station. Paul Eugene [REDACTED] WMA 29 years dob 12-13-39 came to the station. Paul is employed as a welder inspector at Mare Island. He described as 6'1", 160, has long hair, long sideburns, beard and mustache. He states that he has only been to Lake Berryessa once this year. That was in June. Drives a 1965 Cadillac convertible red and white. Has been married but is divorced. Paul states that on 9-27-69 he was around town all day. He in no way resembles composite. (Lynch).

VALLEJO POLICE DEPARTMENT CRIME REPORT SUPPLEMENT FORM 33 6M 10/69			243 146
70. CODE SECTION 187 PC.	71. CRIME MURDER	DATE 7-4-69	72. CLASSIFICATION
73. VICTIM'S NAME – LAST, FIRST, MIDDLE (FIRM IF BUS.) FERRIN, Darlene	74. ADDRESS ☐ RESIDENCE ☐ BUSINESS 1300 Virginia St.		75. PHONE

11-5-69 Letter rec from Sherwood MORRILL, CII, Q.D.E., returning handwriting samples of possible

suspects on this case, William [REDACTED], Bernard [REDACTED], and a third unnamed person. Letter

states "None of the handprinting contained on the material in these documents is that of the

person who wrote the Zodiac material." Handwriting samples kept in Rm 20 with letter.

(Rust)

STATS

REPORTING OFFICERS	RECORDING OFFICER	TYPED BY	DATE AND TIME TYPED	ROUTED BY
Sgt. RUST		Rust	11-7-69 9pm	

COPIES TO: DATE

☐ DETECTIVE

☐ INVEST. COMM.

☐ DIST. ATTNY

☐ CII

☐

☐

DATE

REVIEWED BY	DATE

VALLEJO POLICE DEPARTMENT CRIME REPORT SUPPLEMENT FORM 33 6M 10/69	243 146

70. CODE SECTION	71. CRIME Murder	DATE 11-7-69	72. CLASSIFICATION

73. VICTIM'S NAME – LAST, FIRST, MIDDLE (FIRM IF BUS.)	74. ADDRESS ☐ RESIDENCE ☐ BUSINESS	75. PHONE

On 11-6-69 at 4PM Sgt. Najwoski received a phone call from Deputy Kenney Solano Co. S.O. that a subject had been booked at the branch county jail who resembled composite of murderer "ZODIAC". Suspect's name is GEORGE R. [REDACTED] JR.

11-7-69 11AM

RO contacted jail and arraignments made to talk to [REDACTED]. It was reported by Jailer Albertoni and Deputy Beaver that when [REDACTED] was being booked on a drunk charge he had made the statement that he was "Zodiac".

[REDACTED] taken to Room 27, Vallejo Police Dept. at which time he was advised as to his constitutional rights. He was further advised as to why RO desired to talk to him. [REDACTED] stated he understand his rights and was willing to answer any questions asked. His attitude was polite and cooperative. Stated he was aware of the murders by reading the newspapers but denied all personal knowledge of same. Admitted that he might have made remark that he was Zodiac while he was intoxicated but does not recall having said this. Admits several arrests, most serious charge being that of receiving stolen property for which he is now out on bail. Subject is married and has two children aged five and three. Lives with wife and children at 23000 Arnold Road, Sonoma. Has a 1957 Plymouth 2 dr. sedan, blue in color, Washington license plates, numbers unknown. He is employed as a painter United Pacific Builders and has been so employed for two years.

REPORTING OFFICERS	RECORDING OFFICER	TYPED BY	DATE AND TIME TYPED	ROUTED BY
Sgt. Mulanax				

COPIES TO: DATE		DATE	
☐ DETECTIVE	☐ CII		
☐ INVEST. COMM.	☐		
☐ DIST. ATTNY	☐		

REVIEWED BY	DATE

VALLEJO POLICE DEPARTMENT CRIME REPORT SUPPLEMENT FORM 33 6M 10/69	243 146

70. CODE SECTION	71. CRIME Murder	DATE	72. CLASSIFICATION

73. VICTIM'S NAME – LAST, FIRST, MIDDLE (FIRM IF BUS.)	74. ADDRESS ☐ RESIDENCE ☐ BUSINESS	75. PHONE

[REDACTED] does have a marked resemblance to composite drawing of suspected responsible in San Francisco Zodiac murder case. His physical description is WMA, 29 years, 6 feet, 160, sandy blonde hair, thick horn rimed glasses, same hair line as composite.

Hand writing exemplars obtained, finger prints taken, palm prints taken. Above sent to CII Sacramento for comparison with Zodiac writings and prints obtained by Napa P.D. in their 187 PC case. (Mulanax)

11-10-69 11:30 AM RO took above evidence to CII Sac., hand writing notthe same as on Zodiac letters. [REDACTED] eliminated as suspect. (Mulanax)

REPORTING OFFICERS	RECORDING OFFICER	TYPED BY	DATE AND TIME TYPED	ROUTED BY

COPIES TO: DATE		DATE		
☐ DETECTIVE	☐ CII			
☐ INVEST. COMM.	☐		REVIEWED BY	DATE
☐ DIST. ATTNY	☐			

VALLEJO POLICE DEPARTMENT CRIME REPORT SUPPLEMENT FORM 33 6M 10/69	243 146

70. CODE SECTION	71. CRIME	DATE	72. CLASSIFICATION
187 PC	Murder	7-4-69	

73. VICTIM'S NAME – LAST, FIRST, MIDDLE (FIRM IF BUS.)	74. ADDRESS ☐ RESIDENCE ☐ BUSINESS	75. PHONE
FERRIN, Darlene Elizabeth	1300 Virginia Street	

11-8-69 2:20 AM Officer HOFFMAN brought to the station from the northern end of the parking lot at Blue Rock Springs Robert Leonard [REDACTED] WMA 48 years dob 6-14-21. Robert 5'8 ½", 160, blue eyes, long brown hair with long sideburns. Robert wearing a black Fedora flat, new grey ill fitting suit, white shirt, blue and white checked tie, a reversible vest, navy blueone side, grey checked with blue and red stripes other side. Brown shoes. Has resided at the Sweden House Motel 570 O'Farrell St San Francisco since 8-18-64. This is his permanent address but he has not lived there continuously since that time. Robert is employed at the Rheem Manufacturing Co in San Leandro. He works days 7AM to 3:30PM. Is a janitor. Has an Arizona Drivers License #R 18234 issued 6-6-69. SS 284 12 [REDACTED]. Had $310 in his possession. Drives a 1963 Dodge CXJ 882. Has owned this car for 5 weeks.

Robert states that he worked today and had dinner in San Leandro. After dinner he drove to Sonoma and visited a John [REDACTED] who lives in the [REDACTED] Apts #22. 30 [REDACTED] St Sonoma. States that John is a long time friend of his and he has visited him many times. He left Sonoma around midnight enroute back to San Francisco. He missed the turnoff at Blackpoint and drove down Highway 37 and then onto Columbus parkway. He became tired and when he saw the parking lot he pulled off to take a nap. States that he parked his car and didn't get out. Fell

REPORTING OFFICERS	RECORDING OFFICER	TYPED BY	DATE AND TIME TYPED	ROUTED BY
Sgt. J. Lynch		Lynch	11-9-69 2:40A	

COPIES TO: DATE		DATE	
☐ DETECTIVE	☐ CII		
☐ INVEST. COMM.	☐		
☐ DIST. ATTNY	☐		REVIEWED BY / DATE

VALLEJO POLICE DEPARTMENT CRIME REPORT SUPPLEMENT FORM 33 6M 10/69	243 146

70. CODE SECTION	71. CRIME	DATE	72. CLASSIFICATION
187 PC	Murder	7-4-69	

73. VICTIM'S NAME – LAST, FIRST, MIDDLE (FIRM IF BUS.)	74. ADDRESS ☐ RESIDENCE ☐ BUSINESS	75. PHONE
FERRIN, Darlene Elizabeth	1300 Virginia Street	

asleep and was awakened by the Police Officers and brought to the station.

Robert]had in his possession and envelope that had both writing and printing on both sides. States

that he did this writing and printing today. Also noted on the envelope were 14 symbols, these

all similar. Robert explains these as being "keystones". Some contained numbers others didn't.

The writing and printing did not appear to be the same as Zodiacs.

Robert states that he doesn't smoke or drink. Doesn't own a gun. Has never been in the service.

Has never been arrested. Has never been married. Is a member of the Church of Christ. Claims

that he can speak 5 languages. Spanish, Italian, French, and Portuguese. Robert appears to be

highly intelligent but has never worked at any but menial jobs.

States that he has never been arrested. Denies an interest in Horoscopes or Cryptograms.

States that he frequently makes notes and has kept many of them in his room in San Francisco.

Photocopy made of the envelope.

3:40 AM Robert released. Copy of report to SFPD. (Lynch)

REPORTING OFFICERS	RECORDING OFFICER	TYPED BY	DATE AND TIME TYPED	ROUTED BY
Sgt. J. Lynch		Lynch	11-9-69 2:40A	

COPIES TO: DATE
☐ DETECTIVE
☐ INVEST. COMM.
☐ DIST. ATTNY
☐ CII
☐
☐
DATE

REVIEWED BY | DATE

VALLEJO POLICE DEPARTMENT

CRIME REPORT SUPPLEMENT

243 146

FORM 33 6M 10/69

70. CODE SECTION	71. CRIME	DATE	72. CLASSIFICATION
	Murder	12/12/69	

73. VICTIM'S NAME – LAST, FIRST, MIDDLE (FIRM IF BUS.)	74. ADDRESS ☐ RESIDENCE ☐ BUSINESS	75. PHONE
FERRIN, Darlene E.		

9:30am – Mr. Earl [REDACTED] and his wife Jane, address 3255 [REDACTED] St., Redding, California,

telephone 916-241-[REDACTED], came to the station and stated that they suspected a very distant

relative of theirs being the Zodiac. This subj's name is Norman Russell [REDACTED], dob 10/15/37

address unknown. FBI #537013G. They stated they suspected him as he had written them a letter

indicating that he was a killer for the Mafia and that he was in trouble and needed their help. Mr.

[REDACTED] states that they have never met this subject but brought two pictures of him to the

station. They also brought letters that were written by Norman [REDACTED] to his wife, whose

name is Jane Katherine [REDACTED]. Who lives at 3410 North [REDACTED] St., Chicago, Ill. Phone

312 863- [REDACTED]. These letters were given to him by Mr. Earl [REDACTED]'s son Ronald. Ronald

obtained these letters from the ex-wife of the suspect. These letters indicate that this subject is
a inforcer for the Mafia. Copies of these letters attached to the case report along with the two
pictures of the suspect. John Markey of the FBI was notified and he came to the station and is
handling the investigation of Mr. [REDACTED]. The San Francisco Police Department checked out
the fingerprints of Norman [REDACTED] against theirs on file MMX with the FBI and they came back
negative. The original copy of the letter to the complainant from Norman [REDACTED] is to be sent
by writer to CII and an analysis to be compared with the Zodiac letters.

REPORTING OFFICERS	RECORDING OFFICER	TYPED BY	DATE AND TIME TYPED	ROUTED BY
Sgt. Nilsson	Sgt. Nilsson	pw	12-12-69-5pm	pw

COPIES TO: DATE		DATE	
☐ DETECTIVE ☐ INVEST. COMM. ☐ DIST. ATTNY	☐ CII ☐ ☐		REVIEWED BY	DATE

VALLEJO POLICE DEPARTMENT

CRIME REPORT SUPPLEMENT

243 146

FORM 33 6M 10/69

70. CODE SECTION	71. CRIME	DATE	72. CLASSIFICATION
187 PC	Murder	7-4-69	

73. VICTIM'S NAME – LAST, FIRST, MIDDLE (FIRM IF BUS.)	74. ADDRESS ☒ RESIDENCE ☐ BUSINESS	75. PHONE
FERRIN, Darlene Elizabeth	1300 Virginia Street	

1-22-70 10 AM Information received from Wyman [REDACTED]. He states that he has had

several conversations with a Joseph DE LOUISE 17 [REDACTED] St Room 1525 Chicago, Illinois.

Phone 312 ST 2-3950. Mr DE LOUISE informed him that he has extraordinary powers of Extra

Sensory Perception and has received vibrations that Jim PHILIPPS, Darlenes first husband, may

have knowledge or be involved in her murder. Mr DE LOUISE presently staying at the Stewart

Hotel in San Francisco phone415

Phoned Mr DELOUISE who states that he came to San Francisco and Vallejo to assist in solving

the "Zodiac" murders. States that he has talked to Mrs SUENNEN, Darlenes mother and she told

him that PHILIPPS was formerly in a Mental institution or had been receiving treatment from a

mental health organization. She also told him that PHILIPPS was interested in astrology and

cryptology. He may have worked on cryptograms while he was in the army. Mr DE LOUISE was

informed that he had color photos of Philipps and the address books of Darlenes and they were

available for his inspection. Mr DELOUISE states that he is returning to Chicago tomorrow and he

may not be able to come to Vallejo today as he is very busy.

11:30 AM Called the Daily Republic in Fairfield 425-4646 and was informed that Jim PHILIPPS

worked there for one week on the editorial staff. From January 6, 1967 to January 11, 1967. Gave

his home address as 130 Jordan Street Vallejo. SS # 563 58 4885. No other information available.

REPORTING OFFICERS	RECORDING OFFICER	TYPED BY	DATE AND TIME TYPED	ROUTED BY
Sgt. J. Lynch		Lynch	1-22-70 9PM	

COPIES TO: DATE

☐ DETECTIVE
☐ INVEST. COMM.
☐ DIST. ATTNY

☐ CII
☐
☐

DATE

REVIEWED BY	DATE

	243 146
VALLEJO POLICE DEPARTMENT CRIME REPORT SUPPLEMENT FORM 33 6M 10/69	

70. CODE SECTION	71. CRIME	DATE	72. CLASSIFICATION
187 PC	Murder	7-4-69	

73. VICTIM'S NAME – LAST, FIRST, MIDDLE (FIRM IF BUS.)	74. ADDRESS ☒ RESIDENCE ☐ BUSINESS	75. PHONE
FERRIN, Darlene Elizabeth	1300 Virginia Street	

At the end of the first week he took off. Gave no reason for leaving and did not leave any forwarding address. Shortly after he left the newspaper received several inquiries about him. These inquiries were about money being owed to various people in Fairfield.

Called 916 246 1985 and spoke to [REDACTED] PHILIPPS P.O. Box 801 Project City Calif. [REDACTED] states that Jim PHILIPPS is his step brother. He was adopted by [REDACTED] father when he was a young boy. [REDACTED] states that his father was a California Highway Patrolman but has been dead for approximately one year. [REDACTED] unable to supply a date of birth for Jim. States that he hasn't seen him for approximately 4 months. At that time Jim had long hair and a full beard. At that time was definitely a hippy.

[REDACTED] states that Jim was in the army and was married to a girl in Germany and had a daughter. Believes that he never divorced this woman. He was in some type of trouble in the army and was confined to the stockade in the Presidio in San Francisco. While there he went on a hunger strike and received a dishonorable discharge from the army.

[REDACTED] states that Jim has a High School Education and is very intelligent. Has an IQ of 138. [REDACTED] states that Jim was born in Los Angeles and that his last name is CRABTREE. Jim told him four months ago that he was going to drop the name Philipps and use his true name CRABTREE. [REDACTED] also states that he believes

REPORTING OFFICERS	RECORDING OFFICER	TYPED BY	DATE AND TIME TYPED	ROUTED BY
Sgt. J. Lynch		Lynch	1-23-70 2:50A	

COPIES TO: DATE

☐ DETECTIVE

☐ INVEST. COMM.

☐ DIST. ATTNY

☐ CII

☐

☐

DATE

REVIEWED BY | DATE

VALLEJO POLICE DEPARTMENT

CRIME REPORT SUPPLEMENT

FORM 33 6M 10/69

243 146

70. CODE SECTION	71. CRIME	DATE	72. CLASSIFICATION
187 PC	Murder	7-4-69	

73. VICTIM'S NAME – LAST, FIRST, MIDDLE (FIRM IF BUS.)	74. ADDRESS ☒ RESIDENCE ☐ BUSINESS	75. PHONE
FERRIN, Darlene Elizabeth	1300 Virginia Street	

that Jim is involved with narcotics. Believes that he is living on a ranch in the Watsonville – Santa Cruz area. States he doesn't have any handwriting exemplars of Jims. Believes that Jim is wanted by the Watsonville PD for writing bum checks. Also believes that Jim has written bum checks in the Lake Tahoe Reno area.

Suggests that we contact Judge Dan Reynolds Central Valley Justice Court Central Valley Calif.

Letter written to Judge REYNOLDS requesting information on Jim PHILIPPS background.

1-23-70 Phone call received from Capt. Richard WELCH, Redding P.D. Re Sgt. Lynch's inquiry on James PHILLIPS, C JAMES CRABTREE, this re. C.R. #243 146.

Welch to attempt to locate handwriting of PHILLIPS through research of an old check case and will advise VPD... LWB-hr

REPORTING OFFICERS	RECORDING OFFICER	TYPED BY	DATE AND TIME TYPED	ROUTED BY
Sgt. J. Lynch		Lynch	1-23-70 3:30AM	

COPIES TO: DATE

☐ DETECTIVE

☐ INVEST. COMM.

☐ DIST. ATTNY

☐ CII

☐

☐

DATE

REVIEWED BY

DATE

VALLEJO POLICE DEPARTMENT

CRIME REPORT SUPPLEMENT

FORM 33 6M 10/69

243 146

70. CODE SECTION	71. CRIME	DATE	72. CLASSIFICATION
187 PC	Murder	7-4-69	

73. VICTIM'S NAME – LAST, FIRST, MIDDLE (FIRM IF BUS.)	74. ADDRESS ☐ RESIDENCE ☐ BUSINESS	75. PHONE
FERRIN, Darlene Elizabeth	1300 Virginia Street	

1-23-70 11:30 AM

RO again contacted mother of victim, Mrs. Suennen, 130 Jordan St., re- any possible information she might have which would connect her ex-son-in-law with the death of her daughter as she is alleged to have given to Joseph DeLouise. Mrs. Suennen offered nothing new in way of factual information. Subject is admittedly emotionally upset over daughter's death and further admits that she disliked son-in-law, James Phillips. She could offer very little background information on Phillips and was not in fact around him for any great period of time. Mother stated Darlene had left the family home on Nov. 25, 1965. This happened after a family dispute. The family did not hear from her again until Oct. 1966 when she returned home with her husband, James D. Phillips.. Mother has marriage license which shows couple was married in Reno, Nevada, Jan. 1, 1966. When they came to her home Darlene told them she and her husband had just returned from the Virgin Island where they had spent five months. Phillips told Mrs. Suennen that he "owned" a newspaper in the Virgin Islands and that he was formerly in the U.S. Army as an undercover agent. Subject had no money, no income, no job, and lived off his wife's earnings as a waitress. Couple lived with wife's family. After approximately three weeks Phillips was told to either obtain employment and support his wife or move out. He at this time applied for employment at the Daily Republican Newspaper in Fairfield and was in fact

REPORTING OFFICERS	RECORDING OFFICER	TYPED BY	DATE AND TIME TYPED	ROUTED BY
Mulanax. Sgt		tm		

COPIES TO: DATE ☐ CII DATE

☐ DETECTIVE	☐		
☐ INVEST. COMM.	☐	REVIEWED BY	DATE
☐ DIST. ATTNY			

VALLEJO POLICE DEPARTMENT CRIME REPORT SUPPLEMENT FORM 33 6M 10/69			243 146
70. CODE SECTION 187 PC	71. CRIME Murder	DATE 7-4-69	72. CLASSIFICATION

73. VICTIM'S NAME – LAST, FIRST, MIDDLE (FIRM IF BUS.)	74. ADDRESS ☐ RESIDENCE ☐ BUSINESS	75. PHONE
FERRIN, Darlene Elizabeth	1300 Virginia Street	

hired to assist in writing editorials. Mrs. Suennen stated he worked in this capacity for Approximately three weeks. (Phillips in fact worked five days and did not show up for work again.) Shortly after leaving the paper both Darlene and Phillips left Vallejo and went to Pennsylvania. They spent several months in Pennsylvania and returned to Vallejo. Their marriage was going poorly and Darlene decided to go to Reno and get a divorce. James apparently did not want a divorce but did not contest same. Records show final decree obtained in Reno on June 2, 1967. Shortly afterwards Darlene remarried and Phillips moved to San Francisco. As far as family knows no further contact between Darlene and Phillips until he attended the funeral of Darlene and was seen by two members of the family sitting in the back row during funeral services. He was with an unknown WFA who was pregnant at the time. There was no conversation between Phillips and family.

Mr. DeLouise had indicated to RO that Mrs. Suennen had told him that Phillips was at one time committed to a mental hospital. RO asked her if this was a fact and Mrs. Suennen stated she had "heard" this but did not know it to be a fact. She was also questioned concerning any particular interest Phillips might have had in astrology or cryptograms. Stated she had on one occasion seen him draw up some type of "code".

REPORTING OFFICERS	RECORDING OFFICER	TYPED BY	DATE AND TIME TYPED	ROUTED BY
Sgt. Mulanax		tm		

COPIES TO: DATE		DATE	
☐ DETECTIVE	☐ CII		
☐ INVEST. COMM.	☐		REVIEWED BY
☐ DIST. ATTNY	☐		DATE

VALLEJO POLICE DEPARTMENT

CRIME REPORT SUPPLEMENT

FORM 33 6M 10/69

243 146

70. CODE SECTION	71. CRIME	DATE	72. CLASSIFICATION
187 PC	Murder	7-4-69	

73. VICTIM'S NAME – LAST, FIRST, MIDDLE (FIRM IF BUS.)	74. ADDRESS ☐ RESIDENCE ☐ BUSINESS	75. PHONE
FERRIN, Darlene Elizabeth	1300 Virginia Street	

1-23-70 2:30 PM RO contacted Business Manager of the Daily Republic in Fairfield in an attempt to secure more background information on Phillips and if possible secure printing specimens of his writing. Very little known of Phillips by present employees. No record of his application for employment. An attempt to be made by newspaper to locate federal tax forms made out by Phillips to authorize tax withholding deductions. If located same will be forwarded to the Vallejo P.D. for possible handwriting comparison.

3:00 PM Checked with Fairfield PD re-any record they might have of Phillips. They have an outstanding warrant charging violation 476a P.C. on file since 12-4-67. Also obtained mug shot which was attached to warrant of a James Donald Phillips and a photostatic copy of prints which it is assumed, came from CII. It is opinion of RO that subject shown is not the James Phillips in which we are interested. Subject appears older in photograph and does not wear glasses.

1-26-70 9:30 AM Contacted Mel Nicolai, CII Investigations, by phone. Requested he search his files for any record of a James D. Phillips, WMA, approx. 24-28, and forward mug and rsp sheet if found.

REPORTING OFFICERS	RECORDING OFFICER	TYPED BY	DATE AND TIME TYPED	ROUTED BY
Sgt. Mulanax		tm		

COPIES TO: DATE		DATE	
☐ DETECTIVE ☐ INVEST. COMM. ☐ DIST. ATTNY	☐ CII ☐ ☐		REVIEWED BY / DATE

VALLEJO POLICE DEPARTMENT

CRIME REPORT SUPPLEMENT

243 146

FORM 33 6M 10/69

70. CODE SECTION	71. CRIME	DATE	72. CLASSIFICATION
187 PC	Murder	7-4-69	

73. VICTIM'S NAME – LAST, FIRST, MIDDLE (FIRM IF BUS.)	74. ADDRESS ☐ RESIDENCE ☐ BUSINESS	75. PHONE
FERRIN, Darlene Elizabeth	1300 Virginia Street	

1-26-70 Following Western Union Telegram received from Charis HARRIS:

"CHIEF OF POLICE JACK STILTZ, DON'T FONE, REQ. DIR. A.M.

DEAR CHIEF STILTZ, AM REQUESTING THAT YOU PICK UP JAMES PHILLIPS POSSIBLE SUSPECT IN

CONNECTION WITH ZODIAC CRIMES THIS MORNING I WAS INFORMED THE ZODIAC HAD SHOT

AND CRITICALLY WOUNDED A CAB DRIVER IN SAN FRANCISCO.

PLEASE CALL ME HO 2-1486. CHARIS HARRIS."

Telegram attached to report. No return call made or contemplated. (Mulanax)

REPORTING OFFICERS	RECORDING OFFICER	TYPED BY	DATE AND TIME TYPED	ROUTED BY

COPIES TO: DATE ☐ CII	DATE	

☐ DETECTIVE	☐		
☐ INVEST. COMM.	☐	REVIEWED BY	DATE
☐ DIST. ATTNY			

VALLEJO POLICE DEPARTMENT

CRIME REPORT SUPPLEMENT

243 146

FORM 33 6M 10/69

70. CODE SECTION	71. CRIME	DATE	72. CLASSIFICATION
187 PC	Murder	7-4-69	

73. VICTIM'S NAME – LAST, FIRST, MIDDLE (FIRM IF BUS.)	74. ADDRESS ☐ RESIDENCE ☐ BUSINESS	75. PHONE
FERRIN, Darlene Elizabeth	1300 Virginia Street	

1-27-70 9:30 AM

Phone call from Mel Nicolai, CII Investigator, that he had mailed a rap sheet and mug shot of a James Douglas PHILLIPS to RO. Also had current address on suspect of Rt. 1, Box 521, Boulder Creek, Santa Cruz County, California. Subject is WMA, 5-9, 162, brn. blue, DOB 8-9-44, CII 3523828, FBI 139428F. Mug shot & rap sheet received in morning mail.

10:30 AM Contacted Sgt. Tom LaVarr. Fairfield PD Investigation Divn. It was agreed that this was the Phillips for whom warrant had been issued on checks rather than James Donald Phillips, FBI 785461E. DOB 1933 in Nebr. Record check revealed their warrant invalid as no affidavit had been drawn up on warrant.

1-28-70 8:30 AM

With Deputy District Attorney Charles Meyerherm, RO drove to Santa Cruz. There contacted Lt. Gangloff in charge of Investigation Division, Santa Cruz County S.O., and Detective George Foster. Their records revealed a James Douglas CRABTREE aka PHILLIPS had been booked 1-19-70 on traffic warrants. Gave address at that time as P.O. Box 237, Ben Lomond, Santa Cruz County. Physical description on booking sheet 5-6, 160, brn, blue, DOB 5-8-44. Social Security 563 58

[REDACTED]. (SS given when employed by Solano Daily Republic one digit difference – 563 58
[REDACTED]). CRABTREE aka

REPORTING OFFICERS	RECORDING OFFICER	TYPED BY	DATE AND TIME TYPED	ROUTED BY
Sgt. Mulanax		tm		

COPIES TO: DATE		DATE		
☐ DETECTIVE	☐ CII			
☐ INVEST. COMM.	☐			
☐ DIST. ATTNY	☐		REVIEWED BY	DATE

VALLEJO POLICE DEPARTMENT

CRIME REPORT SUPPLEMENT

FORM 33 6M 10/69

243 146

70. CODE SECTION	71. CRIME	DATE	72. CLASSIFICATION
187 PC	Murder	7-4-69	

73. VICTIM'S NAME – LAST, FIRST, MIDDLE (FIRM IF BUS.)	74. ADDRESS ☐ RESIDENCE ☐ BUSINESS	75. PHONE
FERRIN, Darlene Elizabeth	1300 Virginia Street	

PHILLIPS posted $390 cash bail to appear Santa Cruz Mini Court 2-2-70 9 a.m. Santa Cruz
authorities advised address given by PHILLIPS was a large "hippy" commune & further advised
against attempting to pick him up for fear that subject would skip if word reached him prior to
being picked up. It was decided to come back with Fairfield's warrant when subject appears in
court 2-2-70. Latest photographs taken when subject booked obtained by RO
1-29-70 9:00 AM Photographs of James Douglas CRABTREE shown Mrs. Suennen, 130 Jordan St.

& she stated this is her ex-son-in-law, known to her as John or James D. PHILLIPS. Photographs also shown Pamela GRANT, 117 Jordan St., sister of victim, Ferrin. Mrs. Grant also stated this is person known to her as James Phillips.

10:00 AM Again contacted Fairfield P.D. With Detective Chuck Hess went to District Attorney's Office in Fairfield where Chief Deputy District Attorney Neal McCaslin drew up necessary declaration of affidavit. Warrant of arrest signed by Judge Curtis G. Singleton, Fairfield- Suisun Judicial District, charging violation 476a P.C. for James Douglas Phillips aka Grabtree. Bail set at $10,000 cash. Warrant retained by R.O. (Mulanax)

REPORTING OFFICERS	RECORDING OFFICER	TYPED BY	DATE AND TIME TYPED	ROUTED BY
Sgt. Mulanax		tm		

COPIES TO: DATE
☐ DETECTIVE
☐ INVEST. COMM.
☐ DIST. ATTNY
☐ CII
☐
☐
DATE

REVIEWED BY	DATE

VALLEJO POLICE DEPARTMENT

CRIME REPORT SUPPLEMENT

243 146

FORM 33 6M 10/69

70. CODE SECTION	71. CRIME	DATE	72. CLASSIFICATION

187 PC	Murder	7-4-69	

73. VICTIM'S NAME – LAST, FIRST, MIDDLE (FIRM IF BUS.)	74. ADDRESS ☐ RESIDENCE ☐ BUSINESS	75. PHONE
FERRIN, Darlene Elizabeth	1300 Virginia Street	

2-2-70 7AM

RO and Officer Zander enroute to Muni Court, Santa Cruz. At 10AM James D. Grabtree. aka Phillips appeared on traffic matter. On leaving court room subject was arrested on Fairfield warrant. Detective Foster, Santa Cruz SO. present at time of arrest. Grabtree was in company of his common-law wife. Shirley Irene [REDACTED], WFA, 28, and infant son, Jacob, age 5 weeks. Mother & infant transported to S.O. by Off. Zander while Phillips transported by RO & Detective Foster.

At Santa Cruz S.O. Phillips advised as to his constitutional rights by RO. He was at this time advised also that he was a suspect in a murder. Phillips stated he understood his rights and was willing to answer any questions. He denied any knowledge of ex-wife's death and stated he had not known she was in fact dead until so informed by officers. Subject very cooperative and answered questions without hesitation. Wife also questioned independently from Phillips. Her answers corroborated these given by Phillips. Phillips was asked if he would give permission to search his home. He stated that we had his permission. It was decided to wait until we had returned to Vallejo to take a detailed statement.

With Det. Foster, Phillips & wife, officers drove to his residence located in rural area approx. 20 miles from Santa Cruz. There a search

REPORTING OFFICERS	RECORDING OFFICER	TYPED BY	DATE AND TIME TYPED	ROUTED BY
Sgt. Mulanax		tm	2-3-70	

COPIES TO: DATE		DATE		
☐ DETECTIVE ☐ INVEST. COMM. ☐ DIST. ATTNY	☐ CII ☐ ☐		REVIEWED BY	DATE

VALLEJO POLICE DEPARTMENT

CRIME REPORT SUPPLEMENT

FORM 33 6M 10/69

243 146

70. CODE SECTION	71. CRIME	DATE	72. CLASSIFICATION
187 PC	Murder	7-4-69	

73. VICTIM'S NAME – LAST, FIRST, MIDDLE (FIRM IF BUS.)	74. ADDRESS ☐ RESIDENCE ☐ BUSINESS	75. PHONE
FERRIN, Darlene Elizabeth	1300 Virginia Street	

of his home was conducted for evidence which would tend to connect him with the crime for which he was being investigated. Search proved negative. Hand printed exemplars obtained from letters he had written which were found in house. In opinion of RO printing does not appear to be the same as specimens of Zodiac notes. Printing will be checked through CII at later date.

3:00 PM In Rm. 28 Vallejo Police Department the following information obtained in questioning Phillips.

He had become acquainted with Darlene Suennen while living in San Francisco in the Haight-Ashbury district. Could not recall exact date but it was shortly after his being discharged from the Army in Aug. 65. They started living together and were married in Reno in Jan. 66. Marriage did not go well as he stated his wife was inclined to run around with other men. Couple lived a rather gypay existence and he stated he was not concerned when Darlene decided to terminate the marriage. Denied ever having made the remark that if he could not have her that no one else could.

Was questioned regarding the 63 Chevrolet Corvair, he stated he purchased car from a private

party in Los Angeles, paying $90 down and having a balance of $210. This was in Oct. 66-67, could
not recall which year. Made no further payments on car and in Jan. of next year after buying car
left it parked on a public lot in L.A. and phoned the reg. owner to come pick it up as he was unable
to pay for it. At this time he left for

REPORTING OFFICERS	RECORDING OFFICER	TYPED BY	DATE AND TIME TYPED	ROUTED BY
Sgt. Mulanax		tm	2-3-70	

COPIES TO: DATE		DATE	
☐ DETECTIVE	☐ CII		
☐ INVEST. COMM.	☐		
☐ DIST. ATTNY	☐		REVIEWED BY / DATE

VALLEJO POLICE DEPARTMENT

CRIME REPORT SUPPLEMENT

243 146

FORM 33 6M 10/69

70. CODE SECTION	71. CRIME	DATE	72. CLASSIFICATION
187 PC	Murder	7-4-69	

73. VICTIM'S NAME – LAST, FIRST, MIDDLE (FIRM IF BUS.)	74. ADDRESS ☐ RESIDENCE ☐ BUSINESS	75. PHONE
FERRIN, Darlene Elizabeth	1300 Virginia Street	

Mexico, stayed a few weeks and then returned to San Francisco. Stated Darlene came to visit him
and spent a weekend after he came back but that both decided there was nothing to keep them
together. He wandered around the country after this, working short periods of time at different
jobs and being a part of the "social revolution" as portrayed by the hip generation. He met
[REDACTED] in Jan. 69 and started living with her in S.F. Couple moved to Santa Cruz a short time

later as they had become disenchanted with the scene in S.F. [REDACTED] became pregnant in May.

In early July her father purchased the house in which they are now living for them, paying $11,000

cash.

Stated on July 4, 1969, he recalls going with his wife to a hippy encampment at Boulder Creek and

listening to music. Spent the evening at home. They had no transportation at this time as their old

truck was inoperative. Insists that he had no knowledge of his ex-wife's death until this date.

Stated he had read of the Zodiac but did not connect what he had read as he did not know

Darlene had remarried and did not know her name was Ferrin.

Phillips had in his possession a photostatic copy of his birth certificate showing he was born in L.A.

May 8, 1944. His father was named Crabtree and his mother named Thelma [REDACTED]. He never

knew parents as his mother left him in hospital. He was adopted by a couple named Phillips.

REPORTING OFFICERS	RECORDING OFFICER	TYPED BY	DATE AND TIME TYPED	ROUTED BY
Sgt. Mulanax		tm	2-3-70	

COPIES TO: DATE
☐ DETECTIVE
☐ INVEST. COMM.
☐ DIST. ATTNY
☐ CII
☐
☐
DATE

REVIEWED BY | DATE

VALLEJO POLICE DEPARTMENT

CRIME REPORT SUPPLEMENT

243 146

FORM 33 6M 10/69

70. CODE SECTION	71. CRIME	DATE	72. CLASSIFICATION

187 PC	Murder	7-4-69	

73. VICTIM'S NAME – LAST, FIRST, MIDDLE (FIRM IF BUS.)	74. ADDRESS ☐ RESIDENCE ☐ BUSINESS	75. PHONE
FERRIN, Darlene Elizabeth	1300 Virginia Street	

He recently stated using surname of Crabtree after the death of his foster father who was a CHP officer.

Additional exemplars taken of Phillips' printing. Palm and finger prints taken by John Sparks, I.D. Bureau. Also stand-up photographs, front and profile.

Phillips stated he always wore glasses and unable to see without them. It was observed by RO that glasses were thick lensed and apparently strong. Phillips explained that when Santa Cruz authorities photographed him at the time of his arrest on traffic charges they had requested he remove his glasses while picture was taken.

It is opinion of RO that Phillips is in no way connected with murder of Darlene Ferrin.

Phillips booked enroute Fairfield P.D. on their warrant. Hold from El Dorado Co. S.O. on their warrant directed with Fairfield warrant to Fairfield Police Department. (Mulanax)

REPORTING OFFICERS	RECORDING OFFICER	TYPED BY	DATE AND TIME TYPED	ROUTED BY
Sgt. Mulanax		tm	2-3-70	

COPIES TO: DATE		DATE		
☐ DETECTIVE	☐ CII			
☐ INVEST. COMM.	☐		REVIEWED BY	DATE
☐ DIST. ATTNY	☐			

VALLEJO POLICE DEPARTMENT CRIME REPORT SUPPLEMENT FORM 33 6M 10/69	243 146

70. CODE SECTION	71. CRIME	DATE	72. CLASSIFICATION

73. VICTIM'S NAME – LAST, FIRST, MIDDLE (FIRM IF BUS.)	74. ADDRESS ☐ RESIDENCE ☐ BUSINESS	75. PHONE

6/7/70-7pm

Writer contacted at station a Sandra Karen BETTS, WF, 31 yrs., DOB 8/14/38, presently living at 2157 Navarro St., Napa, no phone, and her girlfriend a Margo Blaine [REDACTED] WF, 22 yrs., DOB 10/13/47, of 150 [REDACTED], Vallejo, she has a phone which has recently been installed and she does not know the number. Both subjects stated that on [UNREADABLE]/6/70 at approx. 10-10:30pm they were at the Coronado Inn on Highway 37 where subject [REDACTED] first observed a WM who was acting strangely. This subject strongly resembled the pictures they had seen of the composite drawing of the "Zodiac." [REDACTED] and BETTS observed this subject for some period of time describing him as a WM, approx. 38 yrs., brown hair which recedes approx to the middle of the head and a bald spot on the back of the head, he had on a nylon sweater shirt with short sleeves, dark pants, black shoes which appeared to be Military type and were extremely shiny. He had somewhat effeminate actions and walked in a swaybacked manner, held his glass with his fingers extended in a feminine way. Subject BETTS danced with this person and determined his name was Paul and that he was stationed in Vallejo. Subject Paul was evasive in his answers to BETTS, however, was determined that his favorite song is "Proud Mary" that he knew the name of the band that had played at the Coronado Inn previously approx. 2 months ago. BETTS and [REDACTED] were both

REPORTING OFFICERS	RECORDING OFFICER	TYPED BY	DATE AND TIME TYPED	ROUTED BY
	Sgt. Bawart	ns	6/7/70-9pm	ns

COPIES TO: DATE		DATE		
☐ DETECTIVE	☐ CII			
☐ INVEST. COMM.	☐		REVIEWED BY	DATE
☐ DIST. ATTNY	☐			

VALLEJO POLICE DEPARTMENT CRIME REPORT SUPPLEMENT FORM 33 6M 10/69	243 146

70. CODE SECTION	71. CRIME	DATE	72. CLASSIFICATION

73. VICTIM'S NAME – LAST, FIRST, MIDDLE (FIRM IF BUS.)	74. ADDRESS ☐ RESIDENCE ☐ BUSINESS	75. PHONE

shown a composite drawing from the San Francisco Police Department and immediately identifying the subject Paul as baring an extremely striking resemblance to the "Zodiac" composite, in fact, BETTS stated "that's him." BETTS and [REDACTED] left at approx. 1am and this subject left at the same time. He was observed to be driving a small black car possibly a Corvette, however subject BETTS was the only one that observed the vehicle and does not know types of cars very well. BETTS drew a picture of subject Paul after leaving the Coronado Inn on the back of a photograph. Picture attached to this supplement. Subject BETTS advises that she frequents the Coronado Inn and if she should observe this subject again will call VPD.

REPORTING OFFICERS	RECORDING OFFICER	TYPED BY	DATE AND TIME TYPED	ROUTED BY
	Sgt. Bawart	ns	6/7/70-9pm	ns

COPIES TO: DATE		DATE	
☐ DETECTIVE	☐ CII		
☐ INVEST. COMM.	☐		
☐ DIST. ATTNY	☐		REVIEWED BY / DATE

VALLEJO POLICE DEPARTMENT CRIME REPORT SUPPLEMENT FORM 33 6M 10/69				243 146

70. CODE SECTION	71. CRIME	DATE	72. CLASSIFICATION

73. VICTIM'S NAME – LAST, FIRST, MIDDLE (FIRM IF BUS.)	74. ADDRESS ☐ RESIDENCE ☐ BUSINESS	75. PHONE

6/16/70 1 am Writer was contacted by Sandra Karen Betts WF 31 yrs., DOB 8/14/38, 2157 Navarro St., Napa in parking lot across from City Hall. She stated that she had contacted V.P.D. in regards to suspect being "Zodiac" and that his vehicle was parked in front of the Ritz Bar 500 block of Captiol. Vehicle described as a Volkswagen Karman Gia black with Florida Lic. 24 D. 1216, Lic. reg. sent for 6/17/70.

6/20/70 Teletype from Fla. shows veh. reg. to a Paul V. [REDACTED] now station at NISMF Mere Island. RO contacted Lt. Never at Kare Island PD. who stated that [REDACTED] applied for a base decal on 3-10-69. Has been issued two decals and has two lic. plate numbers. Decals no. are 23898E & 42452E lic. plate are 24D1216 & 24D3047. However Lt. Never had no information as to how long [REDACTED] has been station here prior to applying for a decal. (Sgt. Blair)

6/22/70 Phoned Insp. MONEZ, M.I. Invst. and he phoned back with info that [REDACTED] IS a Chief Electrician's Mate, Ser. 5189807, with the Naval Inactive Ships Maintenance Facility at M.I. He first arrived at M.I. in March of 1969 and come from the USS Thor ARC-4. He presently has registered to him a 1969 Karmen Ghia with Florida lic. 24D1216 and M.I. decal 42452E. MONEZ States they can met in touch with him for a meet, if necessary; he was requested to obtain where [REDACTED] lives or stays. (Nawojski)

-noted- 6-23-60 AM Phone from MONEZ that [REDACTED] possibly staying aboard the USS Pelius - 646-2101 (Nawojski) – noted – (VW)

REPORTING OFFICERS	RECORDING OFFICER	TYPED BY	DATE AND TIME TYPED	ROUTED BY
	Kollar	mk	6/17/70 6:30a	

COPIES TO: DATE

☐ DETECTIVE
☐ INVEST. COMM.
☐ DIST. ATTNY
☐ CII
☐
☐

DATE

REVIEWED BY	DATE

<table>
<tr><td colspan="5">VALLEJO POLICE DEPARTMENT

CRIME REPORT SUPPLEMENT

FORM 33 6M 1/70</td><td>243 146</td></tr>
<tr><td>70. CODE SECTION
187</td><td>71. CRIME
Murder</td><td>DATE
7/5/69</td><td colspan="3">72. CLASSIFICATION</td></tr>
<tr><td colspan="3">73. VICTIM'S NAME – LAST, FIRST, MIDDLE (FIRM IF BUS.)
FERRIN, Darlene E.</td><td colspan="2">74. ADDRESS ☐ RESIDENCE ☐ BUSINESS</td><td>75. PHONE</td></tr>
</table>

9/8/70-

Information received that a good suspect in the Zodiac murders would be Michael R. [REDACTED], WMA, 30 yrs., 6410, 180-200, residing at 520 [REDACTED] Dr. This suspect wears glasses at times, is single, and to the informants knowledge has never been out with a girl. Constantly walks with his head down. This subject works at Union Oil in Rodeo, he owns a 9 MM automatic and a .45 cal. automatic. The suspects supposedly was involved in a traffic accident on Highway 37 in 1969 in which two people were killed. This subject was prosecuted for manslaughter. The informant indicates that this subject knows a considerable bit about the lake Berryessa area. States that when he gets excited he puts his thumbs to his nose screams. This subject apparently talks quite frequently about the Zodiac murders and he has made statements to the informant about two other persons killed by the Zodiac which have not been reported. He has made statements that the Zodiac would never get caught. Further followup coming. Records at the Sheriff's Office indicate that subject Michael [REDACTED], was booked 11/15/67 for two counts of 192.3A PC and 23102 CVC. Subjects DOB is 4/27/42, residing at 520 [REDACTED]. CII #3083750, no F.B.I. number on subjects prints. [REDACTED] is and inspector at Union Oil. His drivers license #H629605. Print card and booking card obtained from the BCJ and will be sent to F.B.I. for comparison.

REPORTING OFFICERS	RECORDING OFFICER	TYPED BY	DATE AND TIME TYPED	ROUTED BY
	Sgt. Nilsson	ns	10/11/70 - 2:24p	ns

COPIES TO: DATE		DATE	
☐ DETECTIVE	☐ CII		
☐ INVEST. COMM.	☐		REVIEWED BY
☐ DIST. ATTNY	☐		DATE

	69. CASE NO.
VALLEJO POLICE DEPARTMENT CRIME REPORT SUPPLEMENT FORM 33 6M 1/70	#86 243 146

70. CODE SECTION	71. CRIME	DATE	72. CLASSIFICATION
187 PC	Murder	7-5-69	

73. VICTIM'S NAME – LAST, FIRST, MIDDLE (FIRM IF BUS.)	74. ADDRESS ☐ RESIDENCE ☐ BUSINESS	75. PHONE
FERRIN, Darlene E.		

10-3-70 2:20 PM Officer Kinney received a phone call from Sergeant Brown Hot Springs Arkansas Police Dept. Phone number 501 6235551. Brown stated that he wished to speak to an investigator regarding information he has received from Sharon [REDACTED] 631 [REDACTED] Hot Springs Arkansas phone number 501624 [REDACTED]. Refer this case page numbers 43 & 44. 3:00 PM RO phoned Brown and he relayed the following. Sharon [REDACTED], who is in a state of mental break down has been talking of her ex-husband Tommy Southern. The father of Sharon called Brown and stated that he knew that SOUTHERN was a suspect in the murder of Ferrin, and that his daughter has talked of SOUTHERN killing a girl by the name of OLIVIA and her child. The murder was supposed to have been committed in June or July of 1968.

Brown has talked to [REDACTED] on several occasions at her home and he was informed by [REDACTED] that Tommy Southern shot and killed this girl by the name of Olivia and her child with a 30-30 rifle and buried them in the back yard of either 735B Virginia, 436 Capital or 1655 Tuolumne. He further states that she relapses into incoherent states of mind and that he has been slow in questioning her due to this fact. He is sending a complete copy of his report to RO and will continue to send any further information that he receives from the woman. Brown also states that [REDACTED] has on several occasions mentioned Blue Rock Springs.

REPORTING OFFICERS Sgt. Nilsson	RECORDING OFFICER	TYPED BY Nilsson	DATE AND TIME TYPED 10-4-70 - 1:10PM	ROUTED BY DN

COPIES TO: DATE		DATE		
☐ DETECTIVE	☐ CII			
☐ INVEST. COMM.	☐			
☐ DIST. ATTNY	☐		REVIEWED BY	DATE

	69. CASE NO.
VALLEJO POLICE DEPARTMENT CRIME REPORT SUPPLEMENT FORM 33 6M 1/70	#87 243 146

70. CODE SECTION	71. CRIME	DATE	72. CLASSIFICATION
187 PC	Murder	7-5-69	

73. VICTIM'S NAME – LAST, FIRST, MIDDLE (FIRM IF BUS.)	74. ADDRESS ☐ RESIDENCE ☐ BUSINESS	75. PHONE
FERRIN, Darlene E.		

10-4-70 RO contacted informant who originally gave information on Southern. The informant states that the three addresses given are locations where [REDACTED] and Tommy lived while they were married. Southern did have a large garden in the back yard of 735 Virginia St. where he often dug. The informant had information that Southern did go with several different girls while married to [REDACTED], but she knows of no girl by the name of [REDACTED].

Information received from Off. Musted that a girl by the name of Melodie Ann [REDACTED] WFJ 17 yrs dob 2-20-53 620 Corcoran phone number 6425246 lived with Southern for some time and might be able to supply RO with information on SOUTHERN. [REDACTED] in juvenile hall at this time.

2 PM RO contacted Melodie [REDACTED] at juvenile hall. Melodie states that she has been living with SOUTHERN for the past four months. She has never observed any weapons in the possession of Southern. She has never been physically abused by Southern, and she states that he has normal sex drives and has never abused her sexually. He is interested in his own Zodiac sign, but she stated that he doe's not study Astrology. She has never observed him writing criptograms.

She has never heard him mention any girl by the name of OLIVIA.

REPORTING OFFICERS	RECORDING OFFICER	TYPED BY	DATE AND TIME TYPED	ROUTED BY
Sgt. Nilsson		Nilsson	10-4-70 - 3:45PM	DN

COPIES TO: DATE		DATE		
☐ DETECTIVE	☐ CII			
☐ INVEST. COMM.	☐		REVIEWED BY	DATE
☐ DIST. ATTNY	☐			

VALLEJO POLICE DEPARTMENT CRIME REPORT SUPPLEMENT FORM 33 6M 1/70				69. CASE NO. 243 146
70. CODE SECTION 187 PC	71. CRIME	DATE 7-5-69	72. CLASSIFICATION	

73. VICTIM'S NAME – LAST, FIRST, MIDDLE (FIRM IF BUS.)	74. ADDRESS ☐ RESIDENCE ☐ BUSINESS	75. PHONE

10:15 pm RO and Sgt. Blair went to 520 Fairgrounds Dr., Apt 28 and contacted Michael

[REDACTED], WM-28, 4-27-42. Subj was advised that an investigation was being conducted in which

his name had been turned up as a possible suspect and that the police would like his cooperation

in an effort to clear it up. He was told that we would like to obtain printing samples from him

among other things. Subj seemed very surprised and upset about the police coming to his home.

Became very nervous and when RO adv him of his rights he stated that he would prefer to contact

his lawyer, Clinton [REDACTED]prior to any questioning or any other participation, an his part, in the investigation. He stated he will call Mr. [REDACTED] first thing in the morning and then either he or

Mr. [REDACTED] will contact the police dept. tomorrow. RO's left at this time. (Rust-Blair) rst

10-15-71 11pm

10-19-70-11:00PM Michael R. [REDACTED] came to the sta. as requested by RO for hand writing

exemplars and also brought his two 9mm handguns to be tested. Also with him was a Robert H.

[REDACTED] WMA 26 yrs of 112 [REDACTED] way. Mr. [REDACTED] had a 9mm luger Ser. #432 and

wanted to know if it could be tested along with Mr. [REDACTED]'s guns RO advised him it could be.

Ser. numbers of [REDACTED]'s Guns luger Ser. number #3850. P38 Ser. number #305074. These

items and blk cases along with the exemplars were tagged and placed in I.D. lockers. (Sgt. Blair)

Receipts were given to both subjects for their guns.

10-26-70 German Luger S/N 432, German Luger S/N 3850, Walther P-38 S/N 305074, and exemplar
taken to CII for analysis by Sgt. Mulamax. (Waricher)
12-17-70 Card mailed to Michael [REDACTED] to come to station to pick-up weapons that Returned from CII- this date. (Waricher)
12-21-20 I Michael R. [REDACTED] received the above two guns my property.
12/21/70 Postcard mailed to Mr. [REDACTED]

REPORTING OFFICERS	RECORDING OFFICER	TYPED BY	DATE AND TIME TYPED	ROUTED BY
Sgt. Nilsson		Nilsson	10-4-70 - 3:45PM	DN

COPIES TO: DATE		DATE	
☐ DETECTIVE	☐ CII		
☐ INVEST. COMM.	☐		
☐ DIST. ATTNY	☐		REVIEWED BY / DATE

Cecelia Ann Shepard and Bryan Calvin Hartnell

Killed: Shepard, Sept. 29, 1969 (Monday)

Wounded: Hartnell, Sept. 27, 1969 (Saturday)

Case number: 105907

Time of attack: Approximately 6:15 p.m. | Sept. 27, 1969 (Saturday)

Place of attack: The shoreline of Lake Berryessa near Napa, Calif.

Method of attack: Cecelia Shepard, age 22, was stabbed 10 times, five in the front and five in the back. Bryan Hartnell, age 20, was stabbed six times in the back. The knife had a wooden handle and a blade approximately 10 to 12 inches long. There was no indication of robbery or sexual molestation. There were no witnesses.

See more at:

https://zodiackiller.com/confirmed-zodiac-killer-victims-cecelia-shepard-and-bryan-hartnell/

Here is the extensive, 35-page Napa County Sheriff's Department report pertaining to the murder of Cecelia Shepard and wounding of Bryan Hartnell –

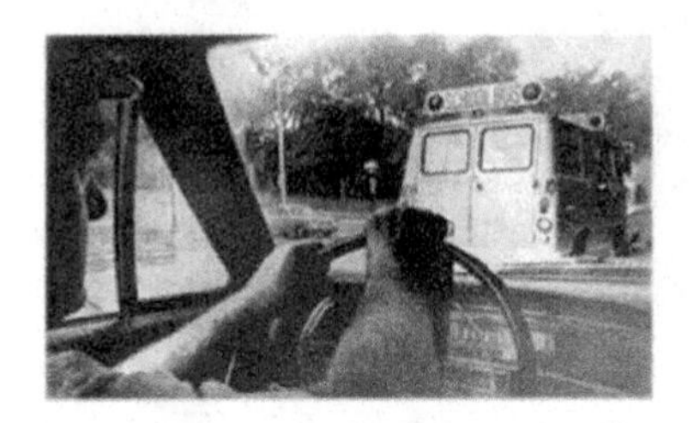

1. CASE NO.
105907

NAPA COUNTY SHERIFF'S DEPARTMENT

Zodiackiller.com

2. CODE SECTION	3. CRIME	4. CLASSIFICATION	5. REPORT AREA
187 P.C.	MURDER	FELONY	Berryessa

6. DATE AND TIME OCCURRED - DAY	7. DATE AND TIME REPORTED	8. LOCATION OF OCCURRENCE
9/27/69, 6:30 PM, Saturday	9/27/69, 7:10 P.M.	Shore line, ½ mile north of Lake Berryessa Park Headquarters

9. VICTIM'S NAME LAST, FIRST, MIDDLE (FIRM IF BUSSINESS)	10. RESIDENCE ADDRESS	11. RES. PHONE
SHEPARD, CECELIA ANN	10733 Mead Lane, Loma Linda, Calif.	976- [REDACTED]

12. OCCUPATION	13. RAGE – SEX	14. AGE	15. DOB	16. BUSINESS ADDRESS (SCHOOL IF JUVENILE)	17. BUS. PHONE
Student	WFA	22	1/1/47		

CODES FOR BOXES 20 AND 30 V=VICTIM W=WITNESS P=PARENT RP= REPORTING PARTY DC= DISCOVERED CRIME	18. CHECK IF MORE NAMES IN CONTINUATION ☐

19. NAME LAS, FIRST, MIDDLE	20. CODE	21. RESIDENCE ADDRESS 503-665-503	22. RESIDENCE PHONE
HARTNELL, BRYAN CALVIN	V	Rt. 2, Box 252, Troutdale, Oregon	

23. OCCUPATION	24. RAGE – SEX	25. AGE	26. DOB	27. BUSINESS ADDRESS (SCHOOL IF JUVENILE)	28. BUSINESS PHONE
Student	WMA	20	7/1/49	Newton Hall, Pacific Union College	965-[REDACTED]

29. NAME – LAST, FIRST, MIDDLE	30. CODE	31. RESIDENCE ADDRESS	32. RESIDENCE PHONE

33. OCCUPATION	34. RAGE - SEX	35. AGE	36. DOB	37. BUSINESS ADDRESS (SCHOOL IF JUVENILE)	38. BUSINESS PHONE

MODUS OPERANDI (SEE INSTRUCTIONS)

39. DESCRIBE CHARACTERISTICS OF PREMISES AND AREA WHERE OFFENSE OCCURRED

Victims were resting on blanket near shore line, remote area, Lake Berryessa.

40. DESCRIBE BRIEFLY HOW OFFENSE WAS COMMITTED

Suspect approached victims with hood over face and shoulders, with automatic pistol, [REDACTED] victims up and then stabbed them multiple times. Victim CECELIA SHEPARD died 9/29/69 4:00 PM

41. DESCRIBE WEAPON, INSTRUMENT, EQUIPMENT, TRICK, DEVICE OR FORCE USED

Gun (automatic pistol) – Knife, thin blade, appeared home-made.

42. MOTIVE - TYPE OF PROPERTY TAKEN OR OTHER REASON FOR OFFENSE

Homicide.

43. ESTIMATED LOSS VALUE AND/OR EXTENT OF INJURIES – MINOR, MAYOR

Victim CECELIA SHEPARD deceased. Victim BRYAN MARTNELL in serious condition.

44. WHAT DID SUSPECT/S SAY – NOTE PECULIARITIES

I want your money and car keys (Not taken).
45. VICTIMS ACTIVITY JUST PRIOR TO AND/OR DURING OFFENSE Lying on blanket – cozy.
46. TRACEMARK – OTHER DISTINCTIVE ACTION OF SUSPECT/S Suspect wore hood with cross hair symbol – even cross over circle.
47. VEHICLE USED – LICENSE NO – ID NO. – YEAR – MAKE – MODEL – COLOR (OTHER IDENTIFYING CHARACTERISTICS) Vehicle unknown – tire casts made of believed suspect vehicle.

48. SUSPECT NO.1 (LAST, FIRST, MIDDLE)	49. RACE-SEX	50. AGE	51. MT	52.WT	53. MARK	54. EYES	55. ID NO. OR DOB	56. ARRESTED
UNKNOWN	W M	30						YES ☐ NO ☐

57. ADDRESS, CLOTHING AND OTHER IDENTIFYING MARKS OR CHARACTERISTICS
Dark cloth hood, dark cloth jacket, dark pants, automatic pistol in holster right hip, knife in sheath left hip.

58. SUSPECT NO.2 (LAST, FIRST, MIDDLE)	59. RACE-SEX	60. AGE	61. MT	62.WT	63. MARK	64. EYES	65. ID NO. OR DOB	66. ARRESTED
								YES ☐ NO ☐

67. ADDRESS, CLOTHING AND OTHER IDENTIFYING MARKS OR CHARACTERISTICS	68. CHECK IF MORE NAMES IN CONTINUATION ☐

REPORTING OFFICERS	RECORDING OFFICER	TYPED BY	DATE AND TIME	ROUTED BY
Det/Sgts. Narlow - Lonergan	K. Narlow-R. Lonergan	M. Feurle	9/29/69, 5:00PM	

FURTHER ACTION		COPIES TO:			
☐ YES	☐ NO	☐ DETECTIVE	☐ CII		
		☐ JUVENILE	☐ PATROL		
		☐ DIST. ATTNY	☐ ____________ OTHER		
		☐ S.O/P.D	☐ ____________ OTHER	REVIEWED BY	DATE

NAPA COUNTY SHERIFF'S DEPARTMENT SUPPLEMENTARY CRIME REPORT				69. CASE NO. 105907
70. CODE SECTION 187 P.C.	71. CRIME MURDER			72. CLASSIFICATION FELONY
73. VICTIM'S NAME – LAST, FIRST, MIDDLE (FIRM IF BUS.)	74. ADDRESS	☒ RESIDENCE	☐ BUSINESS	75. PHONE
SHEPARD, CECELIA ANN	10733 Mead Lane, Loma Linda			

September 27, 1969 – Reporting Officers Det/Sgts. Kenneth Narlow and Richard Lonergan were both contacted by phone at their residences at 2020 hours and advised that a double stabbing had occurred in the Lake Berryessa area and the victims were en route to Queen of the Valley Hospital via Piner's Ambulance. Lonergan and Narlow were requested to proceed to Queen of the Valley Hospital and take over the case for investigative purposes. Det/Sgt. Kenneth Narlow arrived at Queen of the Valley Hospital at 2033 hours; Det/Sgt. Lonergan arrived at the hospital at 2044 hours.

At 2035 hours Sgt. Narlow received information from Station One that a pay phone booth located at the Napa Car Wash, corner of Main and Clinton Streets, was used by a possible responsible in making a phone call to the Napa Police Department. Sgt. Narlow immediately dispatched Det/Sgt. Harold Snook to proceed to the phone booth and process same for physical evidence.

At 2050 hours Piner's Ambulance bearing the two stabbing victims arrived at Queen of the Valley Hospital. The ambulance personnel was MR. EARL [REDACTED] and MR. ROBERT [REDACTED]; both subjects are employed by the Piner Ambulance Company. The two victims were immediately taken into the Emergency Room and were followed by Reporting Officers. At 2055 hours Officers Lonergan and Narlow were asked to leave the Emergency Room by the attending nurses, as both victims appeared to be in critical condition. The victims were identified at that point as

Victim #1 BRYAN CALVIN HARTNELL, WMA, 20 yrs. of age, DOB 7/1/49, a student at Pacific Union College in Angwin, home address Route 2 Box 252, Troutdale, Oregon.

Victim #2 CECELIA ANN SHEPARD, WFA, 22 yrs. of age, DOB 1/1/47. Subject was a student at the University of California at Riverside, home address 10733 Mead Lane, Loma Linda, California.

It was learned from the nurse on duty (unidentified) that attending physicians were a DR. [REDACTED] and a DR. [REDACTED], and that DR. [REDACTED] had been called however had not arrived as yet. This was at approximately 2100 hours.

Reporting Officers were also advised by an unidentified nurse that when hospital officials were attempting to get ID information out of BRYAN HARTNELL, he advised them to contact JUDY [REDACTED] at Pacific Union College in Angwin. He stated she was CECELIA's best friend. Reporting Officers contacted MR. JIM [REDACTED], Chief Security Officer, Pacific Union College, by phone and asked him to attempt to locate MISS

(cont.)

REPORTING OFFICERS	RECORDING OFFICER	TYPED BY	DATE AND TIME	ROUTED BY
Det/Sgts. Narlow and Lonergan	Det/Sgts. Narlow/Lonergan	M. Feurle	10/4/69, 1:15PM	

FURTHER ACTION		COPIES TO:		
	☒ YES		☒ DETECTIVE	☐ GII
	☐ NO		☐ JUVENILE	☐ PATROL
			☐ DIST. ATTNY	☐ ________ OTHER
			☐ S.O/P.D	☐ ________ OTHER

	REVIEWED BY	DATE

NAPA COUNTY SHERIFF'S DEPARTMENT SUPPLEMENTARY CRIME REPORT -------2				69. CASE NO. 105907
70. CODE SECTION	71. CRIME			72. CLASSIFICATION
187 P.C.	MURDER			FELONY
73. VICTIM'S NAME – LAST, FIRST, MIDDLE (FIRM IF BUS.)	74. ADDRESS	☒ RESIDENCE	☐ BUSINESS	75. PHONE
SHEPARD, CECELIA ANN	10733 Mead Lane, Loma Linda			

JUDY [REDACTED]. MR. [REDACTED] advised that MISS [REDACTED] was a student at the college and had left the college earlier in the afternoon, driving a yellow Datsun. At 2135 hours Reporting Officers put out an All Points Bulletin around the City and County of Napa for this above described vehicle. At 2137 hours Officers received permission to interview the victim BRYAN HARTNELL who was taken to the X-Ray Room for x-rays.

Reporting Officer Det/Sgt. Lonergan attempted to interview BRYAN HARTNELL while in the presence of DONALD [REDACTED] and hospital attendant CLIFFORD [REDACTED]. Sgt. Narlow was called away to answer a phone before the interview got under way. HARTNELL appeared to be in extreme pain and also appeared to be in shock. Reporting Officer Lonergan introduced himself to HARTNELL and asked him to give us any information he had on his assailant.

HARTNELL stated that the assailant was wearing a black ceremonial type hood, square on top, and appeared to be heavy-set, between 200 and 250 pounds. He also stated his assailant had approached both him and MISS SHEPARD with a gun but had stabbed them with a long knife. HARTNELL further stated the gun was in a black holster and the knife was in a sheath. He stated that the attacker was wearing dark clothing, dark jacket and dark pants. HARTNELL further stated that the gun was an automatic pistol and the knife had a black handle and appeared to be homemade.

It should be noted that HARTNELL was very groggy and he was very difficult to interview at that time. Subject was re-interviewed the next day by Det/Sgt. Robertson and gave more complete details. (The report of Sgt. Robertson's interview is attached.)

At 2215 hours R/Os Narlow and Lonergan left the Queen of the Valley Hospital after advising Deputy Sheriffs Allen Brambrink and William Munk to take charge of the clothing of the victims and any other evidence from the victims when it was released from the hospital. Munk and Brambrink were also advised to stand by at the hospital as a security measure until other arrangements could be made.

As Reporting Officers Narlow and Lonergan were arriving at the Napa County Sheriff's Office, they were advised by the Napa Police Department that they had located MISS JUDY [REDACTED] in the downtown Napa area and were bringing her to the Napa County Sheriff's Office. MISS [REDACTED] was interviewed by Lonergan and Narlow at the Napa County Sheriff's Office. She was further identified as MISS JUDITH [REDACTED], a student at Pacific Union College, with a permanent residence address of [REDACTED] Sunland Boulevard, Sun Valley, California. MISS [REDACTED] advised that she was with BRYAN

(cont.)

REPORTING OFFICERS	RECORDING OFFICER	TYPED BY	DATE AND TIME	ROUTED BY
Det/Sgts. Narlow and Lonergan	Det/Sgts. Narlow/Lonergan	M. Feurle	10/4/69, 1:15PM	

FURTHER ACTION		COPIES TO:		
☒ YES	☐ NO	☒ DETECTIVE	☐ GII	
		☐ JUVENILE	☐ PATROL	
		☐ DIST. ATTNY	☐ ________ OTHER	
		☐ S.O/P.D	☐ ________ OTHER	

	REVIEWED BY	DATE

NAPA COUNTY SHERIFF'S DEPARTMENT SUPPLEMENTARY CRIME REPORT -------3				69. CASE NO. 105907
70. CODE SECTION 187 P.C.	71. CRIME MURDER			72. CLASSIFICATION FELONY
73. VICTIM'S NAME – LAST, FIRST, MIDDLE (FIRM IF BUS.)	74. ADDRESS	☒ RESIDENCE	☐ BUSINESS	75. PHONE
SHEPARD, CECELIA ANN	10733 Mead Lane, Loma Linda			

HARTNELL and CECELIA SHEPARD earlier in the afternoon. She stated that they all left Pacific Union College together at approximately 1:00 P.M. and went to a rummage sale in the City of St. Helena. She stated that BRYAN had bought a T.V. set at the rummage sale and had to transport it back to his room at Pacific Union College. She stated he left CECELIA at the rummage sale as there was not enough room in his car. MISS [REDACTED] stated BRYAN returned to the St. Helena area and picked up CECELIA at approximately 2:00 P.M. MISS [REDACTED] stated as far as she knew, both BRYAN and CECELIA were planning to go to San Francisco when they left her in St. Helena. MISS [REDACTED] stated she had no knowledge of any plans that BRYAN and CECELIA were making to go to the Lake Berryessa area. MISS [REDACTED] stated the last time she saw BRYAN and CECELIA was approximately 2:00 P.M. in the afternoon. The interview with MISS [REDACTED] was terminated at that point.

Det/Sgts. Lonergan and Narlow then proceeded to Lake Berryessa and arrived at the scene of the crime, which was approximately a mile and a half north of Lake Berryessa Park Headquarters, at 2354 hours. The scene was being preserved by uniformed officers and under the direct control of Deputy Sheriffs David Collins and Ray Land. The investigating officers were briefed by Officers Collins and Land as to what had taken place prior to our arrival.

Officers observed a 1956 white Kharman Ghia with a black vinyl top, Oregon License plate 4 U 2040. Investigating officers were shown footprints in dirt area and tire tracks, both believed to have been left by responsible. Investigating officers awaited the arrival of Sgt. Tom Butler who had been called to take photographs of the crime scene area and Sgt. Hal Snock, criminalist for collection and preservation of physical evidence.

R/Os Narlow and Lonergan were advised by Park Ranger Dennis Land who had also arrived at the scene that it was possible to get to the beach area by vehicle from a locked gate approximately one-half mile south of the victim's vehicle. Officers proceeded to the area and arrived at the footpath approximately halfway between the scene of the crime at the beach and the victim's vehicle on the road. At that point, after a brief examination of the footpath area, officers discovered a similar footprint on the footpath to that found at the scene of the victim's vehicle. At that point, due to the lateness and darkness of the hour, Reporting Officers decided to completely secure the area and make a thorough search of the scene at first light.

Officers then exited the crime scene area in the same manner and locked the afore mentioned gate leading to this vicinity. Investigating officers along with Park Ranger Dennis Land went to Berryessa Park Headquarters. At this time Sgt. Narlow

(cont'd)

REPORTING OFFICERS	RECORDING OFFICER	TYPED BY	DATE AND TIME	ROUTED BY
Det/Sgts. Narlow and Lonergan	Det/Sgts. Narlow/Lonergan	M. Feurle	10/4/69, 1:15PM	

FURTHER ACTION		COPIES TO:		
	☒ YES		☒ DETECTIVE	☐ GII
	☐ NO		☐ JUVENILE	☐ PATROL
			☐ DIST. ATTNY	☐ ________ OTHER
			☐ S.O/P.D	☐ ________ OTHER

	REVIEWED BY	DATE

NAPA COUNTY SHERIFF'S DEPARTMENT SUPPLEMENTARY CRIME REPORT -------4				69. CASE NO. 105907
70. CODE SECTION 187 P.C.	71. CRIME MURDER			72. CLASSIFICATION FELONY
73. VICTIM'S NAME – LAST, FIRST, MIDDLE (FIRM IF BUS.)	74. ADDRESS	☒ RESIDENCE	☐ BUSINESS	75. PHONE
SHEPARD, CECELIA ANN	10733 Mead Lane, Loma Linda			

took into his possession certain items belonging to the victims that were taken into evidence by Ranger Dennis Land. These items consisted of a blanket, a pair of man's shoes, a wallet belonging to BRYAN HARTNELL, eyeglasses, and playing cards. Among the various aforementioned items believed to belong to the victims, were numerous strands of white plastic line cut into various assorted lengths, some of which had what appeared to be bloodstains. These items were subsequently turned over to Det/Sgt. Hal Snook for preservation.

Assigned investigators then proceeded back to the scene where the victim's car was parked and assisted Sgt. Snook in the making of the plaster casts. At approximately 0245 hours Sgt. Lonergan, having previously obtained the keys to the vehicle from BRYAN HARNELL's property at Queen of the Valley Hospital, drove the white Kharman Ghia to the maintenance stop at Berryessa Park Headquarters. The vehicle was parked inside of the maintenance shop building and the building was secured for the evening by investigating officers with the assistance of Park Ranger Dennis Land.

Assigned investigators then returned back to the scene where the victim's vehicle had been previously parked and awaited the arrival of Deputy Sheriffs Allen Brambrink and Mel Fechter who were assigned to security duty in the crime scene area. At approximately 0300 hours officers assumed their duties at the crime scene area and the security was placed under the direction of Deputy Allen Brambrink. Reporting Officers Narlow and Lonergan then returned to their respective residences with plans to continue the investigation at daybreak.

9/28/69 – 0700 hours – R/Os Narlow and Lonergan returned to the scene at Lake Berryessa area, accompanied by Det/Sgt. Harold Snook, Capt. Donald Townsend, and Sgt. James Munk. Officers then assisted Det/Sgt. Snook in tracking the footprints from the vehicle to the scene of the crime by the beach area. (The location and preservation of aforementioned footprints will be detailed in a supplementary evidence report by Sgt. Snook.)

At 0800 hours Reporting Officers Lonergan and Narlow received information via Park Headquarters that a DR. CLIFTON [REDACTED] and his son would like to talk to them at the Spanish Flat Coffee Shop regarding a possible suspect in this crime. At 0912 hours R/Os Narlow and Lonergan contacted Dr. R. CLIFTON [REDACTED] and his 16-yr. old son DAVID LEE [REDACTED] at the Spanish Flat Coffee Shop. DR. [REDACTED] gave a home address of [REDACTED] Cypress Way, Los Gatos, California (phone number [REDACTED]). DR. [REDACTED] stated that about 6:30 P.M. the previous evening he and his son had parked their car north of Park Headquarters in the general area of the

(cont'd)

REPORTING OFFICERS	RECORDING OFFICER	TYPED BY	DATE AND TIME	ROUTED BY
Det/Sgts. Narlow and Lonergan	Det/Sgts. Narlow/Lonergan	M. Feurle	10/4/69, 1:15PM	

FURTHER ACTION		COPIES TO:		
	☒ YES		☒ DETECTIVE	☐ GII
	☐ NO		☐ JUVENILE	☐ PATROL
			☐ DIST. ATTNY	☐ ________ OTHER
			☐ S.O/P.D	☐ ________ OTHER

	REVIEWED BY	DATE

NAPA COUNTY SHERIFF'S DEPARTMENT SUPPLEMENTARY CRIME REPORT -------5					69. CASE NO. 105907
70. CODE SECTION 187 P.C.	71. CRIME MURDER			72. CLASSIFICATION FELONY	
73. VICTIM'S NAME – LAST, FIRST, MIDDLE (FIRM IF BUS.)	74. ADDRESS	☒ RESIDENCE	☐ BUSINESS	75. PHONE	
SHEPARD, CECELIA ANN	10733 Mead Lane, Loma Linda				

crime scene. They stated they went towards the beach area when DAVID noticed a white male adult subject walking in the area, described as about 5'10", heavy build, wearing dark trousers, a dark shirt with red in it, long sleeves. He stated this subject was carrying nothing in his hands and was apparently just walking alongside the hill area about halfway between the road and the lake. DAVID further stated that when the subject observed him he turned around and walked up the hill in a southerly direction. DR. [REDACTED] and his son stated that they did not notice a vehicle in the area of their vehicle and only this subject at a distance of about 100 yards. They also advised there was a man with two young boys in the area shooting B-B guns, but they did not know if this man saw the subject or not. This location was approximately 8/10ths of a mile from the scene of the victim's vehicle. In the opinion of R/Os, it is unlikely, unless this male subject had a vehicle in the immediate area, he could have traversed the area to the scene of the crime on foot. There are four coves of water between the scene of the crime and the area where the doctor saw the subject. The interview with DR. [REDACTED] and his son was terminated at that point.

At 1000 hours R/Os Narlow and Lonergan returned to the scene of the crime and further assisted Sgt. Snook in the collecting and locating of evidence.

At 1320 hours 9/28/69, R/Os interviewed Ranger Sgt. William White at Lake Berryessa Park Headquarters. White was interviewed as to his activities before and during his part in locating the victims the night before. White stated at approximately 1055 hours 9/27/69 he was on routine patrol around the Lake Berryessa area when he received a call from Park Headquarters to proceed to the Rancho Monticello Resort where a person was reporting a possible stabbing. White stated he proceeded to the Rancho Monticello Resort where he was contacted by ARCHIE E. WHITE, MRS. ELIZABETH WHITE, and RONALD FONG. RONALD FONG advised him that he had seen a male and a female victim on the beach area south of Rancho Monticello Resort, hollering that they had been stabbed. Ranger Sgt. White, accompanied by ARCHIE WHITE, ELIZABETH WHITE, and RONALD FONG, proceeded to the beach area via speedboat owned by ARCHIE WHITE. When they arrived on the beach they observed a young female lying on the ground with what appeared to be numerous stabs wounds. Ranger Sgt. White stated that the female appeared to be in a great deal of pain. White stated as they discovered the female victim, Ranger Dennis Land arrived at the scene in his pickup truck, carrying a male victim who also appeared to have numerous stab wounds. White stated he immediately radioed in and had Park Headquarters call the Sheriff's Office to dispatch an ambulance and a Deputy.

White stated he attempted to interview both the boy and girl victims while awaiting

(cont'd)

REPORTING OFFICERS	RECORDING OFFICER	TYPED BY	DATE AND TIME	ROUTED BY
Det/Sgts. Narlow and Lonergan	Det/Sgts. Narlow/Lonergan	M. Feurle	10/5/69, 9 A.M.	

FURTHER ACTION		COPIES TO:		
	☒ YES		☒ DETECTIVE	☐ GII
	☐ NO		☐ JUVENILE	☐ PATROL
			☐ DIST. ATTNY	☐ ________ OTHER
			☐ S.O/P.D	☐ ________ OTHER

	REVIEWED BY	DATE

NAPA COUNTY SHERIFF'S DEPARTMENT SUPPLEMENTARY CRIME REPORT ------------6			69. CASE NO. 105907
70. CODE SECTION 187 P.C.	71. CRIME MURDER		72. CLASSIFICATION FELONY
73. VICTIM'S NAME – LAST, FIRST, MIDDLE (FIRM IF BUS.)	74. ADDRESS ☒ RESIDENCE ☐ BUSINESS		75. PHONE
SHEPARD, CECELIA ANN	10733 Mead Lane, Loma Linda		

arrival of the ambulance. According to White, the male victim said that a male subject approached them, wearing a hood, dressed in dark clothing. The subject was carrying what appeared to be an automatic pistol and stated that he wanted their money and car keys. According to White, the male victim related to him that the subject advised him he was an ex-con out of Colorado and was in route to Mexico. Suspect stated he had to tie them up, and after they were tied the responsible stated, "I'm going to have to stab you." White further related that the male victim advised the responsible, "Stab me first, I can't stand to see her stabbed first." The male victim then advised that the responsible stabbed him numerous times in the back and then stabbed the girl.

The female victim advised White that she could not see the responsible's face as a hood was covering all of his head. She also advised White that the suspect had what appeared to be clip-on sunglasses to cover his eyes.

Ranger Sgt. White stated that this is the most he could get out of either victim as they were both in great shock and pain. White stated that he noticed a lot of blood near the girl's groin area. The interview with Ranger Sgt. White was terminated at that point.

9/28/69 – 1400 hours – Reporting Officers proceeded to the Rancho Monticello Resort and interviewed MR. ARCHIE E. WHITE. (It should be noted that ARCHIE E. WHITE and ELIZABETH WHITE are no relation to Ranger Sgt. White.) ARCHIE E. WHITE is the owner of the Boat Repair Shop at Rancho Monticello Resort. He lives at the Resort and his phone number is [REDACTED]. Also interviewed were MR. WHITE's wife, MRS. ELIZABETH WHITE. MR. and MRS. WHITE advised that they were contacted by RONAL FONG who advised them he had just observed what appeared to be a male and a female subject lying on the beach south of the Rancho Monticello Resort, covered with blood. FONG advised them that the couple had shouted out to him that they had been stabbed and robbed. MRS. WHITE immediately called Park Headquarters and Ranger Sgt. William White arrived at the Resort a short time later. MR. and MRS, accompanied by Ranger Sgt. Bill White and RONALD FONG, proceeded to the scene area in one of MR. WHITE's ski boats.

When they arrived on the scene, they observed a young female wearing a sweater dress, lying on the beach, covered with blood. When they approached the area she was on her elbows and knees, rocking back and forth as if in great pain. MRS. WHITE stated she immediately attempted to make the victim more comfortable and tried to calm her down until the ambulance arrived. MRS. WHITE stated the girl advised him, "He was a man with a hood... His face was covered... He was wearing black pants... It hurts, it

(cont'd)

REPORTING OFFICERS	RECORDING OFFICER	TYPED BY	DATE AND TIME TYPED	ROUTED BY
Det/Sgts. Narlow and Lonergan	Det/Sgts. Narlow/Lonergan	M. Feurle	10/5/69, 9A.M.	

FURTHER ACTION		COPIES TO:		
	☒ YES		☒ DETECTIVE	☐ GII
	☐ NO		☐ JUVENILE	☐ PATROL
			☐ DIST. ATTNY	☐ ______ OTHER
			☐ S.O/P.D	☐ ______ OTHER

	REVIEWED BY	DATE

NAPA COUNTY SHERIFF'S DEPARTMENT SUPPLEMENTARY CRIME REPORT ------------7				69. CASE NO. 105907
70. CODE SECTION 187 P.C.	71. CRIME MURDER			72. CLASSIFICATION FELONY
73. VICTIM'S NAME – LAST, FIRST, MIDDLE (FIRM IF BUS.)	74. ADDRESS	☒ RESIDENCE	☐ BUSINESS	75. PHONE
SHEPARD, CECELIA ANN	10733 Mead Lane, Loma Linda			

hurts." MRS. WHITE then advised after the female had regained her composure, she told her the man had asked for money but didn't take any. She said she hadn't been raped. MRS. WHITE further advised that the female victim told her that the responsible was wearing glasses, with dark clip-on sunglasses over the hood. She told her that the responsible had a black pistol. MR. ARCHIE WHITE stated he overheard the male victim advise someone that the responsible was wearing gloves. MR. and MRS. WHITE further advised that this is the only information either victim gave them on the responsible, and that they spent the balance of the time attempting to make the victim more comfortable until the arrival of the ambulance.

After the interview with MR. and MRS. WHITE, Reporting Officers Narlow and Lonergan returned to the Napa County Sheriff's Office. At 1620 hours R/O Det/Sgt. Narlow was contacted by a DEAN [REDACTED] of the Pacific Union College in Angwin (phone number [REDACTED]). DEAN advised that three young ladies, students at the college, might possibly have information as to a suspect in the attack at Lake Berryessa. The young ladies were identified as MISS JOANNE [REDACTED], MISS LINDA [REDACTED], and MISS LINDA [REDACTED]. DEAN [REDACTED] advised that these girls had been in the Lake Berryessa area from about 3:00 P.M. to 4:30 P.M. the previous Saturday afternoon. They had observed a male subject in a late model, silver blue Chevrolet, two miles north of the A & W Root Beer stand on Knoxville Road. DEAN [REDACTED] advised that the girls had told him they were observed out of the car by this subject while they were sunbathing on the beach. They described the subject as approximately 40 years old, 6 feet tall, dressed in dark clothing. Sgt. Narlow dispatched Deputy Sheriff Raymond Land to interview these three girls that evening. (The report of Land's interview is attached.)

Reporting Officers spent the balance of the day and evening going through their investigative notes and issuing a statewide ALL Points Bulletin.

Monday, 9/29/69 – Reporting Officers Narlow and Lonergan spent the majority of the morning interviewing numerous citizens and officers from other departments regarding this crime and similar crimes. (A general list of possible suspects was begun and they are noted on separate incident reports as to origin of information and description of suspects, attached.)

Reporting Officers were advised by Deputy Sheriff Ray Land who interviewed the three college girls, MISS [REDACTED], MISS [REDACTED], and MISS [REDACTED], that the information appeared to have some merit and advised that the three young ladies would be in the office in the afternoon four further interview.

(cont'd)

REPORTING OFFICERS	RECORDING OFFICER	TYPED BY	DATE AND TIME TYPED	ROUTED BY
Det/Sgts. Narlow and Lonergan	Det/Sgts. Narlow/Lonergan	M. Feurle	10/5/69, 2 P.M.	

FURTHER ACTION		COPIES TO:		
☒ YES	☐ NO	☒ DETECTIVE	☐ GII	
		☐ JUVENILE	☐ PATROL	
		☐ DIST. ATTNY	☐ ______ OTHER	
		☐ S.O/P.D	☐ ______ OTHER	

NAPA COUNTY SHERIFF'S DEPARTMENT	69. CASE NO. 105907
SUPPLEMENTARY CRIME REPORT ------------8	

70. CODE SECTION	71. CRIME	72. CLASSIFICATION
187 P.C.	MURDER	FELONY

73. VICTIM'S NAME – LAST, FIRST, MIDDLE (FIRM IF BUS.)	74. ADDRESS ☒ RESIDENCE ☐ BUSINESS	75. PHONE
SHEPARD, CECELIA ANN	10733 Mead Lane, Loma Linda	

9/29/69 – 1445 hours – The three young ladies came into the office and were interviewed by R/O Sgt. Lonergan, Sgt. Snook, and Capt. Donald Townsend. R/O Lonergan interviewed a MISS JOANNE MARIE [REDACTED], WFA, 21 years of age, DOB 6/4/48. Her address at the college is [REDACTED] Dauphine, Pacific Union College (phone number [REDACTED], Extension 311), home address

[REDACTED] South East 12th, College Place, Washington. MISS [REDACTED] advised R/O that on 9/27/69 at approximately 3:30 P.M. she and her two girlfriends parked their vehicle at a location two miles north of the A & W Root Beer stand on Knoxville Road. When they left their car they noticed a subject driving a late model silver blue Chevrolet, 2-door sedan, pull behind them. What appeared to be a white male adult was sitting in the vehicle. They did not observe this subject leave the vehicle. The girls proceeded to the beach area and were sunbathing in their bikinis. After approximately one-half hour had passed, they observed what appeared to be the same subject standing within 40 or 50 feet of them, apparently observing them. This subject was described as 6' tall, weighting 200/210 lbs., muscular build, rather nice-looking. Subject was wearing dark pants and a dark pull-over shirt. The subject would stare at the three girls but when they looked up at him he would look away. The subject hung around the area for approximately 45 minutes and then the girls observed him walk up the hill. MISS [REDACTED] stated it was very doubtful that from his vantage point in the vehicle the subject could observe the three girls on the beach. She believes he waited in his vehicle and then followed them down after they were on the beach. MISS [REDACTED] further described the car as appearing very conservative. She stated the car did not appear to belong to any young person such as a teenager. She did state the car had California license plates but did not notice the number.

The other two young ladies, MISS [REDACTED] and MISS [REDACTED] were interviewed by Sgt. Snook and Capt. Donald Townsend. MISS LINDA [REDACTED], who was interviewed by R/O Det/Sgt. Snook, is a WFA, DOB 6/29/47, home address [REDACTED] Sunnyside Road, Sanitarium (phone number [REDACTED]. MISS [REDACTED] stated she left the Angwin area with two other girls, JOANNE [REDACTED] and LINDA [REDACTED], at approximately 2:45 P.M. 9/27/69. The girls drove through Pope Valley to Lake Berryesa where they parked their vehicle two mile north of the A & W Root Beer stand. MISS [REDACTED] stated she observed a subject go into the parking lot area to the south. Subject went past their vehicle and backed up so their rear bumpers were nearly touching. Vehicle described as a 1966 or 1967 light blue Chevrolet with California plates. Witness believes the vehicle was a 2-door sedan and described the headlights as being long rather than round. The rear window glass was tinted quite dark.

Another vehicle from Angwin with Arizona plates was in the parking area and witness saw the occupants, a MISS DENISE BROWN and a MR. WAYNE HAIGHT. The three girls went

(cont'd)

REPORTING OFFICERS	RECORDING OFFICER	TYPED BY	DATE AND TIME TYPED	ROUTED BY

Det/Sgts. Narlow and Lonergan	Det/Sgts. Narlow/Lonergan	M. Feurle	10/5/69, 2:00 P.M.	

FURTHER ACTION	☒ YES ☐ NO	COPIES TO:	☒ DETECTIVE ☐ JUVENILE ☐ DIST. ATTNY ☐ S.O/P.D	☐ GII ☐ PATROL ☐ ______ OTHER ☐ ______ OTHER	

NAPA COUNTY SHERIFF'S DEPARTMENT SUPPLEMENTARY CRIME REPORT ------------9	69. CASE NO. 105907

70. CODE SECTION	71. CRIME			72. CLASSIFICATION
187 P.C.	MURDER			FELONY
73. VICTIM'S NAME – LAST, FIRST, MIDDLE (FIRM IF BUS.)	74. ADDRESS	☒ RESIDENCE	☐ BUSINESS	75. PHONE
SHEPARD, CECELIA ANN	10733 Mead Lane, Loma Linda			

to the beach and shortly thereafter noticed the male subject watching them from the edge of the trees. After about 30 minutes the subject came down by the beach and passed within 20 feet of witness [REDACTED] as he walked from south to north. Subject was described by MISS [REDACTED] as approximately 28 years of age, 6' to 6'2" tall, 200/225 lbs., black hair possibly styled, with a part on left, rounded eyes, thin lips, medium nose, straight eyebrows, small ears, well built, rather nice-looking. Subject was wearing a black short-sleeved sweater shirt, bunched up in front, and a white tee shirt hanging out in back, and dark trousers. The three girls left the area about 4:30 P.M. and the subject's vehicle was gone. Witnesses did not observe the subject either leave or get back into his vehicle.

MISS LINDA LEE [REDACTED] was interviewed by R/O Capt. Donald Townsend. MISS [REDACTED] is WFA, DOB 7/8/48, address [REDACTED] Howell Mountain Road, Angwin (telephone number [REDACTED]). MISS [REDACTED] is employed as a secretary of the college press. MISS [REDACTED] observed the same vehicle which was described as a late model Chevrolet, sky blue in color. The rear tail lights appeared to be long rather than round. MISS [REDACTED] stated they parked their vehicle at approximately 2:55 P.M. and observed the subject in his vehicle at that location. The girls proceeded to the beach and she, MISS [REDACTED], again noticed the subject about 30 to 45 minutes after they were at the beach. She noticed him standing on the bank approximately 45 yards from her location. She described the subject as 6 feet tall, stocky build, about 200 lbs., black short-sleeved sweater shirt, dark blue slacks, and straight dark hair neatly combed. She guessed his age at approximately 30 years. Subject had medium color skin and was not wearing glasses. [REDACTED] stated she thought she saw a white belt around his back but it possible was a tee shirt hanging out. She further stated that the man was fairly nice-looking, with a round face. MISS [REDACTED] did not observe the subject leave the area in his vehicle.

9/29/69 – 1600 hours – Reporting Officers Sgt. Narlow and Sgt. Lonergan were advised by Capt. Joseph Page that the female victim, MISS CECELIA SHEPARD, had just died at Queen of the Valley Hospital. Capt. Page, who is Chief Napa County Coroner, stated he would handle the case and contact DR. DE PETRIS who would perform the autopsy the next morning. Capt. Page further advised R/Os that the remains would be removed to Morrison Funeral Home where DR. DE PETRIS would complete the autopsy.

At 1945 hours 9/29/69, R/Os Narlow and Lonergan were contacted by Probation Officer H. B. [REDACTED]. Mr. [REDACTED] had observed the footprint design that R/Os had taken at the scene and stated he had knowledge of a possible similar shoe sole design. Mr. [REDACTED] brought into the office a MR. BASSEL M. [REDACTED], address [REDACTED] Sheveland, Apartment #7, NAPA, California (phone number [REDACTED]). MR. [REDACTED] is employed at Travis

(cont'd)

REPORTING OFFICERS	RECORDING OFFICER	TYPED BY	DATE AND TIME TYPED	ROUTED BY
Det/Sgts. Narlow and Lonergan	Det/Sgts. Narlow/Lonergan	M. Feurle	10/5/69, 2:00 P.M.	

FURTHER ACTION	☒ YES ☐ NO	COPIES TO:	☒ DETECTIVE ☐ JUVENILE ☐ DIST. ATTNY ☐ S.O/P.D	☐ GII ☐ PATROL ☐ ______ OTHER ☐ ______ OTHER

	REVIEWED BY	DATE

NAPA COUNTY SHERIFF'S DEPARTMENT

SUPPLEMENTARY CRIME REPORT ------------10

69. CASE NO. 105907

70. CODE SECTION	71. CRIME	72. CLASSIFICATION

187 P.C.	MURDER			FELONY
73. VICTIM'S NAME – LAST, FIRST, MIDDLE (FIRM IF BUS.)	74. ADDRESS	☒ RESIDENCE	☐ BUSINESS	75. PHONE
SHEPARD, CECELIA ANN	10733 Mead Lane, Loma Linda			

Air Force Base and is a Flight Line Mechanic. He is a retired Master Sergeant in the United States Air Force. MR. [REDACTED] showed R/O a pair of Air Force chukker boots that belonged to him. He described these boots as being Government issue, issued to all Air Force personnel at Lackland Air Force Base, Texas. They are primarily designed as a wing-walker shoe, however according to MR. [REDACTED], most Air Force personnel and many of the civilian personnel employed at Air Force bases had this type of shoe. The sole design of this shoe exactly matched the plaster cast design that Sgt. Snook had taken at the scene of the crime. It should be noted that Det/Sgt John Robertson had attempted to find a similar show design at the local shoe stores in the Napa area, with negative results. (Refer Sgt. Robertson's supplementary report.) MR. [REDACTED] was asked if we could keep his shoes for identification regarding the type of footprint R/Os had discovered had not been released to the press or general public. MR. [REDACTED] stated he would cooperate with R/Os and keep this information confidential.

9/30/69, 0810 hours – R/O Sgt. Lonergan received a telephone call from a MISS MARILYN DENISE [REDACTED], 18 years of age, DOB 4/26/51. MISS [REDACTED] is a student at Pacific Union College and resides at Andre Hall, Room B-3. MISS [REDACTED] stated that about 5:15 P.M. Saturday, 9/27/69 she was in the Lake Berryessa area with a male companion, a MR. JOHN [REDACTED], 22 years of age, also a student at Pacific Union College. She stated at this time they were parked on the Knoxville Road approximately one mile south of the Lake Berryessa Marina. She stated shortly after they parked the vehicle they observed the victims who were known to them, BRYAN HARTNELL and CECELIA SHEPARD, driving south on Knoxville Road in BRYAN's white Kharman Ghia. She stated as the HARTNELL vehicle drove by, BRYAN waved out the window and said, "Hi, John!", referring to MR. [REDACTED]. MISS [REDACTED] stated that they did not see the HARTNELL vehicle any other time that day.

9/30/69, 0900 hours – R/Os Det/Sgt. Narlow and Det/Sgt. Richard Lonergan, accompanied by Sgt. Thomas Butler, proceeded to the Morrison Funeral Home in St. Helena. They were met at the funeral home by Capt. Joseph Page and the owner of the Funeral Home, Mr. Harold [REDACTED]. Shortly after the R/Os arrived, they were met by the pathology surgeons, DR. WILMER A. DE PETRIS and DR. DWIGHT G. STRAUB. DR. DE PETRIS' offices are at 373 Perkings Street, Sonoma (phone number 996-1083). Above mentioned officers witnessed the autopsy of the female victim, MISS

CECELIA SHEPARD, performed by DRS. DE PETRIS and STRAUB. Sgt. Tom Butler took photographs of the deceased both before and during the autopsy. R/O Sgt. Lonergan took notes of the various wounds suffered by the victim. (Complete autopsy report and findings by DRS. DE PETRIS and STRAUB is attached.) The autopsy was concluded at 12:00 noon. Briefly stated, DR. DE PETRIS

(cont'd)

REPORTING OFFICERS	RECORDING OFFICER	TYPED BY	DATE AND TIME TYPED	ROUTED BY
Det/Sgts. Narlow and Lonergan	Det/Sgts. Narlow/Lonergan	M. Feurle	10/5/69, 3 P.M.	

FURTHER ACTION	☒ YES ☐ NO	COPIES TO:	☒ DETECTIVE ☐ JUVENILE ☐ DIST. ATTNY ☐ S.O/P.D	☐ GII ☐ PATROL ☐ ________ OTHER ☐ ________ OTHER	
				REVIEWED BY	DATE

NAPA COUNTY SHERIFF'S DEPARTMENT SUPPLEMENTARY CRIME REPORT ------------11			69. CASE NO. 105907
70. CODE SECTION 187 P.C.	71. CRIME MURDER		72. CLASSIFICATION FELONY
73. VICTIM'S NAME – LAST, FIRST, MIDDLE (FIRM IF BUS.)	74. ADDRESS	☒ RESIDENCE ☐ BUSINESS	75. PHONE
SHEPARD, CECELIA ANN	10733 Mead Lane, Loma Linda		

advised that the cause of death was shock and loss of blood brought on by two main stab wounds.

9/30/69, 1430 hours – R/O Det/Sgt. Kenneth Narlow contacted CAPT. [REDACTED] at Travis Air Force Base and arranged for an interview with COL. [REDACTED], CAPT. [REDACTED], and SGT. [REDACTED] to take place on Wednesday morning, October 1st, 1969, at 9:00 A.M. R/Os wanted to talk to someone at Travis regarding the shoeprints that were found on the scene. The remainder of the day and evening was spent in answering phone calls from people who had possible knowledge of the crime.

Wednesday, 10/1/69 – 0900 hours – Sgts. Lonergan and Narlow went to Travis Air Force Base and were present at an interview in Col. [REDACTED] office, who is Commanding Officer in charge of base security. Also present at this meeting besides the aforementioned officers was LT. COL. [REDACTED] of the Office of Special Investigation. Reporting Officers Narlow and Lonergan advised the Air Force personnel present of the portion of the evidence we had discovered at the crime scene and asked them for assistance in locating where this type of shoe was sold or issued. LT. COL. [REDACTED] advised that this office would assist assigned investigators in attempting to locate the source of the shoe.

Officers were directed to the Base Supply with the assistance of Special Agent DONAL [REDACTED] of O.S.I, at which time it was determined through Base Supply that this shoe in question was of Government issue and that it was not kept in stock at Base Supply, however it was believed that the Sales Store had such an item. It was explained that if a military person or civilian employee was determined to be in need of such an item, he first reported to the Base Supply, at which time he was issued a purchase requisition which he in turn look to the Sales Store and the type of shoe was issued to the individual and they in turn required the individual to sign the purchase requisition showing that he did receive the item. This purchase requisition states the type of shoe that the individual was to receive, however makes no reference as to size.

Assigned investigators, accompanied by Special Agent [REDACTED], proceeded to the Sales Store located on Travis Air Force Base. After a short period of time R/Os located in stock a shoe fitting the identical description of the artist's sketch drawn from the plaster cast which officers had in their possession. The identical shoe with identical tread was found and a shoe bearing the closest measurements in the artist's sketch drawn from the plaster cast was measured and found to be a size 10 ½ R in military styling or a 10 ½ D in civilian equivalent. It was determined through Air Force records that they were unable to furnish officers with the

(cont'd)

REPORTING OFFICERS	RECORDING OFFICER	TYPED BY	DATE AND TIME TYPED	ROUTED BY
Det/Sgts. Narlow and Lonergan	Det/Sgts. Narlow/Lonergan	M. Feurle	10/5/69, 3 P.M.	

FURTHER ACTION		COPIES TO:		
	☒ YES		☒ DETECTIVE	☐ GII
	☐ NO		☐ JUVENILE	☐ PATROL
			☐ DIST. ATTNY	☐ ______ OTHER
			☒ S.O/P.D	☐ ______ OTHER

NAPA COUNTY SHERIFF'S DEPARTMENT SUPPLEMENTARY CRIME REPORT ------------12					69. CASE NO. 105907
70. CODE SECTION 187 P.C.	71. CRIME MURDER			72. CLASSIFICATION FELONY	
73. VICTIM'S NAME – LAST, FIRST, MIDDLE (FIRM IF BUS.)	74. ADDRESS	☒ RESIDENCE	☐ BUSINESS	75. PHONE	
SHEPARD, CECELIA ANN	10733 Mead Lane, Loma Linda				

data regarding the sales of this type shoe due to the fact that no recordings were made of the specific sizes, however purchase records indicate over the past 13 months approximately 100 pairs of this size shoe, namely 10 ½ R, had been purchased and disposed of through sales. Air Force records indicate this type shoe is manufactured by the International Shoe Company, Philadelphia, Pennsylvania, then shipped to Air Force Depot, Ogden, Utah, and from there shipped to the various military installations upon requisition orders.

10/1/69 – 1400 hours – Reporting Officers Narlow and Lonergan then proceeded to the Vallejo Police Department and met with Sgt. Jack Mullanax and Sgt. Duane Nilsson. Officers exchanged information regarding Vallejo's crime of 7/4/69 and our particular incident. Suspect information was exchanged and is listed in the separate suspect file.

Investigating Officers checked to determine the validity of the decoded message and as to how far the original ciphers had been decoded. It was then learned that the message had been decoded by at least two different sources, one being by MR. and MRS. HARDIN of Salinas and the other by the FBI in Washington. It as noted that these cyphers were broken independent of one another and the FBI confirmed the validity of the original decoded message. It as also learned that there was a small portion on the very end of the coded message that had not been decoded for reasons unknown.

The balance of the afternoon and evening Reporting Officers and other investigating officers met to exchange information and further discuss the evidence at hand.

Thursday, October 2nd, 1969, 0845 hours – Reporting Officer Lonergan received a telephone call from Special Agent DONALD [REDACTED], OSI, Travis Air Force Base. Subject called to report that approximately 500 to 1,000 of that type of wing-walker shoe have been sold as surplus on the Base.

This would be over and above those sold at the Sales Store. Agent [REDACTED] further related he has the names of all the subjects who have purchased this item through surplus and will keep these names available to officers upon request.

The balance of the morning was spent searching fingerprints evidence and answering phone calls from possible witnesses.

Thursday, 10/2/69, 1400 hours – R/Os Narlow and Lonergan attended the funeral services for victim CECELIA SHEPARD. These services were held at the Pacific Union College Church, Angwin, California. Sgts. Narlow and Lonergan positioned themselves

(cont'd)

REPORTING OFFICERS	RECORDING OFFICER	TYPED BY	DATE AND TIME TYPED	ROUTED BY
Det/Sgts. Narlow and Lonergan	Det/Sgts. Narlow/Lonergan	M. Feurle	10/5/69, 4 P.M.	

FURTHER ACTION		COPIES TO:		
☒ YES	☐ NO	☒ DETECTIVE	☐ GII	
		☐ JUVENILE	☐ PATROL	
		☐ DIST. ATTNY	☐ ________ OTHER	
		☐ S.O/P.D	☐ ________ OTHER	

	REVIEWED BY	DATE

NAPA COUNTY SHERIFF'S DEPARTMENT SUPPLEMENTARY CRIME REPORT ------------13				69. CASE NO. 105907
70. CODE SECTION 187 P.C.	71. CRIME MURDER			72. CLASSIFICATION FELONY
73. VICTIM'S NAME – LAST, FIRST, MIDDLE (FIRM IF BUS.)	74. ADDRESS	☒ RESIDENCE	☐ BUSINESS	75. PHONE
SHEPARD, CECELIA ANN	10733 Mead Lane, Loma Linda			

inside the church in order to observe all persons who viewed the services and the remains of victim CECELIA SHEPARD. Det/Sgt. Harold Snook, Sgt. Thomas Butler, and Detective Ronald Montgomery of the Napa Police Department positioned themselves outside the church and photographed all persons entering and leaving the services. This included individual photographs and group scenes. Sgts. Lonergan and Narlow also attended the graveside services at the St. Helena Cemetery in St. Helena.

Friday, 10/3/69 – Reporting Officer Det/Sgt. Richard Lonergan contacted JAMES [REDACTED], Napa State Hospital, advised him to set up an interview with a patient who is a possible suspect in our case. The patient is identified as GRIFFIN RAYMOND [REDACTED], WMA, 20 yrs. Of age, DOB 1/11/49, 6'2", 223 lbs. MR. [REDACTED] had previously reported that this subject had left the hospital on a pass Friday evening, 6/26/69, and returned to the hospital Monday afternoon, 9/29/69. This subject also had spent time in the Air Force and was discharged from the Air Force in January 1969 for psychiatric problems. According to the doctors at the hospital, this subject was capable of committing this type of a crime. R/O in the presence of JAMES [REDACTED] and Security Officer PHIL RYAN interviewed subject [REDACTED].

[REDACTED] was very cooperative and talkative to R/O and went over his activities the prior weekend. Briefly stated, MR. [REDACTED], whose parents live in Vallejo, never left the Vallejo area that weekend and stayed around home talking with his mother, stepfather, and three brothers. After interviewing subject, it was the opinion of R/O Sgt. Lonergan that this subject was not the responsible. He had a definite very fast manner of speaking which was completely opposed to the victim's statement concerning the suspect's voice.

R/O also contacted the mother of the suspect, a MRS. OPAL [REDACTED], at [REDACTED] Hollywood Avenue, Vallejo. MRS. [REDACTED] stated more or less the exact same thing that her son had stated as to his whereabouts that weekend. It appears that this subject has a reliable alibi as to his activities and had no access to a vehicle that weekend. This subject was cleared as far as this crime is concerned.

The balance of the morning and afternoon was spent by R/Os Det/Sgts. Narlow and Lonergan going over physical evidence and dictating reports.

Investigation continuing.

(cont'd)

REPORTING OFFICERS	RECORDING OFFICER	TYPED BY	DATE AND TIME TYPED	ROUTED BY
Det/Sgts. Narlow and Lonergan	Det/Sgts. Narlow/Lonergan	M. Feurle	10/5/69, 4 P.M.	

FURTHER ACTION	☒ YES ☐ NO	COPIES TO:	☒ DETECTIVE ☐ JUVENILE ☐ DIST. ATTNY ☐ S.O/P.D	☐ GII ☐ PATROL ☐ ______ OTHER ☐ ______ OTHER

	REVIEWED BY	DATE

NAPA COUNTY SHERIFF'S DEPT. SUPPLEMENT CRIME REPORT				69. CASE NO. 105907
70. CODE SECTION 187 P.C.	71. CRIME MURDER			72. CLASSIFICATION FELONY
73. VICTIM'S NAME – LAST, FIRST, MIDDLE (FIRM IF BUS.)	74. ADDRESS	☒ RESIDENCE	☐ BUSINESS	75. PHONE
CECELIA SHEPARD	10733 Mead Lane, Loma Linda			

At 2020 hours, 9-27-69, Reporting Officer received phone call from the office that there had been a double stabbing at Lake Berryessa, and that an ambulance had been dispatched. Reporting Officer requested Det. Sgt. NARLOW and LONERGAN be called out and that the units at the Lake be instructed to rope off the scene.

Reporting Officer met Det. Sgt. Narlow at Queen of the Valley Hospital at 2045 hours, and was advised the Suspect had made a phone call from a payphone at the Napa Car Wash, Main and Clinton Streets, Napa, and that units were at that scene.

At 2050 hours Reporting Officer met Officer Eric Ronback and Reserve Officer Donald Stanley at the Napa Car Wash. They stated they had secured the area and no one had approached the area that was located on the south wall of a building located at the intersection of Main and Clinton Street.

Color photographs were taken of the scene and the area around the phone searched for physical evidence. No indications were found that the suspect had left at a high rate of speed and tire and foot prints were not observed on the blacktop.

Reporting Officer then approached the phone booth and noted the receiver of the phone was off the hook, and laying on the shelf with the mouth piece directly under the phone unit, the ear piece protruding to the south and the openings on the receiver facing the east wall of the booth. The phone unit was located on the north corner of the east wall of the booth the folding door entrance being the south enclosure of the booth. This scene was photographed to show the receivers position and the phone number 255-9673.

The phone booth was then processed for latent impressions and latent impression lift #1 thru 35 were taken into evidence. The latent impression removed on latent lifts 29, 30 and 31, and the impression lifted on lift 32, impressions photographed approximately three hours after the arrival of Reporting Officer at this scene. Processing of this scene was completed at 2349 at 0020 hours, 9-28-69.

This scene was located on the east side of Knoxville Road, 7/10 mile north of Lake Berryessa Park Headquarters. Processing of this area began with parking area where Victim's 1956 Karmann Ghia, Oregon License 4U2040 was parked. Reporting Officer observed a wooden foot stile over the fence approximately

(cont'd)

REPORTING OFFICERS	RECORDING OFFICER	TYPED BY	DATE AND TIME TYPED	ROUTED BY
Det. Sgt. Hal Snook	Det. Sgt. Hal Snook	S. Ramos	10-5-69	

FURTHER ACTION		COPIES TO:		
☒ YES	☐ NO	☒ DETECTIVE	☒ GII	☐ PATROL
		☐ JUVENILE	☐ ______ OTHER	
		☐ DIST. ATTNY	☐ ______ OTHER	
		☐ S.O/P.D		

	REVIEWED BY	DATE

NAPA COUNTY SHERIFF'S DEPT. SUPPLEMENT CRIME REPORT (cont'd Page -2-)				69. CASE NO. 105907
70. CODE SECTION 187 P.C.	71. CRIME MURDER			72. CLASSIFICATION FELONY
73. VICTIM'S NAME – LAST, FIRST, MIDDLE (FIRM IF BUS.)	74. ADDRESS	☒ RESIDENCE	☐ BUSINESS	75. PHONE
CECELIA SHEPARD	10733 Mead Lane, Loma Linda			

15 feet south of vehicle which separated the parking area from the Lake property.

Reporting Officer observed foot prints leading from the foot stile to the passenger side of the Karmann Ghia, where Suspect had to approach to letter the passenger door of the vehicle. The foot prints measured approximately 13" in length, 4 ½" at the widest point of the sole; heel width 3 ¼ inches and heel length 3 1/7 inches. A parallel bar tread occurred on both the heel and sole inset from the edges approximately ¾ inches.

The foot prints were measured and Sgt. T. Butler photographed the impressions. Sgt. Butler also photographed Reporting Officer pointing to the foot print which was to be cast, said foot print indicating the direction of travel was toward the vehicle. A plaster cast was made of this impression.

Reporting officer observed one set of tire impressions approximately 20 feet to the rear of Victim's vehicle. The Suspect track nearer the fence measured approximately 4 ½" in width and showed a parallel tread design. This tread design was photographed by Sgt. Butler and then a plaster cast was made by Reporting Officer.

The tire impression furtherest from the fence measured approximately 5 ½ inches in width and contained a single straight tread design approximately 1/8 inch width in the center with a herringbone design tread on either at de consisting of three approximately 1/16 inch treads between two approximately 1/8 inch treads. This tire impression was photographed by Sgt. T. Butler and a plaster cast made by Reporting Officer. The distance between the inside of the left tread to the inside of the right tread measured approximately 52 inches.

General scene photographs of the parking area, the Victim's vehicle, and of the writing on the vehicle door was taken by Sgt. Butler.

Reporting Officer observed written on the passenger's door of the Victim's vehicle, a circle with a cross super imposed over it, and below the symbol the words Vallejo, 12-20-68, 7-4-69, Sept. 27, 69 – 6:30, by knife. The writing instrument used appeared to have been a felt type pen approximately 3/16 inch wide on the tip, with black ink. The vehicle was then processed for latent impressions, and latent lifts 36 thru 43 were taken into evidence.

The vehicle was found to be locked and no signs of attempted entry was observed. The vehicle was then impounded and taken to the Lake Berryessa Park Headquarters where it was secured in a locked garage. Sgt. Kenneth Narlow

(cont'd)

REPORTING OFFICERS	RECORDING OFFICER	TYPED BY	DATE AND TIME TYPED	ROUTED BY
Det. Sgt. Hal Snook	Det. Sgt. Hal Snook	S. Ramos	10-5-69	

FURTHER ACTION		COPIES TO:		
	☒ YES		☒ DETECTIVE	☒ GII
	☐ NO		☐ JUVENILE	☐ PATROL
			☐ DIST. ATTNY	☐ ______ OTHER
			☐ S.O/P.D	☐ ______ OTHER

REVIEWED BY	DATE

NAPA COUNTY SHERIFF'S DEPT. SUPPLEMENT CRIME REPORT (cont'd Page -3-)				69. CASE NO. 105907
70. CODE SECTION 187 P.C.	71. CRIME MURDER			72. CLASSIFICATION FELONY
73. VICTIM'S NAME – LAST, FIRST, MIDDLE (FIRM IF BUS.)	74. ADDRESS	☒ RESIDENCE	☐ BUSINESS	75. PHONE
CECELIA SHEPARD	10733 Mead Lane, Loma Linda			

Then turned over to Reporting Officer the following items of evidence, he stated he received from Park Ranger Dennis Land.

#1. One multi colored blanket.

#2. One Army type field jacket.

#3. Several lengths of plastic clothes line, white in color, with a hollow core which appeared to be blood stained.

#4. One

#5. One

These items were tagged for evidence and locked in Reporting Officer vehicle for transportation to the Napa County Sheriff's Department.

At approximately 0800 hours, 9-28-69, Reporting Officer together with Sgt. Richard Lonergan followed the suspected footprints down the hill toward the lake to the point of attack, and then back to the parking area.

Plaster casts were made of a heel print at the bottom of the first hill. Another cast was taken of a complete footprint at the junction of the trail, and a dirt road approximately 50 feet from the point where Park Ranger Land discovered Victim Hartnell. A footprint in the sand approximately 100 ft. from the point of attack, bearing the suspected tread pattern which also showed a circular design in the instep area of the print, was photographed and cast.

General scene photographs were taken by Reporting Officer, and cardboard beer flats were placed over suspected footprints, with the lengthwise portion of the flat paralleling the footprint to show direction of travel toward the scene of the stabbing.

A green bottle was found near a stump on the suspected approach route near the point of attack. This bottle was processed for latent impression and lifts 44 thru 48 were taken into evidence. The bottle was tagged and placed into evidence.

Soil samples were taken from the following locations:

#1. The point where the attack occurred.

#2. From behind the tree the Suspect reportedly had stood to put on the hood.

(cont'd)

REPORTING OFFICERS	RECORDING OFFICER	TYPED BY	DATE AND TIME TYPED	ROUTED BY
Det. Sgt. Hal Snook	Det. Sgt. Hal Snook	S. Ramos	10-5-69	

FURTHER ACTION		COPIES TO:			
	☒ YES		☒ DETECTIVE	☒ GII	
	☐ NO		☐ JUVENILE	☐ PATROL	
			☐ DIST. ATTNY	☐ ___ OTHER	
			☐ S.O/P.D	☐ ___ OTHER	

	REVIEWED BY	DATE

NAPA COUNTY SHERIFF'S DEPT. SUPPLEMENT CRIME REPORT				69. CASE NO. 105907
70. CODE SECTION 187 P.C.	71. CRIME MURDER			72. CLASSIFICATION FELONY
73. VICTIM'S NAME – LAST, FIRST, MIDDLE (FIRM IF BUS.)	74. ADDRESS	☒ RESIDENCE	☐ BUSINESS	75. PHONE
CECELIA SHEPARD	10733 Mead Lane, Loma Linda			

#3. From the parking area beside the Victim's vehicle.

Aerial photographs were ordered by Reporting Officer and Napa Register's Photographer Robert McKenzie took these pictures from an aircraft piloted by Special Deputy Harold Moskowite of the Napa County Sheriff's Dept. Aerial Squadron.

Following a thorough crime scene search Reporting Officer returned to the Napa County Sheriff's Dept. at approximately 1700 hours, 7-28-69. At this time the following items of evidence were taken into Reporting Officers custody from the evidence locker. These items were brought from the Queen of the Valley Hospital emergency room by Officers Allan Brambrink and William Munk.

#1. Shoes and socks of Victim Hartnell.
#2. Trousers, shirt, T-shirt, shorts, and belt of Victim Hartnell.
#3. Wallet, glasses, key, and playing cards belonging to Victim Hartnell.
#4. Dress, slip, panties, and bra, of Victim Shepard.

9-29-69 – The Victim's vehicle was removed from impoundment at Lake Berryesa Park Headquarters, and was brought to the Napa County Corporation Yard where the passenger door was removed, and was taken into evidence by Reporting Officer.

Case continuing.

DET/SGT HAL SNOOK: sr

10-5-69

REPORTING OFFICERS	RECORDING OFFICER	TYPED BY	DATE AND TIME TYPED	ROUTED BY
Det. Sgt. Hal Snook	Det. Sgt. Hal Snook	S. Ramos	10-5-69	

FURTHER ACTION		COPIES TO:		
	☒ YES		☒ DETECTIVE	☒ GII
	☐ NO		☐ JUVENILE	☐ PATROL
			☐ DIST. ATTNY	☐ ___________ OTHER
			☐ S.O/P.D	☐ ___________ OTHER

	REVIEWED BY	DATE

NAPA COUNTY SHERIFF'S DEPARTMENT SUPPLEMENTARY CRIME REPORT					69. CASE NO. 105907
70. CODE SECTION 187 P.C.	71. CRIME MURDER			72. CLASSIFICATION FELONY	
73. VICTIM'S NAME – LAST, FIRST, MIDDLE (FIRM IF BUS.)	74. ADDRESS	☒ RESIDENCE	☐ BUSINESS	75. PHONE	
SHEPARD, CECELIA ANN	10733 Mead Lane, Loma Linda			796-2008	

Sunday, 9/28/69, 10:15 A.M. – R/O contacted MR. ROBERT HILAND SHEPARD, DOB 9/21/21, and MRS. WILMA DOLORES SHEPARD, DOB 7/7/23, address [REDACTED] Head Lane, Loma Linda, San Bernardino County, California (residence phone [REDACTED], business [REDACTED] at the Queen of the Valley Hospital. Above subjects are the parents of MISS CECELIA SHEPARD, victim of a stabbing attack at Lake Berryessa.

Also present was the companion who drove from Southern California with MISS SHEPARD, victim, to Angwin during the past week. Subject's name DALORA LEE [REDACTED] aka LORI, address [REDACTED] Aspen, Loman Linda, California, phone number [REDACTED], Extension 2155.

Victim's parents stated that a former male friend of victim, GARY [REDACTED], 21 years, senior, Pacific Union College, threatened victim when victim started going with BRYAN HARTNELL. This occurred sometime in 1968. However, the parents stated that [REDACTED] was small in stature and that victim HARTNELL knew him quite well.

Other than the above statement by victim's parents, they could offer no other explanation for the attack on their daughter. The parents gave numerous names of persons who knew their daughter.

GWENDOLYN [REDACTED], student at Pacific Union College two years ago (1967) – family resides in Martinez, California.

EDWARD [REDACTED], former Pacific Union College student – did work for mortuary in Lodi, California

MISS ELEANOR [REDACTED], Dean of Girls-Dean of Students, Pacific Union College – presently on leave at the University of Southern California

MADELINE [REDACTED] – residence presently Las Vegas, Nevada – former student Pacific Union College (Sgt. Narlow informed R/O that MISS [REDACTED] presently a student Mills College, Oakland, California)

JERRY [REDACTED], presently a student at Pacific Union College.

R/O interviewed MISS [REDACTED] who could offer no explanation for the assault on her friend, MISS SHEPARD.

The below information received from Sgt. White, Oakland Intelligence Unit, Oakland.

(cont'd)

REPORTING OFFICERS	RECORDING OFFICER	TYPED BY	DATE AND TIME TYPED	ROUTED BY
JOHN ROBERTSON, Det/Sgt.	JOHN ROBERTSON, Det/Sgt.	M. Feurle	9/30/69, 3 P.M.	

FURTHER ACTION		COPIES TO:		
	☒ YES		☒ DETECTIVE	☐ GII
	☐ NO		☐ JUVENILE	☐ PATROL
			☐ DIST. ATTNY	☐ ________ OTHER
			☐ S.O/P.D	☐ ________ OTHER

REVIEWED BY	DATE

NAPA COUNTY SHERIFF'S DEPARTMENT------------------2 SUPPLEMENTARY CRIME REPORT				69. CASE NO. 105907
70. CODE SECTION 187 P.C.	71. CRIME MURDER			72. CLASSIFICATION FELONY
73. VICTIM'S NAME – LAST, FIRST, MIDDLE (FIRM IF BUS.)	74. ADDRESS	☒ RESIDENCE	☐ BUSINESS	75. PHONE
SHEPARD, CECELIA ANN	10733 Mead Lane, Loma Linda			796-2008

Police Department:

9-30-69 2:10 P.M.

Call from Sgt. White, Oakland Intelligence.

MADELINE [REDACTED] 1st yr. student Mills College knows GARY

Sgt. White requesting to know if this guy is prime suspect.
Will advise if GARY contacts MADELINE.]

(Narlow)

REPORTING OFFICERS	RECORDING OFFICER	TYPED BY	DATE AND TIME TYPED	ROUTED BY
JOHN ROBERTSON, Det/Sgt.	JOHN ROBERTSON, Det/Sgt.	M. Feurle	9/30/69, 3 P.M.	

FURTHER ACTION		COPIES TO:			
	☒ YES		☒ DETECTIVE	☐ GII	
	☐ NO		☐ JUVENILE	☐ PATROL	
			☐ DIST. ATTNY	☐ ________ OTHER	
			☐ S.O/P.D	☐ ________ OTHER	

	REVIEWED BY	DATE

NAPA COUNTY SHERIFF'S DEPARTMENT SUPPLEMENTARY CRIME REPORT				69. CASE NO. 105907
70. CODE SECTION 187 P.C.	71. CRIME MURDER			72. CLASSIFICATION FELONY
73. VICTIM'S NAME – LAST, FIRST, MIDDLE (FIRM IF BUS.) CECELIA SHEPARD	74. ADDRESS	☒ RESIDENCE	☐ BUSINESS	75. PHONE

9/29/69 – 2:00 P.M. – Assigned Officer detailed to check men's shoes stores in the Maps area. A/O attempting to locate the manufacturer of a particular tread design from a work shoe or service boot. (Plaster cast of suspect's foot impression taken at scene of crime.)

A/O learned the following information from the twelve shoe stores he canvassed.

1. The imprint could have been made by shoe or boot of foreign import.

2. The imprint size could be approx. size 10 ½ EE.

3. The imprint made possibly by a neoprene sole and heel.

Below a list of stores contacted:

1. Village Shoes, 1101 First Street.

2. Spinning Wheel Shoes, 1129 First Street.

3. Kramers Shoes, 1210 First Street.

4. Schalow Shoes, 1233 First Street.

5. Grande Shoes, 1311 First Street.

6. J.C. Penney Co., 1400 First Street.

7. Gallenkamp's Shoe Co., 1444 First Street.

8. Colonial Saddle Shop, 1043 Main Street.

9. W. H. Springer Shoe Repair (closed), 1140 Main Street.

10. Brewster's Government Surplus, 1146 Main Street.

11. Montgomery Ward & Co., Bel Aire Shopping Center.

12. Bloom Shoes, Bel Aire Shopping Center.

REPORTING OFFICERS	RECORDING OFFICER	TYPED BY	DATE AND TIME TYPED	ROUTED BY
JOHN ROBERTSON, Det/Sgt.	JOHN ROBERTSON, Det/Sgt.	M. Feurle	9/30/69, 11:50 A.M.	

FURTHER ACTION		COPIES TO:		
☒ YES	☐ NO	☒ DETECTIVE	☐ GII	
		☐ JUVENILE	☐ PATROL	
		☐ DIST. ATTNY	☐ ________ OTHER	
		☐ S.O/P.D	☐ ________ OTHER	

REVIEWED BY	DATE

NAPA COUNTY SHERIFF'S DEPARTMENT				69. CASE NO. 105907
				10/1/69 9:14 A.M.
70. CODE SECTION 187 P.C.	71. CRIME MURDER		72. CLASSIFICATION FELONY	
73. VICTIM'S NAME – LAST, FIRST, MIDDLE (FIRM IF BUS.) SHEPARD, CECELIA	74. ADDRESS	☒ RESIDENCE	☐ BUSINESS	75. PHONE

R/O contacted victim BRYAN HARTNELL at Queen of the Valley Hospital. R/O showed victim the following automatic pistols in an attempt to determine if Victim could identify any of the pistols:

Colt automatic .45 cal.

Remington automatic 380 cal.

Colt commander Auto. .45 cal.

Colt auto. .32 cal.

Walther P38 auto. 9mm

Browning auto. 9 mm

Astra auto. (Spain) .25 cal.

Smith & Wesson auto. 9 mm

Luger automatic 9 mm

Astra automatic (Spain) 9 mm

Victim could not identify any of the above pistols.

(NOTE: Sgt. Butler and Deputy D. Bus Catalogued and photographed the above pistols.)

Victim believed the bullet he observed could have been a .45 caliber, but is not certain

1:45 P.M – R/O revisited Victim HARTNELL. The following ammunition was shown to Victim:

.45 cal. autom. Bullet, bullet brass, casing silver

.45 cal. autom. Bullet, bullet brass, casing brass

357 cal. Magnum lead bullet, silver casing

.38 special Wad Cutter lead bullet, brass casing

9 mm Luger hollow point brass bullet, brass casing

9 mm brass bullet, brass casing (autom. bullet)

.25 cal. autom. brass bullet, brass casing

.22 cal. long rifle brass bullet, brass casing

.22 cal. long rifle lead bullet, brass casing

.22 cal. short lead bullet, brass casing

All above ammunition are bullets from automatic pistols, with the exception of the last three items, .22 caliber ammunition.

Victim identified the .45 cal. automatic bullet, brass casing, brass bullet. Victim stated he could not be absolutely certain, however he believes the .45 cal. automatic found is of the same type that the Suspect showed the Victim.

REPORTING OFFICERS	RECORDING OFFICER	TYPED BY	DATE AND TIME TYPED	ROUTED BY
JOHN ROBERTSON, Det/Sgt.	JOHN ROBERTSON, Det/Sgt.	M. Feurle	9/30/69, 11:50 A.M.	

FURTHER ACTION	COPIES TO:		
☒ YES ☐ NO	☒ DETECTIVE ☐ JUVENILE ☐ DIST. ATTNY ☐ S.O/P.D	☐ GII ☐ PATROL ☐ ________ OTHER ☐ ________ OTHER	

	REVIEWED BY	DATE

9/28/69 – 12:30 P.M. – Reporting Officer John Robertson, Det/Sgt., interviewed one of two victims who were each stabbed numerous times by an unknown assailant. Victim CECELIA SHEPARD and victim BRYAN HARKNELL both had been placed in the Queen of the Valley Hospital intensive care unit. Victim SHEPARD had surgery performed on her earlier in the morning (9/28/69) and was unable to be questioned by the Reporting Officer, however Dr. Ludwig gave permission for victim HARKNELL to be interviewed.

Although victim HARKNELL was heavily sedated, he was able to give R/O a verbal statement. (Note: R/O taped electrically the interview with victim HARKNELL.) Victim HARKNELL related the following.

He had known CECELIA SHEPARD for some time, they were good friends, and she had come to the Napa County area to spend the weekend. She and a female companion, DALORA LEE [REDACTED], 25104 [REDACTED], Loma Linda, San Bernardino County, Calif. (phone 796-[REDACTED] Ext. 2155) had driven from Southern California and were to drive back Sunday, 9/28/69. Victim stated he and MISS SHEPARD drove to Lake Berryessa, picked a large tree near the shore line where they decided to lie down and enjoy the scenery. While lying on the ground, victim HARKNELL stated he heard a noise and asked MISS SHEPARD if she could hear anything or see anything behind a tree not far from where the couple were lying. MISS SHEPARD told victim HARKNELL she could see a man behind the tree. HARKNELL asked her what he was doing. MISS SHEPARD stated she couldn't tell. HARKNELL stated he (suspect) the came from behind the tree. MISS SHEPARD said, "Oh my God, he has a gun!" Victim HARKNELL stated the man approached the couple, aiming a black steel automatic pistol. The suspect stated he needed a car and money. Suspect stated his car was "hot" and he wanted victim HARKNELL's car keys.

Victim HARKNELL stated he began talking with the suspect, telling the suspect he had no money, only a small amount of change, also that if the suspect was really in need of assistance HARKNELL would attempt to help him. The suspect told victim to get on the ground. Suspect then had MISS SHEPARD tie HARKNELL's hands behind him. HARKNELL stated he attempted to keep the suspect engaged in conversation while suspect was tying the victims.

HARKNELL further stated the suspect was described as follows: Wearing a black hooded mask (cloth), covering suspect's entire head and shoulders, coming down almost to suspect's waist. Victim stated on front of the four-cornered type mask (similar to paper bag in style) there was a symbol, the symbol described as white approximately 3 x 3 inches in diameter, with a symmetrical cross. Also on the eyelets of the mask was a pair of clip-on sunglasses, the glasses clipped to the eyelets. Victim stated he could also see hair through the mask's eyelets and observed the hair to be dark brown.

Victim stated suspect was wearing a light-weight windbreaker, dark blue or black, pleated slacks (old-fashioned type). Victim could not remember what type of shoes or anything about suspect's hands, could not remember if suspect was wearing gloves.

Victim thought suspect was possible 20 to 30 years of age by voice concept. Victim stated suspect was 5'8" to 6', 225-250 lbs., dark brown hair, eyes unknown, sloppy dresser, stomach hanging over trousers. Suspect spoke with some type of drawl, but victim stated it was not a Southern drawl, did not really know what type of drawl, but thought the man was not well educated, but did not feel he was illiterate either. Victim said suspect's voice was moderate in sound, that is, not high or low pitched.

Suspect told victim he was sent to (?) Lodge State Prison (possibly Deer Lodge State Prison), Montana, for a killing. While there (in prison) he killed a guard while escaping. Suspect also told victims he was heading for Mexico, told victim he was flat broke. Victim observed cut-up rope in suspect's rear pocket (trousers'), also stated he was wearing a knife in a case (on belt) on his right side, near front of trousers. Knife description: Appeared to be a long bread knife, 12" long blade, ¾" wide, hardwood handle, 2 brass rivets holding handle in place, cotton surgical tape wrapped approximately 1" around handle of knife. Knife case possibly made of wood.

Victim asked suspect if suspect's gun was loaded. Suspect removed magazine from handle of pistol and showed victim a bullet removed from gun, bullet described as a possible .45 caliber. Victim did not know what caliber the pistol was.

Suspect had MISS SHEPARD tie HARKNELL's hands behind him, suspect then tied victim SHEPARD's hands, then re-tied HARKNELL's hands, then tied both victim's ankles together, had victims lie on their stomachs. HARKNELL stated suspect said, "I'm getting nervous." This was when suspect was tying MISS SHEPARD's hands, in fact HARKNESS stated suspect got real shaky when he was tying MISS SHEPARD's hands.

Victim HARKNELL then stated that without warning the suspect plunged his knife into the back of HARKNELL. Suspect did this repeatedly, HARKNELL stated he thinks six times. HARKNELL stated he pretended to be dead and the suspect went over to MISS SHEPARD and stabbed MISS SHEPARD repeatedly in the back, and when MISS SHEPARD turned her body over (on back), suspect stabbed her in the lower abdomen. Victim stated suspect stabbed MISS SHEPARD much worse than him. Suspect went into some sort of frenzy when stabbing MISS SHEPARD.

Victim HARKNELL stated suspect left the area after the stabbing. Victim HARKNELL hailed a boat (off shore) and told the man in the boat the couple needed help badly. Victim stated the boat left the area and he (victim) attempted to get help by crawling and walking to the road. (Victim believed he had walked to the road, however had not gone too far from his wounded companion.)

Victim stated he thought suspect had been with the couple for approximately fifteen (15) minutes from time of observing suspect until suspect departed. Victim stated suspect did not take his wallet, although when MISS

SHEPARD was tying victim HARKNELL's hands, she reached in his pocket and threw his wallet to suspect. Suspect did not take the wallet or victim's car keys.

Victim stated a man in a pickup truck found him on the road and called an ambulance. Victim stated he estimated one hour in time was involved between the time he and MISS SHEPARD were stabbed until help arrived.

MISS SHEPARD is listed in critical condition.

MR. HARKNELL is listed in serious condition.

Both victims presently in the intensive care unit of Queen of the Valley Hospital.

Both victims' parents arrived this date and have been at the hospital. Neither parent could offer an explanation of why their children were attacked.

Case pending.

(NOTE: Charles Sims, Official County Court Reporter, took a brief statement from BRYAN HARKNELL, however victim was so heavily sedated he was unable to go into any great detail regarding the case.)

J. ROBERTSON. Det/Sgt.
9/29/69

C: What do you want?

A: Now take it easy – all I want is your money. There is nothing to worry about – all I want is your money.

B: O.K. – whatever you say, I want you to know now that I will cooperate so you don't have to worry – whatever you say we'll do. Do you want us to come up with our hands up or down?

A: Just don't make any fast moves – come up slowly.

B: But we don't have any money – all I have is 75¢.

A: That doesn't matter – every little bit helps (pause) – I'm on my way to Mexico – I escaped from Deer Lodge Prison in Montana, Deer Lodge. I need some money to get there.

B: You're welcome to the money I have, but isn't there something else I can do for you? Give you a check or get some more?

A: No.

B: I can give you my phone number and you can call me.

A: (No reply)

B: I want to get in contact with you. I am a sociology major and maybe I can even offer you more help than you think you need.

A: No.

B: Well, is there any other thing you need?

A: Yes. One more thing – I want your car keys. My car is hot.

B: (Reaching into pockets, then patting first front then back pockets)

I guess in all the excitement I don't remember where I put them. Let's see. Are they in my shirt, in the ignition], on the blanket... Say! Would you answer a question for me? I've always wondered. On T.V. movies and in an article in the Readers Digest they say that thieves really keep their guns loaded. Is yours?

A: (excited slightly) Yes, it is! (then calm and matter-of-fact)

I killed a couple of men before.

B: What? I didn't hear you...

A: I killed a couple of guards getting out of prison. And I'm not afraid to kill again.

C: Bryan – do what he says!

A: Now I want the girl to tie you up.

C: (reaches for rope that he pulls from back pocket)

B: This is really strange. I wonder why someone hasn't thought of this before. I'll bet there's good money in it.

A: (no reply)

B: What was the name of that prison?

A: (no reply)

B: No really, what did you say the name of it was? I'm just curious.

A: (begrudgingly) Deer Lodge in Montana.

(There must have been some dialogue at this point but I can't remember any until we are both tied up)

A: Now I want you both to lay face down so I can tie up your feet.

B: Come on – we could be out here for a long time and it could get cold at night.

A: Come on – get down!

B: Listen, I didn't complain when you tied our hands, but this is ridiculous!

A: I told you...

B: We aren't going anywhere – Anyway, I don't think that it's necessary (or – Aw, come on – we don't want to.)

A: (Pointing gun directly at me at point blank range) I told you to get down!

(He ties me, then her)

B: Your hands are shaking. Are you nervous?

A: Yes, I guess so. (laughed in a very relaxed manner)

B: Well, I suppose that I'd be nervous too.

(Then after we were tied and hog-tied)

B: Now that everything is all said and done, could you show me that your gun is loaded? (Or, and probably this: "Now that all is said and done, was that gun really loaded?")

A: Yes, it was! (or) Sure, I'll show you.

(He then opened cartridge or whatever)

(That was the last thing I remember him saying.)

(signed) BRYAN HARTNELL

CODE SECTION	INCIDENT REPORT	CASE NUMBER
187PC	NAPA COUNTY SHERIFF'S DEPARTMENT NAPA, CALIFORNIA	105907

INCIDENT	DATE OCCURRED	TIME OCCURRED

BEAT	AREA	DATE REPORTED	TIME REPORTED	RECEIVED BY	HOW RECEIVED

COMPAINANT	ADDRESS	PHONE

SUBJECT CODES V=VICTIM W=WITNESS P=PARENT RP=REPORTING PARTY DC=DISCOVERED CRIME

NAME – LAST, FIRST, MIDDLE	CODE	RESIDENCE ADDRESS	RESIDENCE PHONE
LINDA		SUNNYSIDE RD	963-

OCCUPATION	RACE-SEX	AGE	DOB	BUSINESS ADDRESS (SCHOOL IF JUVENILE)	BUSINESS PHONE
STUDENT	W 7		6-28-47		

NAME – LAST, FIRST, MIDDLE	CODE	RESIDENCE ADDRESS	RESIDENCE PHONE

OCCUPATION	RACE-SEX	AGE	DOB	BUSINESS ADDRESS (SCHOOL IF JUVENILE)	BUSINESS PHONE

NAME – LAST, FIRST, MIDDLE	CODE	RESIDENCE ADDRESS	RESIDENCE PHONE

OCCUPATION	RACE-SEX	AGE	DOB	BUSINESS ADDRESS (SCHOOL IF JUVENILE)	BUSINESS PHONE

1. VEHICLE USED – LICENSE NO – ID NO – YEAR – MAKE – MODEL – COLORS (OTHER IDENTIFYING CHARACTERISTICS)

2. VEHICLE USED – LICENSE NO – ID NO – YEAR – MAKE – MODEL – COLORS (OTHER IDENTIFYING CHARACTERISTICS)

SUMMARY:

Stated left Angwin with two other girls Jeanne [REDACTED] and Linda [REDACTED] at approx. 2:25 P.M. 9-27-69 drove through Pope Valley to Lake Berryessa shore they stopped 2 miles north of the A & W (Sugarloaf Park). Suspect pulled into the paring area from the south went past their vehicle then backed up so their rear bumpers were nearly touching.

Suspect vehicle described as 1966-67 sight blue Chevrolet with Calif. Plates. Witness believes the vehicle was a 2-door and described the headlights as being long rather than round – the rear glass was tinted quite dark.

Another vehicle from Angwin with Arizona plates was in the parking area and W. saw the occupants Denise [REDACTED] and Wayne [REDACTED] at the beach. W. went to the beach and shortly there after noticed suspect watching them from the edge of the trees. After about 30 minutes suspect came down by the beach and parked within 20 feet of w. as he walked from south to north.

Suspect desc as approx. 28 yrs 6'-6'2" 200-225 black hair possible styled with parting left, rounded eyes, thin lips, mod. Nose, straight eyebrows, small ears, well built, nice looking, wearing black short sleeve sweater shirt bunched in front, and T-shirt hanging out in back, dark trousers.

W. left area about 4:20 and the vehicle was gone. They drove south to hgw 128 and back to Angwin.

SUSPECT NO. 1 (LAST, FIRST, MIDDLE)	RACE-SEX	AGE	HT.	WT.	HAIR	EYES	ID NO. OR DOB	ARRESTED YES ( ) NO ( )

SUSPECT NO. 1 (LAST, FIRST, MIDDLE)	RACE-SEX	AGE	HT.	WT.	HAIR	EYES	ID NO. OR DOB	ARRESTED YES ( ) NO ( )

ADDRESS, CLOTHING AND OTHER IDENTIFYING MARKS OR CHARACTERISTICS	CHECK IF MORE THAN TWO SUSPECTS ( )

COPIES TO:			ASSIGNED OFFICERS	
( ) OFFICER	( ) ADULT	( ) CLOSED		
( ) DET. DIV.	PROB.	( ) PENDING	SIGNED	DATE
( ) JUV. DIV.	( ) JUV. PROB.	( ) FOLLOW UP		
( ) DIST. ATT.	( ) ________	BY A/D		
	( ) ________	( ) FOLLOW UP BY: ________	REVIEWED BY	DATE

DEPARTMENT OF CALIFORNIA HIGHWAY PA

VEHICLE REPORT	TYPE (CHECK ONE) ☐ IMPOUNDED ☐ RECOVERED ☐ STORED ☐ RELEASED	Use reverse side for stolen or embarked vehicles

REPORTING DEPT.	AREA/DIVISION	DATE	FILE NO.
NAPA SHERRIF DEPT.	LAKE BERRYESSA	9-28-69	105907

DESCRIPTION OF VEHICLE

PLATE	MAKE	BODY TYPE	LICENSE NO	YEAR	STATE	COLOR (COMBINATION)
BIK/WHPS	KARMAN GHIA VOLSKWAGEN	2 DR COUPE	1 402040 2 402040	1970	OREGON	BIK/OREGON

VEHICLE (IDENTIFICATION NO (TIC)	VEH CHECK WITH (X)	VEH APPEAR ALTERED	ENGINE NO.	SPEEDOMETER READING
8641212113	☐ YES ☐ NO	☐ YES ☐ NO		6216

REGISTERED OWNER	ADDRESS	PHONE
BRUCE L. CHRISTIE	3339 NE BROADWAY PORTLAND OREGON	
LEGAL OWNER	**ADDRESS**	**PHONE**
DRIVER OR LAST PERSON IN POSSESSION	**ADDRESS**	**PHONE**
BRYAN HARTNELL	RT 2, BOX 252, BLUE LAKE TROUTDALE, OR	

CIRCUMSTANCES

NAME OF GARAGE	ADDRESS	PHONE
BIAVA MOTORS	466 SOSCOL, NAPA	224-3191

REQUIRED NOTICES SENT TO REGISTERED AND LEGAL OWNERS AND GARAGE (SEC. RAMBA YC)	IF NO IS CHECKED INDICATE REASONS
☐ YES ☒ NO	HELD AS EVIDENCE

TOWED FROM (LOC)	TIME AND DATE TOWED
BERRYESSA SHORE	9-29-69

PERSON REPORTING OCCURRENCE	ADDRESS	PHONE	TIME AND DATE REPORTED
MR. RON FONG	SAN FRANCISCO		9-27-69

CONDITION OF VEHICLE	DRIVABLE	WRECKED	STRIPPED
FAIR	☒ YES ☐ NO	☐ YES ☒ NO	☐ YES ☒ NO

VEH. RETURNED TO OWNER	IF STOLEN, NAME OF REPORTING AGENCY	TELETYPE (RECOVERY)	DATE OF TELETYPE

[UNREADABLE] (IF ARREST IS MDAE, GIVE FULL NAMES, CHARGES, WHERE BOOKED)

VEHICLE INVENTORY								
	YES	NO		YES	NO		CONDITION	LIST PROPERTY TOOLS OTHER ITEMS
CUSHION(FRONT)	X		SPOTLIGHTS(S)		X	L. F. TIRE	POOR	GIRLS RED COAT
CUSHION(REAR)	X		FOGLIGHT(S)		X	R.F. TIRE	POOR	GIRLS SHOES
REAR VIEW MIRROR	X		BUMPER (FRONT)	X		R.R. TIRE	POOR	TOOL BOX
SIDE VIEW MIRROR		X	BUMPER (REAR)	X		L.R. TIRE	POOR	TOOLS
CIGAR LIGHTER	X		MOTOR	X		SPARE TIRE	POOR	1 PR Men's
RADIO	X		BATTERY	X		WHEELS	FAIR	SHOES
CLOCK		X	AIR CONDITIONER		X	FENDERS	FAIR	1 HArtnelll
HEATER		X	HUB CAPS	X		BOOT. HOOD	FAIR	BANK BOOK
KEYS	X		FINDER PARTS		X	TOP	FAIR	
REGISTRATION	X		TRANSMISSION	X		GRILL	FAIR	
WINGSHIELD WIPER	X		JACK	X		Upholstery	FAIR	

OFFICER RECEIVING VEH. STORED (SIGNATURE)	ID. NO. 25.1.8	GARAGE PRINCIPAL OR AGENT STORING VEH. (SIGNATURE)	TIME AND DATE
APPRISING OFFICER'S SIGNATURE [UNREADABLE] x	ID NO.	APPRISED VALUE	TIME AND DATE OF APRRISAL

IMPOUND RELEASE NOTIFICATION		
TO	ADDRESS	DATE
RELEASE VEHICLE TO	ADDRESS	

NATURE PF CLERK OR OFFICER RELEASING	CERTIFICATION: I, the undesigned, do hereby certify that I am legal authorized and entitled to take possession of above described vehicle.
NOTE: This form is furnished by the Highway Patrol to all peace officers. When completed, mail immediately to: California Highway Patrol, P.O. Box 198, Sacramento, California.	SIGNATURE OF OWNER OR LEGAL OWNER OR AGENT OF OWNER

STATE OF CALIFORNIA

DEPARTMENT OF JUSTICE

BUREAU OF CRIMINAL IDENTIFICATION AND INVESTIGATION REPORT

P.O. Box 1859, Sacramento

TYPE OF CASE 187 PC

NUMBER 38-F-5861

	Copies of this report to:	
Subject Cecelia Ann SHEPARD (Victim)HGFFG	SO Napa	(1)
Raymond George (Suspect)	Bureau Files	(2)
CIT 3 818 889 et al		

Requested by: Earl Randol, Sheriff Napa County Date 12-3-69 Time

Reported

Address: 810 Coombs St. Napa, Calif. Telephone

Requested how: By telephone Received by:

Reported

Assigned to: Raymond E. Olsen. Latent FP Examiner Date: Time

Assigned by: A. L. Coffey, Chief of Bureau

Enclosures:

References: Your Case #105907 Atten: Deputy Hal Snook

SYNOPSIS:

Captain Don Townsed of the Napa County Sheriff's Office in a telephone conversation on October 3, 1969, requested the following service of the Latent Fingerprint Unit.

TYPE OF EXAMINATION: To assist in the investigation of the above numbered murder case.

DETAILS OF THE FIELD TRIP: On October 6, 1969, the undersigned along with Supervising Photographer Vern Neuser of this Bureau proceeded to the Napa County Sheriff's Office, arriving at approximately 9:30 a.m. and contacted Captain Don Townsend. A conference was held and the details of the case were discussed. Supervising Special Agent Kenneth Horton and Special Agent Mel Nicolai of this Bureau also attended this meeting.

It was requested that the undersigned copy the usable latent impressions that had been obtained in regard to this crime, and also to compare these latent impressions with the inked impressions of four subject and other subjects that might be developed in the future.

Material received from Deputy Hal Snook is as follows: thirty-five cards bearing forty-five latent lifts, one 8" x 10" photograph of a latent impression, the names of Raymond George [REDACTED], CII 3 818 889, Danny Olon [REDACTED], CII 3 139 751, Raymond Allen [REDACTED], CII 477 035, and Glenn W. [REDACTED], date of birth January 30, 1929. Also received to be delivered to the Questioned Documents Unit of this Bureau was a photograph of an automobile door, five sheets of paper with printing, and a "Charlie Brown" card with printing.

RESULTS AND CONCLUSIONS: The usable latent impressions have been compared to the extent possible with the inked fingerprints of the above-named subjects, as well as subjects submitted by Special Agent Nicolai and the Special Services Section of this Bureau with negative results.

CONTINUED PAGE 2

Several of the latent impressions appear to be a portion of a palm. Since the files of this Bureau do not contain palm impressions of these subjects, a comparison was not possible. Comparisons will continue as the subjects are developed and if an identification is established your Department will be notified.

DISPOSITION OF MATERIAL: The material for the Questioned Documents Unit was given to Questioned Documents Examiner Sherwood Korrill in person on October 7, 1969.

Photographs of the comparable latent impressions have been placed in the files of this Bureau for future reference.

The cards of latent impressions are enclosed along with two sets of photographic copies of the comparable latent impressions for your use. Kindly acknowledge the enclosed evidence receipt by initialing and mailing to this Bureau.

Date: October 9, 1969 Report by RAYMOND E. OLSEN

[UNREADABLE] Title Latent Fingerprint Examiner

NAPA POLICE DEPARTMENT

SUPPLEMENTARY REPORT

OFFENSE ....

COMPLAINANT ....   **ADDRESS** ....

Additional details of offense, progress of investigations, etc.

At 7:40pm, 9-27-69, received a telephone call on line one of the Napa Police Dept. switchboard. I answered with, "Napa Police Dept., Office Slaight."

A male voice, young sounding, possibly early twenties stated calmly, "I want to report a murder, no, a double murder. They are two miles North of Park Headquarters. They were in a white Volkswagen Karmen-Ghia."

There was a pause at which time I ask, "where are you now?" In a voice barely audible came, "I'm the one that did it." I could hear the phone being put down but not hung up. I ask "is anyone there" about twice but received no reply.

I could hear the line was still open because I could hear traffic passing the phone and for some reason I got the impression there were people near or around because I seem to recall hearing feminine voices in the background, however at the time I was in the process of phoning the Napa Sheriff's Office with another phone and with radio transmission it was hard to tell.

I informed the S.O. of the call and then phoned the operator to see if the call could be traced. An operator stated that this was a 255 payphone and that the man had refused to give the number when he placed the call. This lead me to believe that he had dialed the operator and asked for the Police Dept. at which time she ask him for the number he was calling from and he refused to give me the number.

The operator in charge said she would try to find where it came from and she would hold the line open until its origin could be found.

D. Slaight #23

Napa Police Dept.

9-27-69

FEDERAL BUREAU OF INVESTIGATION

Washington, D.C. 20537

REPORT

of the

IDENTIFICATION DIVISION

LATENT FINGERPRINT SECTION

YOUR FILE NO. Case #105907 October 23, 1969

FBI FILE NO.

LATENT CASE NO. A-12397 **AIRMAIL**

TO: Mr. Earl Randol
Sheriff – Coroner of Napa County
Napa, California 94558

Attention: Detective Sergeant Hal Snook

UNKOWN SUBJECT;
RE: BRIAN CALVIN HARTNELL
CECELIA ANN SHEPARD – VICTIMS
LAKE BERRYESSA AREA
NAPA COUNTY, CALIFORNIA
SEPTEMBER 27, 1969
ASSAULT - MURDER

REFERENCE: Letter October 10, 1969

EXAMINATION REQUESTED BY: Addressee

SPECIMENS: Five photographs of latent impressions

Seven latent fingerprints, three latent palm prints, and one latent impression, which is either a fingerprint or a partial palm print, appear in the submitted photographs and are of value for identification purposes.

The latent fingerprints in the captioned case and in the case entitled "Unknown Subject; Vallejo Times Herald, Vallejo, California, Extortion," latent case #A-10042, FBI File #9-49911, Vallejo, California, Police Department Case #243146, are not identical with the fingerprints of the following named individuals:

(Continued on next page)

John Edgar Hoover, Director

THIS REPORT IS FURNISHED FOR OFFICIAL USE ONLY

Griffin Raymond [REDACTED], born
January 11, 1949, in California
Thomas Leonard [REDACTED], born
January 13, 1944, in Texas
(previously named by Vallejo,
California, Police Department)
Aubrey Dwight [REDACTED], FBI #840251C
(previously named by FBI,
San Francisco Division)

The latent impression in the captioned case was compared, with the available fingerprints of these individuals, but no identification was effected. Inked impressions of the side, tip, and lower joint areas of the fingers and pal, prints, which are not contained in our files, are needed to conduct conclusive comparisons. [REDACTED] and [REDACTED] may or may not be the individuals previously named.

On the basis of the information furnished, no identification records were located for victims Hartnell and Shepard.

The latent prints on the captioned case were compared, with the comparable areas of the latent prints in latent case #A-10042, but no identifications were effected.

The submitted photographs of the latent prints have been retained in our files and will be available.

(Continued on next page)

For comparison with the fingerprints of any individuals you name or with any fingerprints or palm prints submitted for that purpose. The submitted copies of case reports have also been retained.

In absence of a specific request, no laboratory examination was conducted with the remaining specimens, which are enclosed. These specimens should be resubmitted to the attention of the Laboratory Division, if laboratory examinations are desired.

A modus operandi file is not maintained in the Identification Division.

Subject: UNKOWN

Case INV 1-15-311-F9-5861

Sgt. ROBERTSON stated that Mr. HARTNELL was heavily sedated but was able to give a verbal statement pertaining to the attack at Lake Berryessa. The interview was taped and reads as follows:

"INTERVIEW OF JOHN ROBERTSON, DET/SGT., NAPA COUNTY SHERIFF'S DEPARTMENT, WITH BRYAN CALVIN HARTNELL (NSO CASE #105907) AT QUEEN OF THE VALLEY HOSPITAL ON SUNDAY, SEPTEMBER 28, 1969 (TRANSCRIBED FROM TAPE RECORDING BY M. FEURLE):

"J.R. Can you give me this fellow's description and tell me what happened?

"B.H. So many people have been asking me... I hope...

"J.R. Well sometimes when we're repetitious, - I know it happens to me, I tell the same thing over and over and over, and sometimes I might vary a little, and if you do...

"B.H Shall I just start out and tell you what happened?

"J.R. I don't want to tire you out.

"B.H. I just don't want this to happen again to anybody... Of course he might have his reasons, - I don't know...

"J.R. Okay. Go right ahead. Start right from the beginning. What happened?

"B.H Okay. This girl came out from school, - I used to go with her two years ago, and she's now going to another school, and she came up to visit some friends and we were having dinner at the school cafeteria, and I said, 'Well, are you doing anything special this afternoon?' and she said, 'Why?', and I said, 'I don't know. We could go out and either go for a walk, go to San Francisco, or, you know, just...', 'cause we used to be good friends. We used to have a good friendship. And so it got too late by the time we got around to what we were going to do. We had to stop in St. Helena for a couple items and then we had to cart a couple kids home and stuff, and by the time we finally got around to it, it was getting late, and I though going to San Francisco 'd rush you, you know, because by the time we got back for worship...

And so we went out to Berryessa, and there was this one place I used to go out... we used to all the time, you know... and I couldn't find it. And so I figured Ah, forget it, and this looks like as good a place as any. So I parked the car, - there were no other cars there. I had a Kharman Ghia, '56, white, with a black vinyl top, and it's in pretty

(Interview of HARTNELL cont'd.)

"good-looking shape. But we parked there on the road's edge and talked Oh it must be about a quarter of a mile to down to the place where we went. We had... (unintelligible)... peninsula, - it's an an island I guess during the wetter season. You can see where it was levee... And so that looked like a lot... there was a big spreading tree up there. There were two of them, really, - one was a little bigger than the other. We took the one that was out on the point.

"It was really beautiful out there. We were sitting on top... I lay down on my back and she lay down on her stomach beside me, you know, kind of resting her head on my shoulder, and we were talking, you know, kind of reminiscing about old times, and stuff. And I heard these rustling leaves, and I said. 'You have your specs on. Why don't you see what the deal is over there?' And she says, 'Oh, it's some man." And I said, 'Is he alone?' and she said, 'Yeah... (unintelligible)... and she says, 'Well he just stepped behind the tree.' And I said, 'What's the idea of that? To take a leak?' You know, 'cause that's the only thing I could think of, - just step behind a tree. And so I says, 'Well, keep looking and tell me what happens,' – and she squeezed my arm and says, 'Oh my God, he's got a gun!'

"And so he came out, and of course still actually I wasn't... There's some things you really wouldn't mind having happen, just for the experience of it. You know I thought, Well I only got fifty cents on me. It's worth all of that having it happen. I didn't think about another angle. So I talked to him, you know. I said, 'Well listen, Mac,' (you know I'm in the sociologist field, you know, I'm pre-law, with history and psych.) You know I've read about the criminal mind and everything, you know. I thought well maybe the guy really does need help, you know. I says, 'There's no strings attached.' I says, 'I don't have any money right now but if you need help that badly I can help you out in another way maybe.' And he says, "Nah... time's running short,' he says, 'cause I just got out of...' – some prison in Montana, I don't know what the name of it is. Feathers? Do you what the name of it is? I'll see if it sounds familiar. Fern of Feathers? It's some double name, like Fern Lock or something...

"J.R. It's Lodge...

(Interview of HARTNELL cont'd.)

"B.H. Oh yeah, yeah, - Lodge. At least we know we're together on that.

"J.R. Mountain Lodge Prison, or something of that nature...

"B.H. Yeah, You know he said he broke out and had to kill a guard getting out. And I said, 'Well, man, I mean actually I don't mean to call your bluff or anything, but wouldn't you rather be stuck on a stealing charge than a threat of homicide? You know? And he says, 'Well just don't start playing hero on me.' You know, 'Don't try to grab the gun,' 'cause I didn't really figure the gun was loaded. I always thought it would be empty. I've heard a lot of times that this is what they do just as a bluff, but I decided not to call his bluff after he really, you know... I told him, 'You know you're really wasting your time with me. I've got a billfold and this much change and that's it.' And he said, he told the girl, 'Go tie him up. I'd feel much better if you were tied up.' And she tied a couple of loose knots on me, so I make it look kind of tight... (unintelligible)... you know, just for a second, and he said 'Go ahead.' And I said, 'Do you mind?' and she got kind of fearful about it, so I figured since there's two lives involved, not just mine, I won't do it.

"So I let her tie me up on the wrists again, and he tied her up, - terribly tight, you know, real... (unintelligible)... put his gun away, and we were talking and all, - bantering, you know, basically. I was thinking, anything I can do to help, by the way just to keep the conversation going... Suddenly he was taking it all seriously, you know... So I was starting out and finally he said. 'Okay, lay down. I've got het tied up', you know... He strung a rope between our ankles in the rear, so we were like this, you know, or our stomachs, tied...

"J.R. You both facing the ground...

"B.H Right. And, oh, this was before. I got sort of ahead. So anyway, he said, 'Get down,' and I said, 'Oh come on! Don't make me lay down! We could be here all night! We could freeze to death!' I said that a couple, three times, and he said, 'GET DOWN! RIGHT NOW!' He got a little pushed off at me. So I got down and then he finished tying her up and clonked her down, - and then he goes.. Sswhooosh (a sound with his mouth)... (unintelligible)

(Interview of HARTNELL cont'd.)

"And so I said, 'Do you have bullets in there?' And so he pulled out the clip and showed me that he did. The bullets were about this long, I can remember, and about this fat, and they had the regular red cap on it, about this long. Maybe that doesn't give you any better description of the gun or not. I don't know. And it came out of the heel, the grip, you know. It slipped out from the bottom.

"And now, to backtrack a bit. I was really trying to see what he looked like, you know. He had on pleated pants, these old type of suit pants, you know, and they were either black or dark blue, I can't remember now. And I can't remember what he was wearing for shoes. But he had on this cotton coat. You've seen the kind, that you just urn the collar up once, there's a zipper down the front, you know. They're real light, super-thin, you know...

"J.R. Kind of a windbreaker...

"B.H. Yeah, like a windbreaker. And it's got this blue, this little collar, sometimes the guys wear them standing up, you know.

"J.R. What color was that?

"B.H. That was dark blue. And I don't know. Maybe he had something in his pouch. I just took it as being a... as being a... you know, he was stout 'cause he looked kind of heavy. I think he was weighing two and a quarter, two fifty, somewhere in there. And I got kind of a look at his hair. His voice... I can remember... almost like I'd heard it before. You know there's some drawls that a lot of people have similar. And... almost as if I'd heard it before... couldn't think where.

"I gave that one up, I just gave it up that angle. I look through his hair. I kind of looked like it was combed, you know, like this... it was a brownish, you know, dark brown hair.

"And this mask he had on. It was ingeniously devised. It was... he had four corners at the top, like the top of a paper sack... black. It came down, came down, with the front panel about to here, and a kind of a thing that came over the shoulders, you know, and then the same thing down the back, straight down. And in the front he had a circle with a symmetrical cross in the middle. You know what I mean by a symmetrical cross?

(Interview of HARTNELL cont'd.)

"J.R. Um hum (affirmative).

"B.H. The ends of the cross hung out about this far on each of the... you know, where it came out. The circle was this much... like this... and then it was like this, you... hung out of the end, over the edge of the circle.

"And he had clip-on sunglasses... it was hard to tell. You know, the sunglasses you clip on when you're wearing glasses, eyeglasses. He had those clipped no. I'm pretty sure.. I don't think he had glasses, though. I think he just had these clipped on to his suit... you know, that little mask.

"And I don't know how tall he was. Maybe 5-8 or maybe 5-10, 6 feet, somewhere in there. I'm a very poor judge of height because of my height. I have no meaning, you know. It's always down, you know. It can never be up...

"And so I saw him put away his gun, and I was turning to say something to Celia, and all of a sudden I felt my back... just... no, I think I saw him pull it out... I don't remember... I think I saw him whip out his knife and just start stabbing me in the back... CHOMP, CHOMP, CHOMP, CHOMP! I was just (makes a guttural sound)... you know that kind of a sound... and Celia turned to see why I was (repeats guttural sound), you know, and she just about fainted. She went hysterical... (unintelligible)... and when he finally stopped... I mean he went over and... The doctor says there's six in the back, six wounds on my back. You ought to confirm that. One I've got went clear through the lung. I've got it draining. I did drain a couple pints of blood out as soon as I got here. I lost an awful lot of blood, I guess.

"We were down... I mean it was absolutely no question in my mind... when a person gets stabbed as many times as we did... we were going to die. I mean there'd be no reason to question it. But somehow I, you know, started (unintelligible)... I just knew there was too much I had to live for. I mean really it does happen... about getting depressed and everything... when you're young you always think about these things... you know you think about it... and when you've got someone forcing your hand, - oh well, there was a lot of things I had to do. And what really kept me going... you know my parents are pretty Christian. I haven't been too much of a Christian myself... but if you believe in the principle you ask God to help you. Another thing, - What was my only strength was knowing two things. One, that I did not want to die, and two, that I felt that whatever was

(Interview of HARTNELL cont'd.)

"going to be was going to be, but I was going to try my damnedest to stay alive. And so, like I say, -before I left her I kissed her, and I said, 'Well,' I says, 'I'm gonna try to get help.'

"There was a boat kept circling around out there in the lake and we started yelling at it and finally it came within about 100 yards of the shore and turned off its motor and stayed there watching us for about fifteen minutes, and we were just screaming hysterically, trying to get their attention, you know, to come over here. Oh, I don't know, I guess they were afraid that the guy might be there in the bushes and they were liable to get choked or something. So finally he came up a little closer. I didn't have my glasses on... I was just swaying, you know... and I had gotten one of her hands free before they came, and so I kept trying to get her to untie me, and she couldn't, she was too weak, she said.

"So finally I just kept hollering and hollering, and she said, 'Turn around and let's see if I can do it again.' She finally got it. My hands and my feet were just pure numbness... they're still numb but I'm sure that will go 'way. But I finally got... (unintelligible)... untie her so she could kind of relax out. 'Cause it was a terrible position, you know, upon our stomachs... (unintelligible)...

"And so I started to go for help. I finally got myself fairly reconciled. I wasn't too worried about dying, if that was what was going to happen, but I knew I had to keep pushing on. I had to force myself into staying alive because it was... I could just see myself... you know, all sort of waves would come over... I just (coughing sound)... (unintelligible)... 'Well, you're not gonna give up this easy', you know. And, like I say, I just kept believing that God would do everything the best, if the thing was gonna happen, but I couldn't see any reason why my dying would be the best good. So I just played along with that.

"I just started to walk to walk toward the road... everything black out on me... my visual... my mid was never blacked out, but my visual was. So I lay down... My eyes started to come open... I just saw a haze of trees, you know. In a little while I got up and wen another twenty feet, and then the same thing happened... (unintelligible)... and sat down. Next thing I went clear... (unintelligible)... the road, and by that time I just fell... I just... I was trying so hard to go far I just went too far. Finally I heard this pickup

(Interview of HARTNELL cont'd.)

"coming... I was just laying alongside the road, and that's where this guy picked me up.

"They weren't in any hurry at all, it didn't seem like, you know, but they finally called an ambulance. About fifteen minutes later it came... (unintelligible)... but I still believe.. I've got feeling... starting to get a little pain to come through. But from the minute that knife baled went in, it was nothing but pure shock from there on. I mean I just did not expect it. I didn't expect that he would do that. That was a variable I had completely left out. And I guess he just took off running after we started running. I don't know. I never saw him before and hope not to see him again... at least outside of a courtroom.

"It's hard for me to explain much more. I'm trying to give you a kind of example of his technique. He had some rope cut up in his back pocket. And he had a... well, I thought it was a police automatic because it was in one of these black leather cases, you know...

"J.R. Was it in a smooth case, or did it have a basket weave like...

"B.H Can I have my glasses? Oh, they're not here. It was a smooth one, though.

"J.R. Did he have this hood down to about the middle of his chest?

"B.H. No, about like... well, I'll show you... Here... his stomach... You know I could see his... (voice fades away)

"J.R. Okay. You said his hair looked dark brown. How could you see his hair?

"B.H 'Cause I saw it from where those goggles fit. I look so closely to find out. And when he turned you know they kind of flittered... I could see his hair. It looked kind of greasy.

"J.R. Now was he as heavy as I am?

"B.H. Well I can't say 'cause he wasn't wearing those type of clothes. They were sloppy clothes, you know. And he just had on this old pair of pleated pants. I don't know... How tall are you?

"J.R. I'm about five eleven.

(Interview of HARTNELL cont'd.)

"B.H. Well, like I say, he was dressed kind of sloppily, you know. His pants real tight up here and his stomach kind of pouched a bit, you know. I don't know... it's hard to say 'cause I can't judge you with being in a suit and all, you know, and him not being professional-looking at all. He could be about the same. It's hard to say. He was so sloppily dressed.

"J.R. Bryan, you also mentioned a drawl. Well not a drawl, an accent.

"B.H. It was just something... I guess his way of talking. It was something I couldn't repeat. It's like a song. Sometimes you know what you're going to say but you just can't sing the melody worth a darn.

"J.R. Did he have a throaty voice or a high pitched?

"B.H. In between. But it was just a unique way of talking.

"J.R. Did he sound like an educated man?

"B.H. Heck no! I don't think so.

"J.R. Did he sound illiterate?

"B.H. No. He didn't sound that way either. He just impressed me as being rather low class. The reason was because of his clothes, you know.

"J.R. Did you lose consciousness when he stabbed you at any time? Did you observe him stab Cecelia?

"B.H. Yeah...

"J.R. What did he say after...

"B.H. He stabbed her a bunch of times in the back. After she turned around, he got her once in the groin and one in the arm I think. He kind of went a little more hog-wild with her than with me. I faked dead... like that... I didn't want him to come back and give me some more.

"J.R. So you were pretty sure he thought you were dead when he finished working on you?

(Interview of HARTNELL cont'd.)

"B.H. I think he kind of thought that. Of course I don't know because we started talking right after he left. It's hard to say... (unintelligible)... I don't think she fainted either.

"J.R. Was she in a lot of pain, did she tell you?

"B.H. Oh yeah. She was more weak at the time... (unintelligible)... from the religious angle. I told her I sure as heck wasn't going to have any deathbed conversion. 'No,' she says... (unintelligible)... I mean it was just like you were gonna die and had a few things to say. But I felt more and more I wasn't losing strength as much... (unintelligible)... that I thought I could cope with...

"J.R. What you did was a courageous thing. It was a terrible thing to have happen to anyone.

"B.H. Well there was nothing we could do. We were kind of at the mercy of him. I mean I wanted to get that gun... (unintelligible)... There was a time I think I could have gotten it...

"J.R. Did it appear to be a .45 to you? An automatic?

"B.H. It was about this long... along the stock... and had a wood edge on it, you know... on either side...

"J.R. Handles.

"B.H. Yeah... yeah...

"J.R. Did the bullet look anything like that?

"B.H. No. It was kind of like this, only it was gold, and this aprt here came out along with this and then round the gold, round the blunt end. Not quite that blunt-ended. Though.

"J.R. Was it fat? Fatter than this?

"B.H. Yeah, I think it was a little fatter. But it was gold, you know. And I didn't see any of this here. There was a part where it crimped... Well, almost like that .22, short, only a lot bigger. It was about like this length, maybe more stubby.

(Interview of HARTNELL cont'd.)

"J.R. Well I'll get a .45 a little later and we can bring it up and let you observe it.

"Let's take the suspect. His hands...

"B.H. I don't remember if they had gloves on or not. I can't remember now. I keep thinking that he had gloves on. I can't figure how he tied us... Let's ask Celia, she probably knows about that.

"J.R. Did he swear? Did he use any profane language or obscenity?

"B.H. I don't think so. If he did it was no more than I was using at the time. I don't think he used any obscenity. He might have used a swear word or something, you know. That wasn't striking to me...

"J.R. Do you have any idea what his motive might have been? Money?

"B.H. Money. He said he was going to go to Mexico and he was flat broke.

"J.R. Did he search you after he...

"B.H. Heck no! Very unprofessional. He didn't even end up taking that loose change and didn't even take my billfold.

"J.R. Why did he stab you when you weren't fighting him off or anything?

"B.H. I couldn't! Even if I'd have wanted to. I was laying on my stomach...

"J.R. So what would have been the purpose of him to stab you, to you think?

"B.H. Well I (unintelligible)... but I think he got rattled... (unintelligible)... very, very nervous. His hands were shaking... (unintelligible)... Are you nervous?

"J.R. I'm just curious. If you could write me that symbol you were telling me about. Do you think you could draw me a picture of that even without your glasses?

"B.H. Um hum (affirmative). (Draws)... kind of like that. I can't see very well...

(Interview of HARTNELL cont'd.)

"J.R. Yes, I see. Okay...

"B.H. ... (unintelligible)... that I could really die...

"J.R. Does this ring a bell?

"B.H. This one here. This is more like it, but I'm not sure. It was distinctly that design. It was thick. More thick marks.

"J.R. Okay. What color was this? Do you recall?

"B.H. Black. And that was white.

"J.R. This was black.

"B.H. No, that was white. It was about this tall.

"J.R. Two and a half, three inches?

"B.H About for by four... three by three...

"J.R. How do you feel? Am I tiring you out too much?

"B.H. No, I've had a couple shots. It's not hurting me at all.

"J.R. Do you think Cecelia could tell me any more than you have already told me? Add anything?

"B.H. (unintelligible)

"J.R. Did he slap you around? Slap her?

"B.H. (unintelligible)... No.

"J.R. He was a much smaller man than you?

"B.H. Not much. About your height I guess. I don't know.

"J.R. Well you're getting kind of sleepy. I'll ease up on you.

"B.H. Have you gotten any clues at all?

"J.R. Yes, we've got some good clues. Before we get this guy it's going to take a lot of work.

"B.H. Remember he said he was headed for Mexico.

(Interview of HARTNELL cont'd.)

"J.R.   He's headed for Mexico?

"B.H.   That's what he said.

"J.R.   I'll leave you my card. It's right up here. I'm going to go down and talk to your mom and dad.

"B.H.   Have the news heard about this at all?

"J.R.   Yes.

"B.H.   Was there anything in the paper today?

"J.R.   No, it wasn't in...

"B.H.   The Napa paper?

"J.R.   Well there's no Napa paper on Sundays. It's been on the news media...

"B.H.   Names? Did they name my name?

"J.R.   I don't know, to tell you the truth.

"B.H.   The reason I asked is my girlfriend lives in Portland and I've got to talk to her before it gets to her...

"J.R.   Okay.

"B.H.   What time is it now?

"J.R.   It's one o'clock

"B.H.   What are the rates now?

"J.R.   Don't you worry about the rates.

"B.H.   Well I should probably give her a call...

"J.R.   You're looking real good. You've got some color...

"B.H.   Is there a phone real close by?

"J.R.   I'll get the nurse...

"B.H.   'Cause I'd like to call her now...

"J.R.   Now if you think of anything that you want to see me about, my card's here. You can have the nurse call me. I'm gonna be up here quite a bit.

"B.H.   You say you have a guard out here?

"J.R.   Yes.

(END OF INTERVIEW)"

Paul Lee Stine

Killed: Oct. 11, 1969 (Saturday)

~~~~~~

Case number: 696314

Time of attack: Approximately 9:55 p.m.

Place of attack: The northeast corner of Washington and Cherry Streets in the Presidio Heights neighborhood of San Francisco, Calif.

Method of attack: Cab driver Paul Stine, age 29, was shot once in the head at point-blank range. The weapon was a 9mm semi-automatic pistol, not the same 9mm used in the Ferrin murder. There were three witnesses from a house on the southeast corner of the intersection.

See more at:

https://zodiackiller.com/zodiac-killer-victims-paul-stine

Here is the two page San Francisco Police Department report pertaining to the murder of Paul Stine, followed by Officer Fouke's report regarding his possible sighting of the Zodiac --
~~~~~~

			HOMICIDE	
69631	HOMICIDE (gun) & Armed Robbery		Sep. 10-11-69	9:58pm
	Washington and Cherry St. G 3 Sat. 10-11-69 approx. 9:55pm			
[REDACTED]	16yrs.	[UNREADABLE]99 Washington St.	[REDACTED] none	
STINE PAUL L.	29yrs.	[UNREADABLE]42 Fell St.	387 3025 6262345	
Yellow taxi cab		Front seat	Money-murder	
Gun		Shoots cab driver-robs same		
see parl.#1	Y17413	Cal Yellow Cab#912	68 Ford	custom
4 dr yellow (cab)			Homicide	
G-84	G-1	909(217) Washington and Cherry Sts.	10-11-69 9:58pm	

#1 Upon responding to the above location officers Peda and Felissetti found Yellow Cab #912 parked at the northeast corner of Washington St. at the corner of Cherry St. The reportee together with two other witnesses, [REDACTED], age 14, and [REDACTED], age 13, same address and phone as reportee, stated that they saw the below described suspect in the front seat of the Yellow cab, mid to passenger side, with the victim slumped partially over his lap. The suspect appeared to be searching the victim's pockets. (Witnesses never heard a gunshot). The suspect then appeared to be wiping (fingerprints) on the interior of the cab, leaning over the victim to the driver's compartment. The suspect then exited the cab by the passenger side front door, also wiping with a white rag, possibly a handkerchief. The suspect then walked around the cab to the driver's side and proceeded to wipe the [~~STRIKETHROUGH~~] exterior of the left door area. The suspect then fled (walking) north on Cherry St. toward the Presidio of S.F. R/Os immediately checked the interior of the cab and found the victim to be slurped over the front seat with his upper torso in the passenger side, head resting on the floorboard, facing north. Ambulance was summoned, Code three, and other units were requested for an immediate search of the area. Description was obtained from reportees, whose observation point was directly across the street (50ft.) and unobstructed. Description was broadcast and numerous units responded to institute a search of the area. P.E.H. ambulance #82 responded, steward Dousette, victim was examined and pronounced dead at 10:10pm. Inspector Krake responded and summoned dog units and a fire department "spotlight" vehicle to assist in the search. R/Os called for the Crime Lab, Coroner, Yellow cab officials, and a tow.

Assistant traffic manager of Yellow Cab, LeRoy Sweet responded and gave reporting officers the victim's identification. Mr. Sweet further stated the last dispatch given the victim was at 9:45pm to 500 9th Ave. apt. #1. Victim allegedly never arrived at the above location... contd.pg.2

[UNREADABLE]			[UNREADABLE]	Crime Lab
10-12-69 12:30am Sullivan		#225	not	Homicide
[UNREADABLE]			[UNREADABLE]	Robbery Taxi det.
Armond Pelissetti	2	1879	Pelissetti 1879	

Frank Peda	2	212	[UNREADABLE]	LT.	#534

INCIDENT REPORT FORM

69631

CONTD.	Richmond #1	HOMICIDE
HOMICIDE (gun) & Armed Robbery		10-11-69 9:58pm
STINE, PAUL L.	1842 Fell St.	Washington & Cherry Sts.

Continued.Page-2	G-84	G-1	909(217) Washington and Cherry	10-11-69 9:58pm

As the dispatch was reassigned to another cab at 9:58pm. R/Os noted that the meter of the cab was running, indicating that the victim possibly picked up another fare (suspect) en route to his original assignment. (The meter read $6.25 at exactly 10:46pm) A check with the Yellow Cab Co. revealed the victim arrived at work at approximately 8:45pm and had only one fare prior, that being from Pier 64 to the Air Terminal. Sgt. Falk responded in G-10. Homicide inspectors Armstrong and Toschi responded and took charge. G-40, Lt. Kiel also responded. The military police headquarters of the Presidio of S.F. was notified and an intense search of the Julius Kahn area was made by seven dog units, other Richmond and C.P. units-to no avail. The coroner responded, Deputy Schultz and Kindred and took charge of the deceased. Coroner's receipt attached this report. Crime lab responded and to necessary photographs of the preserved scene-Dagitz and Kirkindal- all physical evidence was retained by crime lab for I.D. The auto, Yellow Cab #912 Calif. Lic. Y17413, was towed to the Hall, impounded for homicide for prints Tow slip attached this report. Room 100 was notified, given description, and advised to have broadcast continuous throughout the morning as per insp Armstrong's direction. Crime lab's initial investigation showed that the victim was devoid of any U.S. Currency, nor did he have the possession of a wallet; the ignition keys for the cab were also missing.

#2 SUSPECT: WMA, in his early forties, 5'8", heavy build, reddish-blond "crew-cut" hair, wearing eyeglasses, dark brown trousers, dark (navy blue or black) "Parka" jacket, dark shoes. Suspect should have many blood stains on his person and clothing, suspect may also be in possession of the keys to the Yellow Cab, possibly has wallet belonging to the victim. Suspect is armed with a gun. Last seen walking north on Cherry St. from Washington St.

#3 LOSS to be determined. All property of the victim in possession

Physical evidence property retained by crime lab.

Yellow Cab #912 towed to Hall for homicide for prints.

#4 N/A.

#5 N/A.

#6 N/A.

[SIGNATURE] Armond Pelissetti	2	1879	not			Crime Lab Homicide
Frank Peda	2	212	Pelissetti	LT.	#534	Robbery Taxi det.

SIGNATURE

SAN FRACISCO POLICE DEPARTMENT	INTRA-DEPARTMENTAL MEMORANDUM	
	DIST. BUR. DET. Richmond	DAY & DATE Wed. 11/12/69
Insp. Armstrong & Toschi Homicide Detail	SUBJECT: Information re: Stein murder Possible Zodiac suspect	

Sir;

I respectfully wish to report the following, that while responding to the area of Cherry and Washington Streets a suspect fitting the description of the Zodiac killer was observed by officer Fouke walking in an easterly direction on Jackson street and then turn north on Maple street. This subject was not stopped as the description received from communication was that of a negro male. When the right description was broadcast reporting officer informed communications that a possible suspect had been seen going north on Maple Street into the Presidio. The area of Julius Kahn playground and a search was started which had negative results.

The suspect that was observed by officer Fouke was a WMA 35-45 Yrs about 5'10", 180-200 lbs Medium heavy build – Barrel chested – Medium complexion – Light colored hair possibly graying in rear (May have been lighting that caused this effect.) Grey cut – Wearing glasses – Dressed in dark XXXX blue waist length zipper type jacket (Navy or royal blue) Elastic cuffs and waist band zipped part way up. Brown wool pants pleated type baggy in rear (Rust brown) May have been wearing low cut shoes.

Subject at no time appeared to be in a hurry walked with a shuffling lope, slightly bent forward head down. The subject's general appearance to classify him as a group would be that he might be of Welsh ancestors.

My partner that night was officer E. Zelms # 1348 of Richmond station. I do not know if he observed this subject or not.

Respectfully submitted

FROM		APPROVED BY:		REFER TO
Donald G. Fouke				
RANK Patrolman	STAR 847	RANK	STAR	

Next: Supplemental case overview prepared by the California Department of Justice:

Zodiac Killer Case Overview Prepared by

California Department of Justice

BUREAU OF CRMINAL IDENTIFICATION AND INVESTIGATION REPORT

P.O. Box 1859, Sacramento

TYPE OF CASE HOMICIDE NUMBER 1-15-311-F9-5861

Subject HGFFG	Copies of this report to: (1) Requesting Agency (1) Deputy Director (1) AAG Harris (3) Bureau

Requested by: Earl Randol, Sheriff Date 10-3-69 Time

Reported

Address: SO Napa Co., 810 Coombs, Napa. Telephone 255-5500

Requested how: Telephone Received by:

Reported

Assigned to: Melvin H. Nicolai, Special Agent Date: 10-3-69 Time

Assigned by: Kenneth Horton, Supervising Special Agent

Enclosures:

SYNOPSIS:

On September 27, 1969 CECELIA ANN SHEPARD and BRYAN CALVIN HARTNELL were attacked and stabbed numerous times by an unknown assailant. The attack occurred at approximately 1830 hours on the shoreline of Lake Berryessa in the County of Napa. On September 29th Miss SHEPARD died as a result of the stabbing. Mr. HARTNELL survived and subsequently reported they had been attacked by a heavyset man wearing a dark hood over his head and shoulders. The hood bore a white crosshair design on the front.

The suspect had handprinted numbers and letters on the passenger door of victim HARTNELL's vehicle. Additional investigation revealed that the person who had printed on the car door was the same individual who had sent letters to the Vallejo Times Herald, San Francisco Examiner and San Francisco Chronicle claiming to have killed three people in Solano County.

On December 20, 1968 BETTY LOU JENSEN and DAVID L. FARRADAY were shot and killed in Solano County by an unknown assailant. On July 5, 1969 DARLENE E. FERRIN and MICHAEL R. MAGEAU were shot within the city limits of Vallejo, Solano County. Mrs. FERRIN died as a result of the attack. Mr. MAGEAU survived.

In a subsequent letter the killer identified himself as "Zodiac" and on October 11, 1969 shot and killed PAUL STINE, Yellow Cab driver in the city of San Francisco.

In a letter dated April 20, 1970 the "Zodiac" killer indicated he had killed ten people, however, law enforcement agencies can only account for five.

Combines efforts by law enforcement agencies have failed to uncover the identity of the "Zodiac" killer.

Hour expended: 903

Date report written:	April 29, 1970	Report by:	MELVIN H. NICOLAI
Sec. 8704	MHN: 1m	Title	Special Agent

Subject: UNKNOWN Case INV 1-15-311-F9-5861

Details

At the request of EARL RANDOL, Sheriff of Napa County, reporting agent was assigned by Supervising Special Agent KENNETH HORTON to assist the Napa County Sheriff's Office in the investigation of the murder of CECELIA ANN SHEPARD and the attempt to murder BRYAN CALVIN HARTNELL.

On October 6, 1969 at 1000 hours Supervising Special Agent KENNETH HORTON, RAY OLSEN, Latent Fingerprint Examiner, VERNON MEUSER, Photography Unit, and the reporting agent conferred with Napa County Undersheriff TOM JOHNSON, Captain DONALD TOWNSED, Detective Sergeants KENNETH NARLOW, RICHARD LONERGAN AND HAL SNOOK at the Napa County Sheriff's Office relative to the murder and attempted murder.

Reporting agent was furnished with Napa County crime report #105907 which advised that on September 27, 1969 at 1910 hours Lake Berryessa Park Headquarters reported a double stabbing had occurred approximately one-half mile north of their headquarters office. A report by Deputy DAVE COLLINS advises that he was dispatched at 1913 hours to investigate the report of the double stabbing and states that on arrival at the crime scene he was joined by Park Ranger DENNIS LAND and Deputy RAY LAND of the Napa County Sheriff's Office.

Deputy COLLINS advised the victims, a male and female, told him they had been laying on a blanket near the shore line, the girl with her head on the boy's lap, when they noticed a subject approach them wearing a dark hood over his entire head and shoulders and on the front of the hood at approximately the center of the chest was a crosshair symbol. The victims reported the subject appeared to have dark glasses on and a portion of brown hair was observed through the eye opening in the hood.

The victims reported the suspect said, "I want your money and your car keys. I'm an ex-con from Montana Deer Lodge. I have a stolen car and I've nothing to lose." The victims reported that the suspect was armed with what appeared to be an automatic handgun. The male victim advised that he stood up but was told by the suspect to get back down on the blanket. The male victim stated he refused to lay down and the suspect then moved closer, pointing the gun at him and ordering him back down on the blanket.

The victims stated the suspect then removed several pieces of what appeared to be plastic clothesline in lengths approximately two and a half to three feet from his jacket, giving several of these pieces to the female victim and ordered her to tie up her boyfriend, which she did but not very tight. The victims advised the suspect then tied the female securely and retied the male victim.

The male victim stated the suspect then began stabbing him in the back but stopped when he feigned dead. The suspect then began stabbing the female victim in the back and on the front after she had somehow turned over. After stabbing the female victim several times the suspect without further conversation walked away.

The male victim stated they laid quietly for a short time and then began untying the plastic material they had been bound with. The male victim advised that after removing their bonds they both became faint from loss of blood and realized the seriousness of their wounds. The male victim stated he began yelling for help and after approximately fifteen or twenty minutes a fisherman in a boat approached the shore line and asked what the trouble was. The male victim related he told the fisherman they had been stabbed and robbed and the fisherman then left to get aid.

Deputy COLLINS advised the fisherman is identified as RONAL HENRY FONG, DOB 4-26-30, [REDACTED] Avenue, San Francisco.

Mr. FONG reported he had waited ten to fifteen minutes after hearing the cries for help before ascertaining whether or nor they were legitimate and after learning of the injuries inflicted on the victims, he immediately proceeded to the Rancho Monticello Resort where he notified the owner, Mr. ARCHIE WHITE.

Deputy COLLINS stated that ARCHIE [REDACTED] and his wife, BETH, Park Ranger BILL WHITE and Mr. RONALD FONG left the resort by boat and proceeded to the scene of the crime. Deputy COLLINS advised that Park Ranger DENNIS LAND departed from park headquarters by vehicle and enroute to the crime scene picked up the male victim who was lying beside the trail approximately three hundred yards from the main road. Park Ranger LAND then transported the male victim back to the scene of the crime. Deputy COLLINS advises the victims were subsequently transported by ambulance to the Queen of the Valley Hospital in Napa.

Deputy COLLINS stated that while enroute to Lake Berryessa the Napa Police Department had issued a radio all points bulleting at 1940 hours reporting their department had received a phone call from an unknown male with a youthful sounding voice, possibly in the early twenties, who told the police dispatcher, "I want to report a murder, no a double murder. They are two miles north of park headquarters. They were in a white Volkswagen Karmann Ghia."

Deputy COLLINS advised that after securing the scene of the

stabbing, the assigned officers then began a search of Knoxville Road in an effort to locate the white Karmann Ghia which was found by the officers approximately three-quarters of a mile from the location where the attack occurred.

Deputy COLLINS reported the vehicle bore Oregon license #RU2040 and further examination revealed the door had a crosshair symbol drawn on the upper middle portion and words and dates printed below. Deputy COLLINS advised the message read as follows:

"Vallejo 12-20-68
7-4-69
September 27, 1969 6:30 by knife"

Deputy COLLINS related the printing was apparently done with a felt pen, black in color.

Deputy COLLINS stated that a preliminary examination was conducted in the vicinity of the vehicle and as a result distinctive footprints were found leading to the passenger side of the car. Deputy COLLINS advised he remained at the scene until the arrival of the detectives assigned to investigate the attack on the victims

A report by Officer DAVE SLAIGHT of the Napa Police Department reads as follows:

"At 7:30pm, 9-27-69, received a telephone call on line one of the Napa Police Dept. switchboard. I answered with, 'Napa Police Dept., Officer Slaight'. A male voice, young sounding, possibly early twenties stated calmly, 'I want to report a murder, no, a double murder. They are two miles North of Park Headquarters. They were in a white Volkswagen Karman-Ghia.'

"There was a pause at which time I ask, 'where are you now' In a voice barely audible came, 'I'm the one that did it.' I could hear the phone being put down but not hung up. I ask, 'Is anyone there?' about twice but received no reply.

"I could hear the line was still open because I could hear traffic passing the phone and for some reason I got the impression there were people near or around because I seem to recall hearing feminine voices in the background, however at the time I was in the process of phoning the Napa Sheriff's Office with another phone and with radio transmission it was hard to tell.

(Officer SLAIGHT´s report cont'd.)

"I informed the S.O. of the call and then phoned the operator to see if the call could be traced. An operator stated that this a 255 payphone and that the man had refused to give the number when he placed the call. This lead me to believe that he had dialed the operator and asked for the Police Dept. at which time she ask him for the number he was calling from and he refused to give the number"

"The operator in charge said she would try to find where it came from and she would hold the line open until its origin could be found.

A report by Detective Sgt. NARLOW advises that he and Detective Sgt. LONERGAN were contacted by phone on September 27th at 2020 hours and assigned to contact the victims at the Queen of the Valley Hospital and conduct the investigation relative to the attack. Sgt. NARLOW stated he arrived at the hospital at 2033 hours and at 2035 hours received information from Station One to the effect that a pay phone booth located at the Napa Car Wash, corner of Main and Clinton Streets, had been used to make the phone call to the Napa Police Department. Sgt. NARLOW advised he immediately dispatched Detective Sgt. SNOOK to the phone booth to process the scene for physical evidence. Sgt. NARLOW stated that Piner's Ambulance arrived at the hospital at 2050 hours with the stabbing victims who were taken directly to the emergency room.

Sgt. NARLOW reported the victims were identified as BRYAN CALVIN HARTNELL, male, Caucasian, 20 years, DOB 7-1-49, student at Pacific Union College, Angwin, California, home address Route 2, Box 252, Troutdale, Oregon, and CECELIA ANN SHEPARD, female, Caucasian, 22 years, DOB 1-1-47, student at University of California, Riverside, home address 10733 Mead Lane, Loma Linda, California.

Sgt. NARLOW advised that an unidentified nurse told him that when hospital officials were attempting to get the identification from BRYAN HARTNELL he had told then to contact JUDY [REDACTED] in Angwin as she was one of CECELIA's best friends. Sgt. NARLOW reported he contacted Mr. JIM [redacted, Chief Security Officer, Pacific Union College, by phone and requested Mr. [REDACTED] to attempt to locate Miss [REDACTED] was a student at the college but had left early in the afternoon driving a yellow Datsun. A routine all points bulletin was then issued by Sgt. NARLOW in an effort to locate Miss [REDACTED].

Sgt. LONERGAN advises that a 2137 hours he interviewed the victim BRYAN HARTNELL who appeared to be in extreme pain and in a state of shock.

Mr. HARTNELL stated the assailant was wearing a black ceremonial type hood, square on the top, and said he appeared to be heavyset, weighing two hundred to two hundred and fifty pounds. The victim related that the attacker had approached both he and Miss SHEPARD armed with a gun but had stabbed them with a long knife. Mr. HARTNELL further stated that the gun was in a black holster and the knife was in a sheath. The victim further stated the suspect was wearing dark clothing and that the knife as having a black handle and a homemade appearance.

Victim HARTNELL had been stabbed in the back six times by his assailant.

Sgts. NARLOW and LONERGAN advise they left the Queen of the Valley Hospital at 2215 hours and proceeded to the Sheriff's Office where they interviewed Miss JUDITH [REDACTED] who had been located by the Napa Police Department.

Miss [REDACTED] advised that she was a student at Pacific Union College and had a residence address of [REDACTED] Sunland Boulevard, Sun Valley, California.

Miss [REDACTED] stated that she was with BRYAN HARTNELL and CECELIA SHEPARD earlier in the afternoon. She stated they all left Pacific Union College together at approximately 1300 hours and went to a rummage sale in the city of St. Helena. Miss [REDACTED] reported that Mr. HARTNELL had purchased a TV at the rummage sale and had to transport it back to his room at the college. Miss [REDACTED] stated that Mr. HARTNELL had left Mrs. SHEPARD at the rummage sale as there was not enough room for her in his vehicle. Miss [REDACTED] advised that Mr. HARTNELL returned to St. Helena and picked up Miss SHEPARD at approximately 1400 hours.

Miss [REDACTED] stated it was her understanding that Miss SHEPARD and Mr. HARTNELL were planning to go to San Francisco when they left her in St. Helena. Miss [REDACTED] advised she had no knowledge of any plans pertaining to Miss SHEPARD and Mr. HARTNELL going to the Lake Berryessa area.

Sgts. NARLOW and LONERGAN advise they proceeded to Lake Berryessa, arriving at the scene of the crime at 2354 hours. They stated they observed the 1956 white Karmann Ghia with the black vinyl top and were shown footprints and tire tracks, both believed to have been left by the responsible.

Sgts. NARLOW and LONERGAN advised they were told by Park Ranger DENNIS LAND that it was possible to get to the beach area by vehicle through a locked gate approximately one-half mile south of the victim's vehicle. They report they proceeded to the area, arriving at footpath approximately half between the scene of the crime at the beach and the victims' vehicle on the road. Sgt. NARLOW advised that a brief examination was conducted of the footpath area and as a result the officers discovered a footprint on the footpath similar to the footprints found at the scene of the victims' vehicle. Sgt. NARLOW stated that after finding the footprints they decided to completely secure the area and make a thorough search at daylight.

Sgt. NARLOW stated they left the crime scene area and proceeded to Berryessa Park Headquarters where he took into his possession several items of evidence that had been in the custody of Park Ranger DENNIS LAND. The items are listed as follows:

One blanket
One pair men's shoes
One wallet, property of victim HARTNELL
One pair of sun glasses
Playing cards
Numerous strands of white plastic line of various lengths, some appearing to be bloodstained.

Sgt. NARLOW advised the aforementioned items were subsequently submitted to Sgt. SNOOK for preservation.

Sgt. NARLOW reports that after receiving the evidence he and Sgt. LONERGAN returned to the area of the victims' vehicle and assisted Sgt. SNOOK in the making of plaster casts. Sgt. LONERGAN advised that after completing the casts he drove the victims' vehicle to the maintenance shop at Berryessa Park Headquarters where it was secured inside the shop by Park Ranger DENNIS LAND.

Sgt. NARLOW advised that Deputy ALLEN BRAMBANK was assigned to maintain the security of the crime scene until daybreak.

Sgts. NARLOW and LONERGAN stated they returned to the crime scene at Lake Berryessa at 0700 hours on the 28th accompanied by Captain TOWNSEND, Sgt. SNOOK and Sgt. JAMES MUNK. The investigating officers assisted Sgt. SNOOK tracing the footprints from the victim's vehicle to the scene of the crime by the beach area. Sgt. NARLOW advised that at 0800 hours he received information from Park Headquarters that Spanish Flat Coffee Shop regarding a possible suspect in the crime.

Dr. CLIFTON R. [REDACTED], [REDACTED] Cypress Way, Los Gatos, California, phone [REDACTED]-1309, and his son, DAVID LEE [REDACTED], 16 years, were interviewed by Sgts. NARLOW and LONERGAN at the Spanish Flat Coffee Shop, Lake Berryessa, at 0912 hours.

Dr. [REDACTED] reported that the previous evening at approximately 1830 hours he and his son parked their vehicle north of the Park Headquarters in the general area. DAVID [REDACTED] stated that while enroute to the beach area he observed a white male subject described as 5-10, heavy build, wearing dark trousers and a long sleeved dark shirt with red coloring. DAVID stated that the subject was not carrying anything and was apparently just out for a walk. DAVID further related that the subject was walking along the hillside about half way between the road and the lake. DAVID further reported that when the subject saw him he, the subject, turned and walked up the hill in a southerly direction.

Dr. [REDACTED] and his son both stated they had not observed a vehicle parked in the area of their car and had only noticed the subject at a distance of approximately one hundred yards. Dr. [REDACTED] did report that there was a man with two young boys in the area shooting beebee guns but does not know whether or not they may have seen the same subject.

Sgts. NARLOW and LONERGAN advised that the location where the doctor had parked his vehicle was approximately eight-tenths of a mile from where the victims' car had been parked.

A report by Sgt. HAL SNOOK advises that he contacted Sgt. NARLOW at the Queen of the Valley Hospital on September 27th at 2045 hours and was told by Sgt. NARLOW that the suspect had made a phone call to the Napa Police Department from a pay phone located at the Napa Car Wash, Main and Clinton Streets, and that police units were standing by. Sgt. SNOOK stated he proceeded to the Napa Car Wash, arriving at 2050 hours, where he contacted Officer ERIC RONBACK and Reserve Officer DONALD STANLEY who had secured the area prior to his arrival.

Officer SNOOK reports color photos were taken of the scene and the vicinity of the phone searched for physical evidence. Sgt. SNOOK advised there was no evidence found that would tend to indicate the subject left the scene at a high rate of speed and no tire marks or footprints were observed on the blacktop surface.

Sgt. SNOOK states he approached the phone booth and noted the receiver was laying on the small shelf with the mouthpiece directly under the phone unit. The earpiece was protruding to the south and the openings on the receiver facing the east wall of the booth. The complete phone unit was located on the north corner of the east wall of the booth, the folding door entrance being the southern enclosure of the booth. The inside of the booth was photographed to show the receiver position and the phone number, 255-9673.

Sgt. SNOOK advised the phone booth was processed for latent impressions and latent impressions lifts I through 35 were removed and held as evidence. The latent impressions numbered 29 through 32 were photographed prior to lifting. Sgt. SNOOK states that heavy beads of moisture remained on the photographed impressions for approximately three hours after his arrival. Sgt. SNOOK reports he completed processing the scene at 2349 hours and then proceeded to Lake Berryessa, arriving at 0020 hours on the 28th.

Sgt. SNOOK advises he began a search for physical evidence in the area of the victims' vehicle which had been parked on the east side of Knoxville Road seven-tenths of a mile north of Lake Berryessa Park Headquarters. The parking lot and state property are separated by a fence and a footstile through the fence is located approximately fifteen feet south of the victims' vehicle. Footprints were observed leading from the footstile to the passenger door of the victims' vehicle.

The footprints measured approximately 13" in length, 4 1/2" at widest part of the sole with the heel measuring 3 1/4" in width and 3 1/7" in length. The footprint bore parallel tread bar design on both the sole and the heel which was inset from the edges approximately three-quarters of an inch. Sgt. SNOOK reports the shoe impressions were photographed by Sgt. TOM BUTLER and a plaster cast was made of one of the footprints leading from the footstile to the passenger side of the victims' vehicle.

Sgt. SNOOK further advises that he observed a set of tire impressions approximately twenty feet to the rear of the victims' vehicle. The track nearest the fence measured approximately 4 1/2" in width and bore a parallel tread design. The tread was photographed by Sgt. BUTLER and a plaster cast was made by Sgt. SNOOK. the tire impressions furthest from the fence measured approximately 5 1/2" in width with a single straight tread design approximately 1/8" wide in the center with a herringbone tread design on both sides consisting of three 1/16" treads between two 1/8" treads. Photographs and a cast were also made of this impression. The distance between the inside of the left tread and the inside of the right tread measured approximately 52".

Sgt. SNOOK advised hat after photographs of the area and the vehicle had been taken the vehicle was then processed for latent impressions. As a result latent lifts 36 through 43 were removed and retained as evidence. After the processing the vehicle was driven to Lake Berryessa Park Headquarters by Sgt. LONERGAN where it was secured inside of a garage

Sgt. SNOOK states that he and Sgt. LONERGAN followed the suspect footprints down the hill toward the lake to the point where the two victims were attacked and back to the parking area. The distance from the parking lot where the attack occurred was found to be approximately 510 yards.

Sgt. SNOOK reports that plaster casts were made of a heel print at the bottom of the first hill, a footprint at the junction of the trail and a dirt road approximately fifty feet from the point where Park Ranger DENNIS LAND found the victim HARTNELL and a footprint in the sand approximately one hundred feet from the scene of the attack. The latter footprint bore the same tread design and also showed a circular design in the instep area. The general area was photographed by Sgt. SNOOK.

Sgt. SNOOK states that during the search for physical evidence a green bottle was found near a stump close to the scene of the attack. The bottle was processed for latent impressions and lifts 44 through 48 were removed and along with the bottle were retained as evidence.

Sgt. SNOOK reports soil samples were taken from the point where the attack occurred, from behind a tree were the suspect had reportedly stood to put on the hood and from the parking are beside the victims' vehicle.

Aerial photographs were taken by ROBERT MC KENZIE, Photographer for the Napa Register, from an aircraft piloted by HAROLD MOSKOWITE, Napa County Special Deputy.

Sgt. SNOOK advises he returned to the Napa County Sheriff's Office at 1700 hours and upon arrival removed from the evidence locker the following listed items:

1 – Shoes and socks of victim HARTNELL

2 – Trousers, shirt, T-shirt, shorts and belt of victim HARTNELL

3 – Wallet, glasses, key and playing cards, property of victim HARTNELL

4 – Dress, slip, panties and brassiere of victim SHEPARD.

Sgt. SNOOK reports that on September 29th the victims' vehicle was removed from Lake Berryessa Park Headquarters and brought to the Napa County corporation yard where the passenger door was removed and retained as evidence by the Sheriff's Office.

A report by Detective Sgt. JOHN ROBERTSON advises that he interviewed victim HARTNELL t the Queen of the Valley Hospital on September 28th at 1230 hours.

Sgt. ROBERTSON advised that Miss SHEPARD had been in surgery earlier in the morning and could not be interviewed.

Sgt. NARLOW and LONERGAN advised they interviewed Park Ranger Sgt. WILLIAM WHITE at Lake Berryessa Park Headquarters on September 28th at 1320.

Sgt. WHITE stated that while on routine patrol on September 17th he had received a dispatch at approximately 1855 hours from Park Headquarters directing him to proceed to the Rancho Monticello Resort where a citizen was in the process of reporting a possible stabbing. Sgt. WHITE advised he proceed to the resort where he met Mr. and Mrs. ARCHIE [REDACTED] and Mr. HENRY FONG.

Mr. FONG told him he had seen a male and female on the beach area south of the Rancho Monticello Resort yelling that they had been stabbed. Sgt. WHITE advised that he, Mr. and Mrs. ARCHIE [REDACTED] and Mr. FONG then proceed to the beach area in a speed boat owned by Mr. ARCHIE [redacted.

Sgt. WHITE states that upon arrival he observed a young female with what appeared to be numerous stab wounds lying on the ground. Sgt. WHITE advised that shortly after their arrival Park Ranger DENNIS LAND arrived at the scene in his pickup truck accompanied by a young male who also appeared to have numerous stab wounds. Sgt. WHITE states he then radioed park headquarters advising them to notify the Sheriff's Office and send an ambulance.

Sgt. WHITE advised he attempted to interview the victims prior to the arrival of the ambulance and said the male victim told him they had been approached by a male subject wearing a hood, dark clothing, and carrying what appeared to be an automatic pistol. The victim told Sgt. WHITE that the suspect had said he wanted their money and car keys. The victim further related hat the suspect had said he was an ex-con out of Colorado and was enroute to Mexico. The victim reported that the suspect told them he had to tie them up and after they had been tied the suspect said, “I’m going to have to stab you.” The male victim then told the suspect, “Stab me first, I can’t stand to see her stabbed first.” Sgt. WHITE states the male victim told him that the suspect stabbed him numerous times in the back and then stabbed the girl.

Sgt. WHITE advised the female victim told him she could not see the responsible’s face as a hood was covering his entire head. She also told Sgt. WHITE that the suspect had on what appeared to be clip-on sunglasses to cover his eyes. Sgt. WHITE stated he could get no further information from the victims as they were in a state of shock and suffering from severe pain.

Sgts. NARLOW and LONERGAN advise they interviewed Mr. ARCHIE [REDACTED], owner of the boat repair shop at the Rancho Monticello Resort, phone [REDACTED]-2216, and his wife, ELIZABETH, at the resort on September 28t at 1400 hours.

Mr. [REDACTED] stated that he and his wife were contacted by Mr. FONG who told he had just observed what appeared to be a male and a female covered with blood lying on the beach south of the Rancho Monticello Resort. Mr. [REDACTED] stated that Mr. FONG further told him that the victims were shouting they had been stabbed and robbed.

Mrs. [REDACTED] states she notified park headquarters and Park Ranger Sgt. WHITE arrived at the resort a short time later. Mr. ARCHIE [REDACTED] stated he then proceeded to the scene of the crime in one of his ski boats accompanied by his wife, Mr. FONG and Sgt. WILLIAM WHITE.

Mr. ARCHIE [REDACTED] reported that upon arrival at the scene he observed a young female wearing a sweater dress covered with blood, rocking back and forth on her elbows and knees as if in great pain.

MRS. [REDACTED] related that she immediately attempted to make the victim more comfortable and tried to calm her down until the ambulance arrived, Mrs. [REDACTED] stated the female victim told her, “He was a man with a hood. His face was covered. He was wearing black pants, it hurts, it hurts.” Mrs. [REDACTED] stated the female victim told her the suspect was wearing glasses with dark clip-on sunglasses over the hood and had a black pistol.

Mrs. ARCHIE [REDACTED] advised he heard the male victim tell someone that the suspect was wearing gloves

Mr. and Mrs. [REDACTED] reported that was all the information they had obtained from the victims.

A report by Park Ranger DENNIS LAND advises that on September 27th after being notified of the attack he proceeded to the scene of the crime from Rancho Monticello by vehicle. Ranger LAND stated that after turning off of the main county road and while enroute to the lake shore he observed a male subject sitting in the grass on the right side of the lake access road. Ranger LAND reported the subject was very bloody on his back and abdomen and was saying, "Help me, help me." Ranger LAND advised he stopped his vehicle and got out and talked to the subject who said "Don't bother with me, my girlfriend is hurt much worse." The subject told Ranger LAND he had been stabbed in the back. Ranger LAND stated that he loaded the victim into his vehicle and proceeded to the scene of the crime, Ranger LAND advised that he did not get any information from either of the victim.

Sgts. NARLOW and LONERGAN advised that after interviewing Mr. and Mrs. WHITE they returned to the Napa County Sheriff's Office and at 1620 hours Sgt. NARLOW was contacted by a Mr. DEAN [REDACTED] of Pacific Union College, Angwin, phone [REDACTED]-2421, who told him that three young female students may have information pertaining to a suspect in the attack at Lake Berryessa. The three students were identified as Miss JOANNE [REDACTED], Miss LINDA [REDACTED] and Miss LINDA [REDACTED].

Sgt. NARLOW related that Mr. [REDACTED] told him the three girls had been in the Lake Berryessa are on September 27th from about 1500 to 1630 hours and during that time had observed a male subject in a late model silver blue Chevrolet approximately two miles north of the A&W Root Beer stand on Knoxville Road.

Mr. [REDACTED] reported the girls told him that the man was watching them sunbathing on the beach and described him as approximately forty years of age, six foot tall and dressed in dark clothing.

Sgt. NARLOW advised he assigned Deputy RAY LAND to interview the three students at the college. Sgt. NARLOW states that on September 29th Deputy LAND told him that after interviewing the three students, he felt their information may be pertinent and had asked them to report to the Sheriff's Office for additional interview by the investigators.

A report by Sgt. ROBERTSON states that he contacted the local shoe stores in an effort to identify the manufacturer of the suspect's shoe with negative results.

Miss JOANNE MARIE [REDACTED], DOB 6-4-[REDACTED] Dauphin Street, Pacific Union College, phone [REDACTED]-2421, extension 311, home address [REDACTED] [REDACTED] Southeast 12th Street, College Place, Washington, was interviewed by Sgt. LONERGAN on September 29th at 1445 hours.

Miss [REDACTED] stated that on September 27th at approximately 1530 hours she and her two girlfriends parked their vehicle at a location two miles north of A&W Root Beer stand on Knoxville Road and when they left their car they noticed a white male subject in a late model silver blue Chevrolet two door sedan drive into the lot behind them. Miss [REDACTED] related that she and her friends proceeded to the beach area where they were sunbathing in their bikinis and after approximately a half hour they observed what appeared to be the same subject who had parked the car, watching them.

Miss [REDACTED] described the man as being 6' tall, weighing 200 to 210 pounds, muscular build, nice looking, wearing dark pants and a dark pullover shirt. Miss [REDACTED] advised the subject was approximately 40 to 50 feet from them and when they would look at him, he would turn away.

Miss [REDACTED] realted the subject stayed around the area for approximately forty-five minutes and then walked back to the hill. Miss [REDACTED] stated that it was very doubtful that from his vantage point in the vehicle he could observe them on the beach. She believes he waited in his vehicle and them followed them to the beach area.

Miss [REDACTED] described the car the subject was driving as being very conservative and did not appear to belong to a young person. Miss [REDACTED] advised the vehicle had California license plates but she did not notice the number.

Miss LINDA [REDACTED], DOB 6-29-[REDACTED], home address [REDACTED] Sunnyside Road, Sanitarium, phone [REDACTED]-2329, was interviewed by Sgt. SNOOK on September 29th at 1445 hours.

Miss [REDACTED] stated she left the Argwin area with her two female friends, JOANNE [REDACTED] and Linda [REDACTED], at approximately 1445 hours on September 27th. Miss [REDACTED] related they drove through Pope Valley to Lake Berryessa where they parked their vehicle two miles north of the A&W Root Beer stand. Miss [REDACTED] stated that a white male subject operating a 1966 or 1967 light blue Chevrolet with California license plates drove into the parking lot and backed up toward their vehicle until the bumpers were nearly touching. Miss [REDACTED] advised she thought the vehicle was a two tone sedan and described the headlights as being long rather than round. She stated the vehicle also had a tinted rear window glass.

Miss [REDACTED] related that she and her friends went to the beach area and shortly thereafter observed the male subject who had been operating the vehicle watching them from the edge of the trees. Miss [REDACTED] stated that after about thirty minutes the subject came down by the beach and passed within twenty feet of her, walking from south to north.

Miss [REDACTED] described the subject as being approximately 28 years of age, 6' to 6'2", 200 to 225 pounds, black hair, possibly styled, with the part on the left, rounded eyes, thin lips, medium nose, straight eyebrows, small ears, well built and rather nice looking. Subject was wearing black short sleeved sweater shirt, punched up in the front, a white T-shirt handging out in back and black trousers.

Miss [REDACTED] advised that she and her friends left the beach area at approximately 1630 hours and at that time the subject's vehicle was gone.

Miss LINDA LEE [REDACTED], DOB 7-8-[REDACTED], [REDACTED] Howell Mountain Road, Angwin, phone [REDACTED]-2721, employed as a secretary by the College Press, was interviewed by Captain DONAL TOWNSEND on September 29th at 1445 hours.

Miss [REDACTED] stated she had observed a late model Chevrolet, sky blue in color with rear tail lights appearing to be long rather than round, in the Lake Berryessa parking area where she and her friends parked their car at approximately 1455 hours on September 27th.

Miss [REDACTED] stated that she and her friends proceeded to the beach and after they had been there for thirty to forty-five minutes she observed the subject who had been operating the vehicle standing on the bank approximately forty-five yards from her location.

Miss [REDACTED] described the subject as approximately 30 years of age, 6" tall, stocky build, wearing black short sleeved sweater shirt, dark blue slacks and straight dark hair neatly combed. She stated the subject had medium colored skin and was no wearing glasses. Miss [REDACTED] further advised she thought she saw a white belt around his back but it might be possibly have been his T-shirt hanging out. She related that the man was fairly nice looking and had a round face. She reported she did not observe the subject leave in his vehicle.

Sgts. NARLOW and LONERGAN advised that on September 29th at 1600 hours they were notified by Captain JOE page, Chief Napa County Coroner, that the female victim, Miss CECELIA SHEPARD, had just died at Queen of the Valley Hospital. Captain PAGE informed Sgts. NARLOW and LONERGAN that he would contact a Dr. DE PETRIS relative to performing an autopsy the following day. Captain PAGE further reported the body would be taken to the Morrison Funeral Home in St. Helena.

Sgt. NARLOW and LONERGA advised that on September 29th at 1945 hours they were contacted by Probation Officer H.B. SCHOTTE who had previously observed the plaster cast of the footprint design found at the scene. Mr. SCHOTT told them he had knowledge of a possible similar shoe sole design and brought into their office a Mr. BASSELL M. [REDACTED], [REDACTED] Sheverland Street, Apartment #7, Napa, phone [REDACTED]-6560.

Mr. [REDACTED] reported that he is a retired Air Force Master Sargent currently employed as a flight line mechanic at Travis Air Force Base. Mr. [REDACTED] produced a pair of Air Force chukker boots which he stated were issued to all Air Force personnel at Lackland Air Force Base, Texas. Mr. [REDACTED] stated the shoes are primarily designed as a wing walker shoe, however, most Air Force personnel and many of the civilian personnel employed at Air Force bases have this type of shoe.

Sgt. NARLOW advised that the design on the sole of the she brought in by Mr. [REDACTED] exactly matched the cast design of the footprint made at the scene of the crime.

The shoe has a circular design 1 1/4" in width on the outside instep of the sole. Inside of the design is printed:

"Avon

Oil Resistant

Super wear

AUYNA"

Sgt. LONERGAN advised that on September 30th at 0810 hours he received a telephone call from a Miss MARILYN DENISE [REDACTED], 18 years, student at Pacific Union College, currently residing in Andre Hall, Room B3.

Miss [REDACTED] reported that she was in the Lake Berryessa area on September 27th with a male companion, JOHN [REDACTED], age 22 years, also a student at Pacific Union College, Miss [REDACTED] stated they had parked their vehicle on Knoxville Road approximately one mile south of the Lake Berryessa Marina. At approximately 1715 hours they observed the victims BRYAN HARTNELL and CECELIA SHEPARD driving south on Knoxville Road in BRYAN's white Karmann Ghia. Miss [REDACTED] stated as the vehicle passed by BRYAN waved out of the window and said, "Hi JOHN," referring to Mr. [REDACTED], Miss [REDACTED] related that she had not seen the HARTNELL vehicle at any other time on that day.

Sgts. NARLOW and LONERGAN advised that on September 30th at 0900 hours they proceeded to the Morrison Funeral Home in St. Helena accompanied by Sgt. THOMAS BUTLER where they were met by two pathologists, Dr. WILMER A. DE PETRIS and DWIGHT G. STRAUB.

Sgt. NARLOW states that Sgt. BUTLER photographed the deceased before, during and after autopsy. Sgt. LONERGAN took notes of the various wounds suffered by the victim.

Dr. DE PETRIS advised the cause of death to be shock and loss of blood brought on by two main stab wounds. The autopsy report reads as follows:

"To the

CORONER OF NAPA COUNTY CAN 69-66

SHEPARD, Cecelia Date of Autopsy: 9-30-69

"REPORT OF AUTPSY OR POST MORTEM

"EXTERNAL EXAMINATION

"The body is that of a young female who measures 65 inches and weighs approximately 100 pounds.

"POSTERIOR SOFT TISSUE LESIONS

1. Immediately below the inferior border of the right scapula, 8-1/2 inches from the plane of the shoulder and 1-1/2 inches from the mid-line, is a 1,7cm. incision which extends for a depth of 1.7cm. to the rib. (1)
2. A 1.0 cm. incision, approximately 4-1/4 inches from the midline at the inferior border of the left scapula, 8-1/2 inches from the plan of the shoulder, extends for a depth of 1.2 cm. to the depth of the rib. (2)
3. A 2.0 cm. incision, 2.0 cm. in depth, approximately 2-1/2 inches from the mid-line, and 3-1/2 inches cephalad from the right iliac crest which hits the eleventh rib posteriorly. (3)
4. Six inches from the shoulder on the posterolateral aspect of the left arm is a slash-type incision, 2.2 cm, in width with a depth of 1.9 cm. (4)
5. Two inches posteriorly and 2 inches cephalad to the previous slash-type incision is a 2.0 cm. bruise. (5)
6. On the dorsum of the right hand is a 1-inch slash-type incision. (21)

(Autopsy report cont'd.)

"ANTERIOR SOFT TISSUE LESIONS

1. Bilaterally in both subclavicular spaces are two approximately 2.5 cm. wide drain tubes. (2,8)
2. A 10-inch sutured incision extends anteriority from the posterior axillary line toward the mid-line in the vicinity of the fourth inter-space. (12)
3. For inches laterally on a plane with the nipple is a 4.0 cm. incision into the depth to the chest wall. (10)
4. A 10-inch, somewhat S-shaped, sutured right perimedian incision extends from 2 inches below the umbilicus to 1-1/2 inches above the xyphoid. (11)
5. A 1-1/2 inch, somewhat irregular incision begins 2 inches left laterally from the umbilicus at the plane of the umbilicus, extends anteromedially and antero-right laterally. (9)
6. Immediately deep to this incision, there is a tear in the sheath of the right rectus muscle leading to a defect extending 12. Cm. along the sheath of the rectus muscle with the defect ending in another tear of the muscle sheath.

NOTE: Numbers in parantheses refer to soft tissue lesions on attached diagram with those circled in red being those apparently inflicted by the attacker.

7. Bilaterally in the femoral regions are two 1-1/2 inch wide sutures incisions containing intercaths. (13,14)
8. Two 1-inch sutured cut-down incisions are preset, one in the left medial ankle region, the other in the right medial ankle region. (15,16)
9. Left antecubital fossae, 4.0 cm. slash-type wound with irregular cutting, subcutaneous tissues, though both skin edges re sharp. Extends to plane of muscle sheath. (6)

"CHEST STRUCTURE

1. A sutured defect is present in the fourth right interspace from the anterior axillary line to the sternum. (17)
2. A 2-1/2 inch defect is present in the left seventh interspace 2-1/2 inches from the costal cartilage which does not penetrate the chest wall. (18)

"DIAPHRAGM

There is a suture defect in left anterior medial disphragm.

(Autopsy report cont'd.)

"LUNGS

The left lower lobe anteriorly shows a 3.0 cm. tear above the diaphragmatic defect. The posterior aspect of the right lower lobe shows a 4.0 cm. sharp incision. There is bilateral pulmonary edema and hemorrhage.

"LIVER

A small nick is present in the dome of the right lobe of the liver due to (9). There are minimal to moderate fatty changes

"CENTRTAL NERVOUS SYSTEM

The brain shows flattened convolutions, is moderately edematous with moderate generalized hyperemia and diffuse moderate encephalomalacia.

"G.I. RACT, KIDNEYS, BLADDER, UTERUS

No significant gross abnormalities identified.

"ANATOMICAL DIAGNOSES

"A. SEVERE BRAIN DAMAGE

B. DUE TO SEVERE CEREBRAL ANOXIA

C. DUE TO SEVERE INTERNAL AND EXTERNAL HEMORRHAGE

D. DUE TO MULTIPLE KNIFE-STAB WOUNDS.

"Note: There were multiple surgical repairs of the stab wound involving the back and abdomen. There was also found contusion (laceration) of the liver secondary to a stab wound.

/s/ W. DePetris, M.D.

Wilmer De Petris, M.D"

Dr. DE PETRIS further stated that after examining the wounds inflicted on Miss SHEPARD it was his opinion that the weapon used would be from nine to eleven inches in length, one inch in width and possibly sharpened on both sides on the top of the blade similar to a bayonet type weapon. In addition the wounds indicated it would be a heavy or sturdy type blade.

Subject: UNKNOWN Case INV 1-15-311-F9-5861

Sgts. NARLOW and LONERGAN advised that on October 1st t 0900 hours they interviewed Colonel BENDER, Officer in Charge of Base Security at Travis Air Force Base. Also present during the interview was Lt. Col. LAVERICK representing the office of Special Investigation. Sgt. NARLOW stated the Air Force officers were informed of the type of shoeprint found at the scene of the crime and requested assistance in locating where the type of shoe skid or issued.

Sgts. NARLOW and LONERGAN advised they were directed to the base supply accompanied by OSI Special Agent DONALD SANTINI who had been assigned to assist them in the investigation.

Investigating officers were informed at base supply that the shoe in question was government issue but was not kept in stock at base supply. However, the officers were told that the sales store may possibly stock the shoes.

Investigating officers were informed that if a military person or civilian employee was determined to be in need of such type of shoes, the first step would be to contact base supply where a purchase requisition would be issued which would them be presented to the sales store. The sales store would issue the shoe and, in turn, would require a person receiving the shoes to sign the purchase requisition indicating that they had received the item. The purchase requisition indicating the type of shoe but bears no indication as to the size.

Investigation officers proceeded to the sales store located on Travis Air Force Base and after a brief search located a shoe fitting the identical description of the footprint found at the scene of the crime. The measurements taken from the plaster cast indicated the shoe size to be 10 1/2R in military styling or a 10 1/2D civilian equivalent. Purchase records revealed that one hundred pair of 10 1/2R shoes had been purchased and disposed of through sales over the past thirteen months, however, as previously reported, individual requisition record do not show the shoe size.

Investigating officers stated that Air Force personnel records indicate the type shoe in question is manufactured by the International Shoe Company, Philadelphia, Pennsylvania. The shoes are then shipped to the Air Force Depot in Ogden, Utah, where they are sent to various military installations upon requisition order.

A report by Sgt. ROBERTSON advises that on October 1, 1969 he interviewed victim BRYAN HARTNELL at the Queen of the Valley Hospital and showed him the following listed automatic handguns for purposes of identification:

Colt automatic .45 cal.

Remington automatic 380 cal.

Colt Commander Auto. .45 cal.

Colt auto. .32 cal.

Walther P38 auto. 9 mm

Browning auto. 9 mm

Astra auto. (Spain) .25 cal.

Smith & Wesson auto. 9 mm

Luger automatic 9 mm

Astra automatic (Spain) 9 mm

Sgt. ROBERTSON reports that Mr. HARTNELL could not identify any of the weapons as being the same as possessed by the suspect on September 27th.

Sgt. ROBERTSON advised that Mr. HARTNELL also viewed the following reported automatic pistol ammunition for identification purposes:

.45 cal. autom. Bullet, bullet brass, casing silver

.45 cal. autom. Bullet, bullet brass, casing brass

357 cal. Magnum lead bullet, silver casing

.38 special Wad Cutter lead bullet, brass casing

9 mm Luger hollow point brass bullet, brass casing

9 mm brass bullet, brass casing (autom. Bullet)

.25 cal. autom. Brass bullet, brass casing

.22 cal. Long rifle brass bullet, brass casing

.22 cal. long rifle lead bullet, brass casing

.22 cal. Short lead bullet, brass casing

Mr. HARTNELL reported that the .45 caliber automatic cartridge with brass casing and brass colored bullet appeared to be the same as shown to him by the suspect on September 27th.

Sgt. LONERGAN states that on October 1st he received a phone call from Special Agent DONALD SANTINI, OSI, Travis, who reported that some 500 to 1000 pairs of wing walker shoes had been sold as surplus on the air base. This would be in addition to those sold at the sales store. Agent SANTINI further told Sgt. LONERGAN that he had the names of the persons who had purchased the shoes through surplus and would make them available upon request.

Sgts. NARLOW and LONERGAN advise that on October 2nd at 1400 hours they attended the funeral services for Miss CECELIA SHEPARD which were held at Pacific Union College, Angwin.

Sgts. NARLOW and LONERGAN stated they positioned themselves inside the church in order to observe all persons in attendance. Sgt. NARLOW reported that Sgt. SNOOK, Sgt. BUTLER and Detective RONALD MONTGOMERY of the Napa Police Department positioned themselves outside the church and photographed all persons entering and leaving the services.

Sgt. NARLOW further stated that he and Sgt. LONERGAN attended the graveside services at the St. Helena Cemetery in St. Helena.

Sgt. LONERGAN advised that on October 3rd he contacted JAMES [REDACTED], Administrative Assistant, Napa State Hospital, regarding a possible suspect in their homicide case.

The subject is described as GRIFFIN RAYMOND [REDACTED], DOB 1-11-[REDACTED], 6-2, 223 pounds. Mr. [REDACTED] had previously reported that this subject had left the hospital on Friday evening, September 26th, and returned Monday afternoon, September 29th.

Hospital records indicated that Mr. [REDACTED] had been in the Air Force but had received a discharge in January of 1969 due to psychiatric problems. According to the doctors at the hospital Mr. [REDACTED] would be capable of committing the type of crime that occurred at Lake Berryessa.

Sgt. LONERGAN states he interviewed Mr. [REDACTED] in the presence of JAMES [REDACTED] and Security Officer PHIL [REDACTED]. Sgt. LONERGAN advises that Mr. [REDACTED] told him he had gone to Vallejo to visit his mother, stepfather and three brothers over the weekend of the 27th and had not left Vallejo until Monday, the 29th, at which time he returned to hospital.

Sgt. LONERGAN advised that he interviewed Mr. [REDACTED] mother, Mrs. OPAL [REDACTED], [REDACTED] Hollywood Avenue, Vallejo, who corroborated her son's activities over the weekend of the 27th. Sgt. LONERGAN also reported that Mr. [REDACTED] did not have access to a vehicle.

Sgt. NARLOW advised that the Montana State Prison at Deer Lodge, Montana, had been contacted pertaining to any recent escapes from their institution where in a guard had been killed and he was informed there had been no such incidents when any of the personnel had been murdered.

Sgt. NARLOW advised he conducted a further investigation into the type of shoes possibly worn by the suspect and as a result learned that several companies manufacture the same shoe on government contract. Also, that approximately 100,000 pair of the shoes had been manufactured and shipped to the west coast to be distributed to the AAIR Force and Navy since 1966.

On October 7, 1969 Mr. SHERWOOD MORRILL, Questioned Document Examiner, advised that the person who had printed the message on the victim's vehicle at Lake Berryessa was the same individual who had sent handprinted letters to the Vallejo Times Herald, San Francisco Chronicle and San Francisco Examiner claiming to have murdered three persons in Solano County.

A report by Detective Sgt. LES LUNDBLAD, Solano County Sheriff's Office, advises that on December 20, 1968 between 2314 and 2320 hours two teenagers identified as BETTY LOU JENSEN, female, Caucasian, 16 years, and DAVID L. FARRADAY, male, Caucasian, 17 years, were shot and killed by an unknown assailant.

Sgt. LUNDBLAD stated the two homicides were committed in an isolated area frequently used by lovers and located approximately five miles east of the City of Vallejo on Lake Herman Road. Sgt. LUNDBLAD advised the victims traveled to the are in a 1960 Rambler four door station wagon and that the female victim was found lying face down in a pool of blood 28'6" west of the rear bumper of the vehicle. She had been pronounced dead at the scene by Dr. BRYAN SANFORD. The male victim was lying on his back, face up, with his feet pointing toward the right rear wheel of the vehicle and his head to the south away from the car. The victim was transported to the Vallejo General Hospital where he was pronounced dead on arrival by Dr. SIEBERT.

Sgt. LUNDBLAD advised that ten empty .22 caliber Super-X cartridge cases were found at the scene of the crime and that eight of the shots fired had been accounted for. The female victim had been shot five times on the right side of the back. The male victim had been shot once behind the left ear, one shot had been fired into the top of the Rambler and one through the rear window.

A subsequent examination by Criminalist DAVID Q. BURD, CII, revealed that the ten empty casings had possibly been fired from the same weapon and that they correspond with tests fired in a J.C Higgins Model 80 .22 automatic pistol.

Sgt. LUNDBLAD stated that there was no evidence to indicate the female had been molested in any manner and that investigators were unable to establish a motive for the crime.

Vallejo Police Department crime report #243146 advises that on July 5, 1969 at 0010 hours a female citizen reported two juveniles being shot at the Blue Rock Springs parking lot. A subsequent investigation by the Vallejo Police Department revealed that DARLENE E. FERRIN, female, Caucasian, 22 years, and MICHAEL R. MAGEAU had been shot by an unknown assailant while sitting in their vehicle in a parking lot at Blue Rock Springs. The parking lot is located on a secluded country road and is often used by young lovers.

The female victim was shot five times and was pronounced dead on arrival at the Kaiser Hospital in Vallejo. The male victim was shot four times and recovered from the attack.

Investigators of the Vallejo Police Department found nine empty 9 millimeter casings at the scene of the crime and recovered eight of the bullets.

Victim MAGEAU advised investigating officers that while he and the female victim were parked in the lot another car drove up and parked approximately twelve feet behind them. Mr. MAGEAU reported that a man carrying a handle type flashlight approached their car on the passenger side, flashed the light inside the car and without warning fired four or five shots, hitting both he and his female companion. Mr. MAGEAU stated the assailant did not say anything and after the shots started to walk away. Mr. MAGEAU related he screamed and the assailant then returned and shot he and his companion each two additional times.

Mr. MAGEAU described the suspect as a young male, Caucasian, 5'9", heavyset, beefy type face, light brown hair and believed he was operating a Ford Mustang or Chevrolet Corvair, medium light brown in color.

A report by NANCY L. SLOVER, Vallejo Police Department radio dispatcher, advises that on July 5th at 0400 hours she received a phone call from a unidentified male subject who stated, "I called to report a double murder. If you will go one mile east on Columbus Park Way to the public park you will find the kids in a brown car. They were shot with a 9 millimeter Luger. I also killed those kids last year. Goodbye."

Mrs. SLOVER stated that she could not distinguish any accent in the caller's voice and said he seemed to be reading or had rehearsed what he was saying. She further related that the suspect spoke in an even consistent voice, rather soft but forceful.

Vallejo Police Department investigators advise they were unable to establish a motive for the assault and murder.

On August 1, 1969 the Vallejo Police Department received a letter and portion of a cryptogram from the Vallejo Times Herald which had been sent to the newspaper by an unknown person. The envelope was postmarked in San Francisco and dated July 31st. two additional letters had been sent to the San Francisco Chronicle and the other to the San Francisco Examiner, each containing a portion of cryptogram. These letters had also been mailed in San Francisco.

The letter received by the Vallejo Times Herald reads follows:

"Dear Editor:

"I am the killer of the two teenagers last Christmas at Lake Herman and the girl las 4th of July. To prove this I shall state some facts which only I and the police know.

"Christmas.

"1. Brand name of ammo – Super X.

2. Ten shots fired.

3. Boy was on back, feet to car.
4. Girl was lyeing on right side, feet to west.

"4th of July.

"1. Girl was wearing patterned pants.

2. Boy was also shot in knee.

3. Brand name of ammo was Western.

"Here is a cipher, or that is part of one. The other two parts have been mailed to the San Francisco Examiner and the San Francisco Chronicle. I want you to print this cipher on the front page by Fri. afternoon August 1, 1969. If you do not this I will go on a kill rampage Fry night that will last the whole weekend. I will cruse around and pick of all stray people or couples that are alone, then move on to kill some more until I have killed over a dozen people."

The three portions of the cryptogram were deciphered by a Mr. and Mrs. DONALD HARDEN, [REDACTED] Street, Salinas, California, and states as follows:

"I like killing people because it is so much fun. It is more fun than killing wild game in the forest because man is the most dangerous animal of all. To kill something gives me the most thrilling experience. It is even better than getting your rocks of with a girl. The best part of it is that when I died I will be reborn in paradise and all the I have killed will try to slow down or stop my collecting of slaves for my after life."

A subsequent letter was mailed to the San Francisco chronicle on August 15th and reads as follows:

"Dear editor

"This is the Zodiac speaking. In answer to your asking for more details about the good times I have had in Vallejo, I shall be very happy to supply even more material. By the way, are the police having a good time with the code? If not, tell them to cheer up; when they do crack it they will have me.

"On the 4th of july:

"I did not open the car door, the window was rolled down all ready. The boy was origionaly sitting in the front seat when I began fireing. When I fired the first shot at his head, he leaped backwards at the same time thus spoiling my aim. He ended up on the back seat then the floor in back troshing out very violently with his legs; thats how I shot him in the knee. I did not leave the cene of the killing with squealing tires & raceing engine as described in the Vallejo paper. I drove away quite slowly so as not to draw attention to my car.

"The man who told the police that my car was brown was a negro about 40-45 rather shabbly dressed. I was at this phone boot having some fun with the Vallejo cop when he was walking by. When I hung the phone up the dam X O thing began to ring & that drew his attention to me & my car.

"Last Christmas

"In that epasode the police were wondering as to how I could shoot & hit my victims in the dark. They did not openly state

(Zodiac letter cont'd.)

"this, but implied this by saying it was a well lit night & I could see the silowets on the horizon. Bull shit that area is srounded by high hills & trees. What I did was tape a small pencel flash light to the barrel of my gun. If you notice, in the center of the beam of light if you aim it at a wall or ceiling you will see a black or darck speck in the center of the circle of light about 3 to 6 in. across. When taped to a gun barrel, the bullet will strike exactly in the center of the black dot in the light...(not legible)

"To prove that I am the zodiac, ask the Vallejo cop about my electric gun sight which I used to start my collecting of slaves."

On October 9, 1969 at 1300 hours reporting agent and Detective Sgt. NARLOW met with investigators of the Vallejo Police Department, Solano County Sheriff's Office and California Highway Patrol at the Vallejo Police Department. The aforementioned homicides were discussed and all investigators were made aware of the evidence that existed.

BRYAN CALVIN HARTNEEL was reinterviewed at Pacific Union College by reporting agent and Sgt. NARLOW on October 10th at 1345 hours.

Mr. HARTNELL was unable to furnish any additional information relative to the attack at Lake Berryessa.

San Francisco crime report #696314 by Officer ARMOND PELLISSETTI advises that on October 11, 1969 at approximately 2155 hours PAUL L. STINE, a driver for yellow cab, was shot and killed by an unknown assailant at Washington and Cherry Streets.

The victim was shot once in the right temple with a 9 millimeter automatic pistol. Officer PELLISSETTI's report advises that three teenagers had observed the suspect in the front seat of the Yellow cab with the victim slumped partially over his lap. They reported the suspect appeared to be searching the victim's pockets and after finishing began wiping on the interior of the cab. They reported the suspect then exited the cab on the passenger side, wiped the outside area with what appeared to be a white piece of cloth and then proceeded to the driver's side where he wiped the exterior of the door.

The suspect then walked north on Cherry Street toward the Presidio of San Francisco.

The witnesses had observed the suspect from a residence directly across the street from the cab and described him as male, Caucasia, 35 to 40 years, 5'8", heavy build, short brown hair, wearing eye glasses, dark navy blue or black parka jacket, dark brown trousers and dark shoes. The witnesses reported they had not heard a gunshot.

Officer PELISSETTI's report advises that a thorough search was conducted inside the Presidio grounds by the San Francisco Police Department, Military Police and seven dog units with negative results.

Officer PELISSETTI's report also advises that the victim's black leather wallet and keys to the cab were missing.

On October 14th the Sn Francisco Chronicle received a letter and a piece of cloth material from an unknown individual who identified himself as "ZODIAC" and saying he was the person who had murdered the cab driver.

The letter was postmarked in San Francisco on October 13th and states as follows:

"This is the Zodiac speaking. I am the murderer of the taxi driver over by Washington St. & Maple St last night, to prove this here is a blood stained piece of his shirt. I am the same man who did in the people in the north bay area.

"The S.F. Police could have caught me last night if they had searched the park properly instead of holding road races with their motorcicles seeing who could make the most noise. The car drivers should have just parked their cars & sat there quietly waiting for me to come out of cover.

"School children make nice targets, I think I shall wipe out a school bus some morning. Just shoot out the front tire $ then pick off the kiddies as they come bouncing out."

On October 14th at 2100 hours reporting agent, Captain DON TWONSEND and Sgt. NARLOW conferred with Inspectors WILLIAM ARMSTRONG and DAVE TOSCHI of the San Francisco Police Department at the Napa County Sheriff's Office.

Inspector ARMSTRONG advised that the piece of cloth material contained in the letter to the Chronicle was identified as being a portion of the murdered cab driver's shirt. The suspect had torn a piece of material from the victim's shirt at the time of the homicide and had included a portion of the torn material with the letter.

Inspector ARMSTRONG further stated that as a result of a ballistics test it had been determined that the 9 millimeter weapon used in the San Francisco homicide was not the same gun that had been used in the homicide in Vallejo on July 5th.

On October 20th at 1300 hours a conference was held at the San Francisco Police Department among investigators assigned to the so-called "Zodiac" case.

Investigators were made aware of what evidence and information each department had available.

On October 22nd an individual who identified himself as the "Zodiac" made several phone calls to the Jim Dunbar Show at KGO TV, Channel 7, San Francisco, and also talked with San Francisco Attorney MELVIN BELLI on the same program. The caller had indicated that he desired to surrender himself to Mr. BELLI.

Arrangements were made for a meeting between the caller and Mr. BELLI but the caller failed to keep the appointment.

On October 22nd Officer DAVID SLAIGHT, Napa Police Department, Mrs. NANCY SLOVER, Vallejo Radio Operator, and BRYAN HARTNELL, Napa County victim, were transported to KGO TV, Channel 7, by reporting agent, Captain TOWNSEND and Sgt. NARLOW for the purpose of listening to the recordings of the calls made by the person who identified himself as "ZODIAC."

At 1300 hours the three witnesses listened to the recordings, Officer SLAIGHT and Mrs. SLOVER both stated they did not believe the caller was the same person who had phoned their respective departments relative to the homicides. Mr. HARTNELL stated the caller did not sound like the same person who had attacked him at Lake Berryessa.

Inspector BILL ARMSTRONG, San Francisco Police Department, reported that the portion of the shirt mailed to Mr. BELLI had been identified as part of the murdered cab driver's shirt.

On April 20, 1970 the San Francisco Chronicle received a letter postmarked in San Francisco from the self-identified "Zodiac" which states as follows:

"This is the Zodiac speaking By the way have you cracked the last cipher I sent you? My name is ----

"I am mildly cerous as to how much money you have on my head now. I hope you do not think that I was the one who wiped out that blue meannie with a bomb at the cop station. Even though I talked about killing school children with one. It just wouldn't doo to move in on someone elses territory. But there is more glory in killing a cop than a cid because a cop can shoot back. I have killed ten people to date. It would have been a lot more except that my bus bomb was a dud. I was swamped out by the rain we had a while back.

"The new bomb is set up like this

"Sun light in early morning

"A&B are photo electric swiches when sun beam is broken A closes circuit

" B opens "

which makes B the
cloudy day discon-
ect so the bomb
wont go off by acid.

"PS I hope you have fun trying
To figgure out who I killed

10 SFPD-0"

Subsequent to September 27, 1969, 481 suspects have been eliminated as a result of investigation, handprinting and latent print examinations compared with latents relative to the Napa County and Sn Francisco homicides. The names of the suspects and reporting agency or person are contained in a separate file maintained in the Investigation unit.

Names of possible suspects have been furnished by private citizens, various institutions, law enforcement and military agencies. In addition, Modus Operandi files and dealer's records of sales of handguns have been searched relative to suspects. California Highway Patrol citations and oil company credit card purchases that were issued or used in Napa County on September 27th have been obtained and investigated.

During the investigation information was received to the effect that the concept that persons killed will be the killer's slaves in the life hereafter originated in South East Asia and particularly in Mindanao in the southern Philippines. Suspects from groups having similar beliefs were investigated, including all male members of the CHARLES MANSON Family.

Combined efforts by law enforcement agencies have failed to uncover the identity of the "Zodiac" killer.

MELVIN H. NICOLAI
Special Agent

MHN: 1m

STATE OF CALIFORNIA

DEPARTMENT OF JUSTICE

BUREAU OF CRIMINAL IDENTIFICATION AND INVESTIGATION REPORT

P.O. Box 1859, Sacramento

SUPPLEMENTAL #1

TYPE OF CASE HOMICIDE NUMBER 1-15-311-F9-58

Subject UNKNOWNFDJHFHJDFHSJDFDHGFFG	Copies of this report to: (1) Requesting Agency (1) Deputy Director (1) AAG Harris (3) Bureau

Requested by: Earl Randol, Sheriff ghkjgkjfk Date 10-3-69 Time haghagdhggh

Reported

Address: SO Napa CO., 810 Coombs, Napa Telephone 255-5500 DDDDDDDDDDD

Requested how: Telephonehhhhhhhhhhnh Received by: Chief of Bureau hjjhggfgjgjgggggggg

Reported

Assigned to: Melvin H. Nicolai, Special Agent Date: 10-3-69kk jj kk l

Assigned by: Kenneth Horton, Supervising Special

Enclosures:

References:

SYNOPSIS:

Subsequent to April 20, 1970 the Zodiac killer sent several additional letters and cards to the San Francisco Chronicle. In a letter sent to the Chronicle on July 26, 1970 the Zodiac claimed thirteen victims. Law enforcement agencies had definitely linked him to only five.

On November 16, 1970 Mr. SHERWOOD MORRILL, Questioned Document Examiner, identified printing contained in letters sent to the Riverside Police Department, Press Enterprise and a Mr. JOSEPH BATES as being printed by the same person who prepared the Zodiac letters. The letters were postmarked April 30, 1967 and referred to the murder of CHERI JO BATES, 18 years, an unsolved homicide that occurred in Riverside on October 30, 1966.

Investigating agencies are in the process of obtaining data relative to suspects in the Riverside case in an effort to eliminate or identify the Zodiac killer.

Hours expended: 1505

Date report written January 22, 1971 Report by: MELVIN H. NICOLAI

Sec. 8704 MHN:1m Title Special Agent

Investigation by the Riverside Police Department revealed that the victim had been at the riverside City College Library on Sunday, October 30th, at 1800 hours. The victim's vehicle, a 1960 Volkswagen, was found parked in front of the library on the morning of the thirty-first and the examination of the car revealed that the coil wire had been pulled out of the distributor socket.

Evidence found at the scene of the crime consisted of a Timex wrist watch with the fastener on one side of the strap torn off and a heel print. The heel print was identified as a B.F Goodrich waffle design, men's four-eights inch washer type half feel. The B.F. Goodrich Products Division of Akron, Ohio, reported that this type heel is only sold to the Federal prison industries at Leavenworth, Kansas. It was subsequently learned that Federal prison industries made low quarter military type shoes and supplied them to all of the armed services using black dress shoes. The measurement of the heel indicated that it would have been attached to an eight to ten shoe. Shoes bearing the same type heel were issued and sold at the PX at March Air Force Base at Riverside.

On November 29, 1966 an unstamped envelope addressed to the Homicide Detail, Riverside, was removed from the collection box in the main post office at 1700 hours. The lettering on the envelope appeared to have been drawn using a heavy felt pen. The envelope contained a typewritten titled "The Confession" and reads as follows:

"SHE WAS YOUNG AND BEAUTIFUL. BUT NOW SHE IS BATTERED AND DEAD. SHE IS NOT THE FIRST AND SHE WILL NOT BE THE LAST. I LAY AWAKE NIGHTS THINKING ABOUT MY NEXT VICTOM. MAYBE SHE WILL BE THE BEATIFUL BLOND BABY SITS NEAR THE LITTLE STORE AND WALKS DOWN THE DARK ALLEY EACH EVENING ABOUT EVEN. OR MAYBE SHE WILL BE THE SHPELY BLUE EYED BRUNETTE THAT SAID NO WHEN I ASKED FOR A DATE IN HIGH SCHOOL. BUT MAYBE IT WILL NOT BE EITHER. BUT I SHALL CUT OFF HER FEMALE PARTS AND DEPOSITE THEM FOR THE WHOLE CITY TO SEE. SO DON'T MAKE IT EASY FOR ME. KEEP YPUR SISTERS, DAUGHTERS, AND WIVES OFF THE STREETS AND ALLEYS. MISS BATES WAS STUPID. SHE WENT TO THE SLAUGHTER LIKE A LAMB. SHE DID NOT PUT UP A STRUGGLE. BUT I DID. IT WAS A BALL. I FIRST PULLED THE MIDDLE WIRE FROM THE DISTRIBUTOR. THEN I WAITED FOR HER IN THE LIBRARY AND FOLLOWED HER OUT AFTER ABOUT TWO MINUTES. THE BATTERY MUST HAVE BEEN DEAD BY THEN. I THEN OFFERED TO HELP. SHE WAS THEN VERY WILLING TO TALK WITH ME. I TOLD HER THAT MY CAR WAS DOWN THE STREET AND THAT I WOULD GIVE HER A LIFT HOME. WHEN WE WERE AWAY FROM THE LIBRARY WALKING. I SAID IT WAS ABOUT TIME. SHE ASKED ME ABOUT TIME FOR WHAT. I SID IT WAS ABOUT TIME FOR HER TO DIE. I GRABBED HER AROUND THE NECK WITH MY HAND OVER HER MOUTH AND MY OTHER HAND WITH

(Letter cont'd)

"A SMALL KNIFE AT HER THROAT. SHE WENT VERY WILLINGLY. HER HREAST FELT VERY WARM AND FIRM UNDER MY HANDS, BUT ONLY ONE THING WAS ON MY MIND. MAKING HER PAY FOR THE BRUSH OFF THAT SHE HAD GIVEN ME DURING THE YEAR PRIOR. SHE DIED HARD. SHE SQUIRMED AND I KICKED HER IN THE HEAD TO SHUT HER UP. I PLUNGED THE KNIFE INTO HER AND IT BROKE. I THEN FINISHED THE JOB CUTTING HER THROAT. I AM NOT SICK. I AM INSANE. BUT THAT WILL NOT STOP THE GAME. THIS LETTER SHOULD BE PUBLISHED FOR ALL TO READ IT. IT JUST MIGHT SAVE THAT GIRL IN THE ALLEY. BUT THAT'S UP TO YOU. IT WILL BE ON YOUR CONSCIENCE, NOT MINE. YES I DID MAKE THAT CALL TO YOU ALSO. IT WAS JUST A WARNING PERIOD. BEWARE I AM STALKING YOUR GIRLS NOW."

On November 30th the Riverside newspaper Daily Enterprise received an unstamped envelope containing a copy of the confession letter that had been sent o thee police department. Efforts to locate the source of the paper the confession letter was typed on and the identity of the typewriter proved negative.

During the month of December 1966 while removing several desks from the Riverside City College Library one of the custodians observed a poem written on one of the desks which reads as follows:

"Sick of living/unwilling to die

cut
clean
if read
clean
blood spurting,
        dripping,
        spilling;
all over her new
dress.
oh well,
it was red
anyway.
life draining into an

uncertain death.

she won't

die

this time

Someone ll find her.

Just wait till

next time.

rh"

The poem appeared to have been written with a ballpoint pen.

On April 30, 1967 an unknown person mailed three letters in the City of Riverside that were addressed as follows:

1 – Joseph BATES, 4195 Via San Jose, Riverside, California

2 – Riverside Police Department, Riverside, California

3 – Press Enterprise, 3512 14th Street, Riverside, California.

Letter #1 contained the following handprinted message: "She had to die. There will be more."

Letters #2 and #3 contained identical handprinted messages: "Bates had to die. There will be more."

The letters had been printed on ordinary loose leaf binder paper.

Mr. SHERWOOD MORRILL concluded that three envelopes and letters along with the printed poem on the desk had been prepared by the same person responsible for the Zodiac letters.

On November 18, 1970, Inspector DAVE TOSCHI, San Francisco Police Department, Sgt. KEN NARLOW, Napa County Sheriff's Office, and the reporting agent conferred with Captain I.L. CROSS and Sgt. DAVID BONINE AT THE Riverside Police Department relative to the Zodiac murders.

All information and evidence was exchanged. Handprinting exemplars and prints of suspects relative to the CHERI BATES homicide are being obtained and compared with the evidence relating to the current Zodiac homicides. Names of suspected persons and results of comparisons are maintained in a file in the Investigation Section.

Investigation continuing.

MELVIN H. NICOLAI

Special Agent

MHN:1m

Next: After it was concluded that Cheri Jo Bates was indeed a victim of the Zodiac killer, the California Department of Justice prepared a report that was distributed to both police and sheriff departments throughout California --

TOP SECRET REPORT

CALIFORNIA DEPARTMENT OF JUSTICE/DIVISION OF LAW ENFORCEMENT/BUREAU OF INVESTIGATION

SPECIAL REPORT

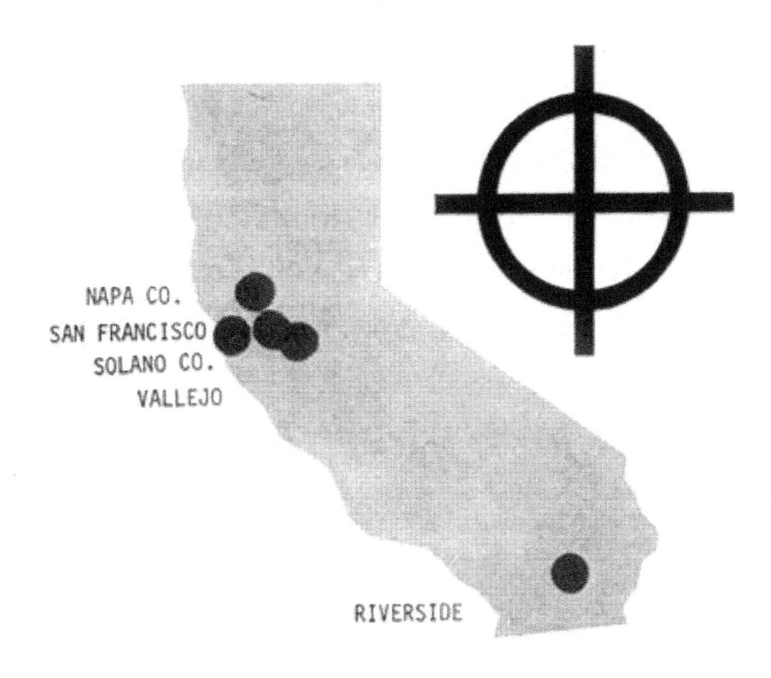

ZODIAC HOMICIDES

FOR LAW ENFORCEMENT USE ONLY

Date: October 30th, 1966 – Sunday night

Time: Approximately 6:15 PM

Victim: Cheri Jo Bates – Female Caucasian, 18 years

Riverside City College freshman

Location: Riverside City College campus

Victim parked her vehicle in front of Riverside City College library just prior to 6 PM and entered library building. Suspect disabled victim's vehicle by removing coil wire and evidently waited for victim to return. Suspect then either forced or enticed her approximately 300 feet to an unpaved parking area between two vacant houses where he attacked her with a small knife having a blade approximately 3 ½" in length and ½" in width. Victim suffered seven lacerations on her throat and death was due to hemorrhage of the right carotid artery. There was no evidence of sexual molestation. No witnesses.

Heelprints identical to those worn by Air Force personnel and a Timex wrist watch indicating that the suspect had a 7" wrist circumference were found at the scene of the crime.

Suspect mailed typewritten confession letter from Riverside to the Police Department and Riverside Enterprise newspaper on November 29th, 1966, claiming to be the perpetrator of the crime.

Three additional handprinted letters were mailed in Riverside by the suspect on April 30th, 1967, again claiming the Bates homicide and indicating there would be more.

Evidence:

Handprinting

Latents

Military heelprints

Timex wrist watch

Typewritten confession letter

Riverside Police Department case "352-481

Investigating officer: Captain I.L. Cross

4201 Orange St. – 92502

Phone 714-787-7011

★★★★★★★★★★★

Date: December 20th, 1968 – Friday night

Time: Between 11:14 and 11:20 PM

Victims: Betty Lou Jensen – Female Caucasian, 16 years (student)

David Farraday – Male Caucasian, 17 years (student)

Location: Isolated lover's lane are approximately five miles east of Vallejo

Victims were evidently in their vehicle when suspect approached. Male victim shot in head through left ear at contact range and was found on ground on passenger side of vehicle. Female victim shot five times right side of back and was found lying 28'6" from right rear bumper. No statements from victims no witnesses. No evidence of sexual molestation.

Weapon: .22 caliber semi-automatic. Possibilities – J.C. Higgins

Model 80 or High Standard Model 101.

Ammunition: .22 caliber Super X copper coated long rifle.

Evidence:

.22 caliber bullets and casings

Handprinting

Solano County Sheriff's Office case #V-25564

Investigating Officer: Sgt. Les Lundblad

1350 Virginia St. – 94590

Phone 707-643-6495

★★★★★★★★★★

Date: July 4th, 960 – Friday night

Time: Approximately midnight

Victims: Darlene Ferrin – Female Caucasian, 22 years (waitress)

Michael Mageau – Male Caucasian, 19 years (laborer)

Location: Blue Rock Springs Park approximately 4 miles northeast of downtown Vallejo. An area frequented by overs during evening and early morning hours.

Victims were sitting in vehicle in parking lot. Suspect parked his vehicle approximately 10' to rear of victims' and left headlights on. Suspect approached victims' vehicle on passenger side with large handle type flashlight directed into victims' faces. Suspect fired five shots into vehicle striking male and them female. When suspect started to walk away the male victim screamed and suspect returned and fired four more shots into vehicle. The suspect did not say anything to the victims prior to the shooting.

Female victim suffered multiple bullet wounds and was DOA at hospital.

Male victim shot in left knee and face, survived the attack.

Male victim described suspect as Male Caucasian, 26-30 years, 5' 8", 200 pounds, light brown hair, no glasses or mustache. Described suspect vehicle as brown and shaped like a Corvair.

Weapon: 9mm semi- automatic

Possibilities regarding manufacture of weapon:

Browing
Smith & Wesson
Star
Astra
Llama
Neuhausen
Zebrojoka
Husqvarna
Esperanza

Ammunition: 9mm Winchester Western

Suspect phoned the Vallejo Police Department from downtown Vallejo at 12:40 AM on July 5, 1969. Stated he had just committed a double murder, gave location and also claimed the killings on December 20th, 1968. Call made from pay phone through operator. No distinguishable voice characteristics.

Suspect sent letters and cryptogram to newspaper subsequent to the crime claiming credit for the Vallejo and Solano County homicides. Cryptogram was deciphered and suspect indicated that killing people was more fun than sexual relations and that the people he killed would be his slaves in his after life. (See attached cryptogram).

Evidence:

9mm casings and bullets
Handprinted letters

Vallejo Police Department case #243146

Investigating officer: Detective Sgt. Jack Mulanax

P.O. Box 1031 – 94590

Phone 707-643-5661

★★★★★★★★★★★

Date: September 27, 1969 – Saturday (daylight)

Time: Approximately 6:15 PM

Victims: Cecelia Shepard – Female Caucasian, 22 years (college student)
Bryan Hartnell – Male Caucasian, 20 years (college student)

Location: Shoreline of Lake Berryessa in Napa County

Victims parked their vehicle alongside main highway and walked 510 yards to shoreline where they laid down on a blanket. Female victim observed suspect step behind tree. When suspect emerged and approached victims he was wearing a black hood with white circle and cross hair in center. Suspect step behind tree. Suspect was armed with what appeared to be a semi-automatic pistol. He told the victims that he was an escapee from Deer Lodge Prison, Montana, was enroute to Mexico and wanted their car keys and money. Suspect carried on a rather lengthy conversation with male victim, then had female tie male with pre-cut clothes line. He then tied female and retied male. Suspect placed gun in holster, took a large knife out of a sheath, stabbed male victim six times in back, then stabbed female victim both back and front. Male victim feigned death and suspect departed. Did not take money or car keys. After the attack suspect departed. Did not take money or car keys. After the attack suspect printed message on right passenger door of victim's vehicle, again indicating he was responsible for the Solano County, Vallejo and Napa County homicides.

Approximately one hour and ten minutes after the crime the suspect phoned the Napa Police Department from downtown Napa reporting a double murder and giving the location. The call was placed through an operator and the suspect did not hang up the phone. No distinguishable speech characteristics were noted.

Female victim died on September 29th.

Male victim survived.

Male victim described suspect as Male Caucasian, 20-30 years, 5'10" – 6'2", 220 pounds, brown hair, (visible through eye slots in hood) wearing black hood, lightweight windbreaker dark blue or black, dark baggy pleated slacks, very sloppily dressed with protruding stomach. No distinguishable speech characteristics.

Hood described as black in color with four corners at the top similar to a paper sack, sleeveless with the front panel coming down just below the chest with white circle and cross hair middle of chest. Appeared well made, well sewn with clip on sunglasses on the outside. Victim not positive suspect had sunglasses on the outside. Victim not positive suspect had glasses on under hood. Gun described as blue steel semi-automatic pistol, possibly .45 caliber, carried in a plain black holster with flap.

Knife described as having blade approximately 12" in length, 1" in width Possibly sharpened on both sides similar to a bayonet. Appeared to have a wooden handle with two brass rivets and 1" white adhesive tape wrapped around the handle where the guard would normally be. (May be encased in wooden sheath.)

Shoeprints identical to military "Wing Walker Boots" were tracked from the road to the scene of the crime and back to the passenger side of the victim's car. (See attached photos).

Evidence:

Latents

Handprinting

White plastic clothes line, hollow core

Military shoeprints

Napa County Sheriff's Office case #105907

Investigating Officer: Captain Ken Narlow
810 Coombs St. – 94558
Phoned 707-255-5500

★★★★★★★★★★

Date: October 11th, 1969 – Saturday

Time: 9:55 PM

Victim: Paul Stine, Male Caucasian, 29 years (Yellow Cab driver)

Location: Washington & Cherry Streets, San Francisco

Victim picked up suspect at Mason and Geary Streets, proceeded to Washington and Cherry where suspect shot victim once behind right ear at contact range. Suspect took victim's wallet, taxi keys and tore a portion from the back of his shirt. Witnesses observed suspect wipe inside of cab with a cloth, then walk nonchalantly away from the cab toward the Presidio, an army installation.

Witnesses described suspect as Male Caucasian, 35-45 years, 5'10", 190 pounds, crew cut reddish blonde hair, eye glasses with plastic frames, wearing parka type jacket, navy blue or black, dark baggy trousers and paunchy stomach.

Weapon: 9mm semi-automatic, possibly new model Browning. (Not same 9mm as used in Vallejo Police Department case.)

Ammunition: 9mm Winchester Western

Evidence:

Two portions of victim's shirt (white with black stripe)

Handprinting

Latents

9mm bullet and casing

Black leather men's gloves size 7

Subsequent to the homicide the suspect mailed a series of post cards and letters, two which contained a portion of the cab driver's shirt.

San Francisco Police Department case #696314

Investigating officers: Inspectors William Armstrong & Dave Toschi
850 Bryant St. – 94103
Phone 415-553-1145

★★★★★★★★★★

All homicides have been committed on weekends, Friday through Sunday.

All letters the Zodiac has mailed in Northern California have been postmarked in San Francisco with the exception of one that was mailed in Pleasanton to the Los Angeles Times on March 13, 1971. In the letter he acknowledged he had committed the Riverside homicide in 1966. This being the only time the Zodiac has reference to this particular murder. The last correspondence received from the Zodiac was March 22nd, 1971.

All letters are handprinted, over posted with stamps on sideways ore inverted. Suspect misspells simple words apparently on purpose.

Contents of letters tend to indicate the suspect may possess knowledge of the following:

Crypotography
Meteorology
Explosive devices
Charts and terminology used in conjunction with the compass
Latent print identification. (Wiped down cab and claimed he used clear plastic cement on fingers.9
Typewriter identification. (Mailed fourth or fifth carbon copy of confession letter in Riverside.)
Light opera. (one letter contained excerpts from opera "Mikado.")

Conclusions that may be drawn from suspect's activities:

Likes publicity

Enjoys ridiculing police

Claims to be crack proof (egotist)

Cultist (States persons killed will be slave in after life.)

Does not panic in stress situations

Suspect may possess the following:

(2) 9mm semi-automatic pistols of different manufacture

.22 caliber semi-automatic pistol

9mm Winchester Western ammunition

.22 caliber Super X copper coated long rifle ammunition

.45 caliber blue steel semi-automatic

Portion of cab driver's shirt – white with black stripe

Victim Stine's wallet and taxi keys

Black hood with white circle and cross

Clip on sunglasses

Windbreaker – dark blue or black

Pleated baggy slacks – dark in color

Large knife having blade approximately 12" in length, 1" in width, wooden handle with two brass rivets ad 1" wide adhesive tape around handle. May be encased in wooden sheath.

White plastic clothes lines – hollow core

Portable Royal typewriter – Elite type – canterbury shaded

Black Wing Walker Boots 10 ½ R

Handle type flashlight

Small knife with blade 3 ½" in length, 1" in width. May have broken tip.

Felt pens

Complete newspaper and magazine article accounts of Zodiac homicides

This bulletin has been compiled in conjunction with the investigating agencies and distributed by the State Department of Justice, Law Enforcement Division, Bureau of Investigation. The Bureau of Investigation maintains a file of all suspects that have been eliminated as a result of handprinting comparisons. Pending receipt of any additional evidence, handprinting is the most positive method of identification or elimination of suspects. Identity of suspects that have been eliminated may be obtained by contacting Special Agent Mel Nicolai, California Department of Justice, Bureau of Investigation, P.O. Box 13327, Sacramento, California 95813, phone 916-445-9002.

ZODIAC KILLER CIPHERS

1. TIMES HERALD 8/1/69

2. CHRONICLE 8/1/69

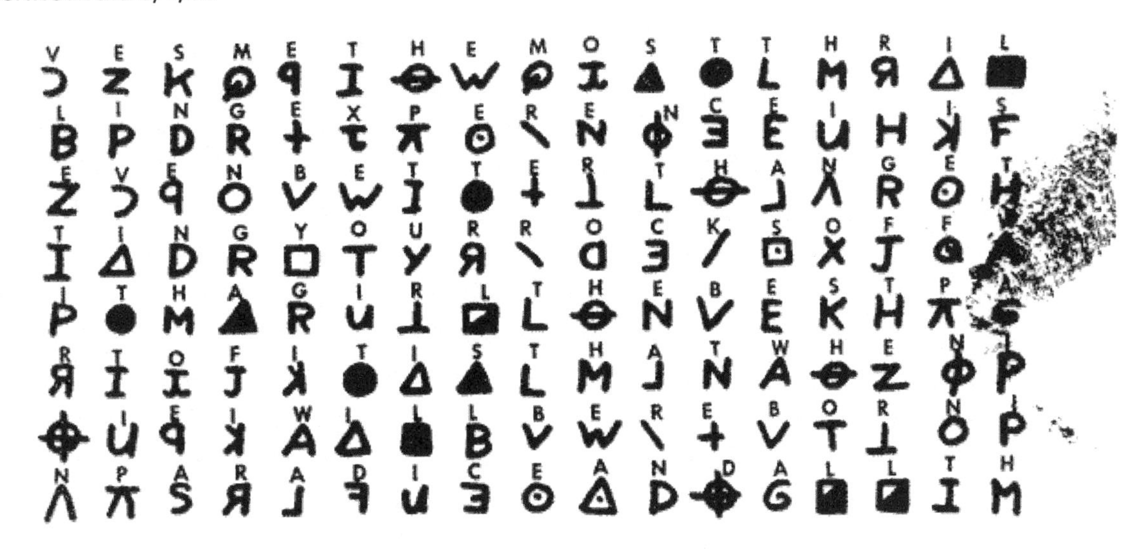

3. EXAMINER 8/1/69

WING WALKER SHOE PHOTOS

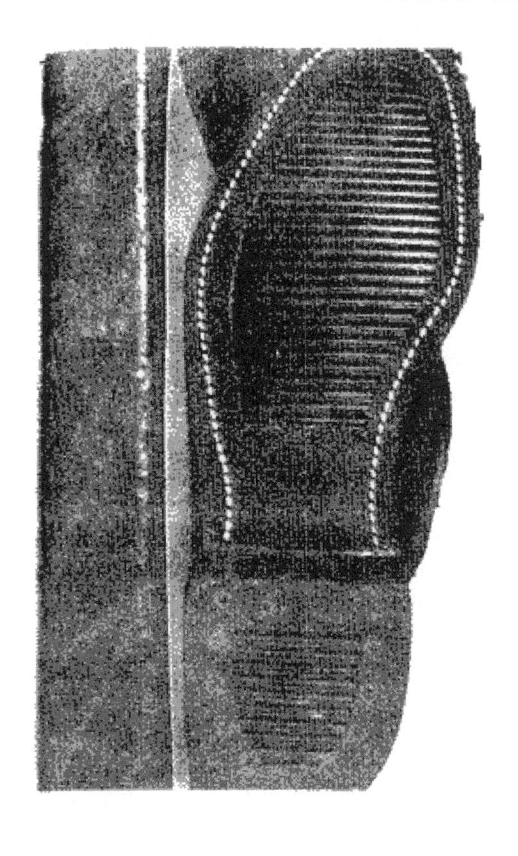

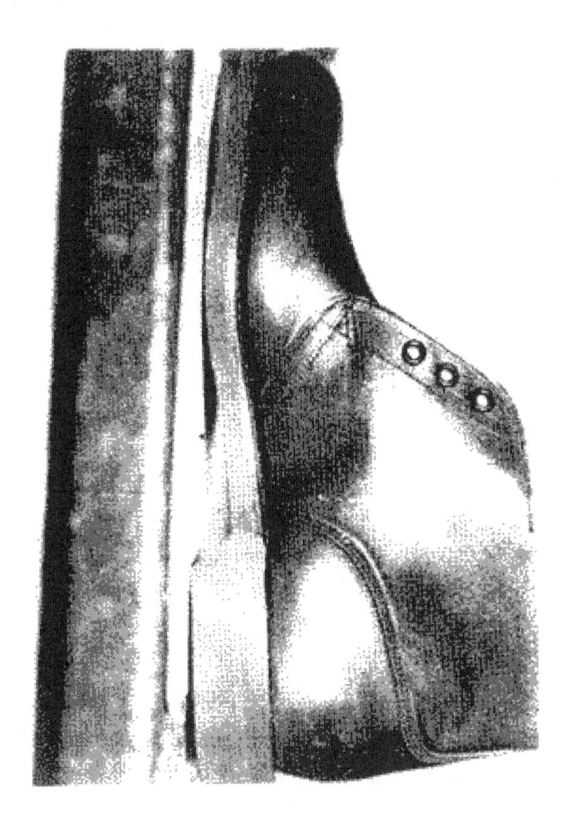

Wing Walker shoe- uppers manu-
Factured by Weinbrenner Shoe Company, Merrill, Winsconsin. Soles manufactured by Avon, Avon, Massachusetts. Over one million manufactured as per a government contract in 1966. Both Air Force and Navy issue. 103,700 pairs shipped to Ogden, Utah and subsequently distributed to military installations on the west coast.

INDEX

A&W Root Beer stand, 294, 295
Albertoni, Jailer, 162
Allen, Arthur Lee, 159
American Cryptograph Association, 140
Amik, Bill, 158
Armstrong, Insp. William, 278, 311, 312, 313
Ashley, Mr. & Mrs., 153
Balmer, Thomas D., 10
Barrus, Agt., 143
Bates, Cheri J., 3
Bates, Cheri Jo, 3, 4, 315, 317, 320, 322
Bates, Joseph, 320
Bawart, Sgt., 157, 190, 192
Beaver, Deputy, 162
Belli, Melvin, 312
Benicia Police, 10, 18, 20, 24
Benicia Water Pumping Station, 20, 22, 24, 28, 29, 31, 34, 37, 40, 44, 45, 47, 49, 51, 52, 54, 55, 56, 59, 64, 70, 73, 75, 76, 77, 80, 81, 82
Betts, Sandra Karen, 189, 191, 193
Bidou, Sgt. Pierre, 157
Bird, Capt., 91, 135, 139, 141, 148, 150
Black, Dr., 108
Blackpoint, CA, 166
Blair, Sgt., 193, 201
Blue Rock Springs, 75, 86, 87, 91, 92, 95, 97, 99, 104, 106, 108, 111, 114, 116, 121, 122, 127, 131, 144, 158, 166, 197, 307, 324
Blue Rock Springs Golf Course, 92
Borges Ranch, 30, 44, 85
Borges, Stella, 9
Boulder Creek, California, 180
Brambrink, Allan, 236
Brambrink, Allen, 208, 212
Brown, Denise, 220
Brown, Sgt., 197
Burd, David Q., 306
Burton, Richard, 60
Bus, Deputy D., 244
Butler, Sgt. Thomas, 210, 223, 224, 228, 232, 244, 290, 299, 305
Butterbach, Det. Sgt., 10, 12, 13, 17, 22, 27, 28, 29, 31, 32, 33, 37, 39, 40, 42, 43, 44, 49, 50, 51, 52, 53, 54, 55, 56, 57, 58, 60, 61, 62, 63, 68, 72, 74, 75, 76, 77, 78, 79, 82
Cahill, Thomas J., 2
California Highway Patrol, 255, 310, 314
Captain, Benicia, 16
Central Valley, California, 173
Cherry Street, 276, 277, 278, 279, 310, 328
Chicago, Illinois, 171
Christie, Bruce L., 254
Cipher. *See* Cryptogram
Ciphers. *See* Cryptogram
Code. *See* Cryptogram
Coffey, A. L., 256
Collins, David, 210
Colonial Chapels, 18
Columbus Parkway, 75, 91, 92, 95, 104, 113, 122, 166, 307
Crabtree, James, 187
Crabtree, Jim, 172, 173, 180, 181, 182, 183, 186
Cross, Capt. I.L., 322
Cryptogram, 135, 137, 138, 140, 141, 152, 154, 157, 168, 171, 176, 226, 308, 309, 313, 325
Cunningham, Sgt., 10, 12, 13, 18, 19, 22, 24, 27, 28, 29, 34, 37, 40, 44, 45, 47, 49, 50, 51, 52, 54, 55, 56, 58, 59, 64, 68, 69, 70, 73, 75, 76, 77, 80, 81, 82
Daily Enterprise, 318
Daily Republic, 171, 177, 181
Daily Republican Newspaper, 175
Daisy, Arkansas, 153
De Louise, Joseph, 171
De Petris, Wilmer, 222, 223, 297, 299, 301
DEAN, 218, 294
Dean, Lee Y., 59, 60
Dean, Sue, 107
Decoded, 138, 226
Deer Lodge Prison, 249, 250, 327
DeLouise, Joseph, 175
Dennan, Paul, 135
Dotta Ranch, 41
El Dorado Co., 187
Elmer Cave School, 159
Fairfield Daily Republic, 10
Fairfield Police Department, 177, 180, 187
Faraday, David Arthur, 9, 11, 16, 18, 19, 20, 26, 36, 47, 50, 51, 52, 66, 68, 73, 282, 323
Faraday, Debbie, 76

Faraday, Jean L., 76
FBI, 6, 8, 109, 138, 139, 143, 152, 153, 154, 158, 169, 170, 180, 195, 226, 260, 261, 262
Ferrin, Darlene E., 86, 87, 89, 93, 94, 106, 108, 114, 117, 125, 143, 144, 146, 166, 168, 169, 170, 172, 173, 174, 176, 177, 178, 180, 181, 183, 184, 185, 187, 195, 197, 199, 323
Ferrin, Darlene, E., 86
Feurle, M., 205, 207, 209, 211, 213, 215, 217, 219, 221, 222, 224, 225, 227, 229, 239, 241, 243, 245
Flanders, Lt., 138
Fong, Henry, 284, 292
Fong, Ronald, 214, 216, 217, 254, 284
Fort Lewis, Washington, 137
Foster, Det., 183
Foster, Detective, 183
Fouke, Donald G., 280
Fouke, Officer, 280
GallenKamp's store, 57, 64
GallenKamp's store, 58
Gasser Ranch, 37, 40, 42, 83
Gasser, Frank, 37, 83
Gasser, Mr., 43
Geary Blvd, 328
George Washington High School, 157
George, Raymond, 256, 257
Grabtree, James. *See* Crabtree, Jim
Grant, Pamela, 141, 182
Haight, Wayne, 220
Harden, Donald, 137, 138
Hardin, Mr. and Mrs., 226
Harris, Charis, 179
Hartnell, Bryan Calvin, 203, 204, 206, 207, 208, 210, 212, 223, 234, 238, 244, 246, 247, 249, 251, 254, 260, 264, 265, 266, 267, 268, 269, 270, 271, 272, 273, 274, 275, 281, 283, 286, 287, 288, 291, 298, 299, 302, 303, 304, 310, 312, 327
Hogan High School, 50, 52, 54, 71, 148, 149
Homsher, H.L., 8
Hoover, John Edgar, 261
Horan, Dan, 18, 20, 64
Horton, Kenneth, 256, 281, 315
Hot Springs, Arkansas, 197
Humble Oil Company, 32
Idaho Falls, Idaho, 144, 145
International Shoe Company, 226, 302
Jacks Hangout, 144
Jackson Street, 280
Jantzen, Dr., 108
Jensen, Betty Lou, 9, 10, 16, 18, 19, 20, 47, 50, 51, 52, 55, 56, 59, 60, 66, 68, 70, 282, 306, 323
Jensen, Mrs., 50, 72, 73, 74, 83
Jensen, Vincent, 69
Jim Dunbar Show, 312
Jobe, Melody, 69, 70, 72, 84
Kaiser Hospital, 94, 96, 104, 105, 108, 111, 114, 307
Kaiser Steel, 78, 79, 118, 129
Kammer, Gaven, 158
Kare Island Police Department, 193
Kindred, Deputy, 278
Kinkead, L. T., 8
Korrill, Sherwood, 258
Krake, Inspector, 278
Kramer, Sgt., 146
Lackland Air Force Base, 223, 297
Lake Berryessa, 157, 158, 159, 195, 203, 204, 206, 210, 212, 214, 218, 223, 230, 231, 233, 238, 246, 252, 264, 281, 283, 284, 287, 288, 289, 290, 291, 292, 294, 295, 296, 298, 305, 306, 310, 312, 327
Lake Berryessa Marina, 223, 298
Lake Berryessa Park Headquarters, 204, 210, 214, 231, 233, 283, 290, 291, 292
Lake Herman Road/Area, 9, 10, 12, 13, 16, 18, 19, 20, 22, 24, 26, 27, 28, 29, 31, 32, 33, 34, 37, 39, 40, 42, 43, 44, 45, 47, 49, 50, 51, 52, 54, 55, 56, 58, 59, 60, 61, 62, 63, 64, 66, 67, 68, 69, 70, 73, 75, 76, 77, 78, 80, 81, 82, 83, 85, 119, 123, 135, 137, 306
Land, Dennis, 210, 211, 212, 215, 234, 283, 284, 288, 291, 292, 294
Land, Ray, 210, 219
Leo SUENNEN, 106, 108
Little, Lt., 10, 18
Little, Lt. George, 143
Lodge State Prison, 247
Loma Linda, California, 204, 206, 208, 210, 212, 214, 216, 218, 219, 221, 223, 224, 226, 228, 230, 232, 234, 236, 238, 240, 246, 286
Lonegran, Det. Sgt., 230, 283, 286, 287, 288, 289, 290, 291, 292, 293, 294, 295, 297, 299, 302, 304, 305
Lonergan, Det. Sgt., 205, 206, 207, 208, 209, 210, 211, 212, 213, 214, 215, 217, 218, 219, 221, 222, 223, 224, 225, 226, 227, 228, 229, 234
Los Angeles, California, 103, 185, 186
Los Gatos, California, 213, 289
Lowe, Barbara, 12

Lundblad, Det. Sgt., 12, 17, 19, 21, 22, 24, 26, 27, 29, 34, 36, 37, 39, 40, 42, 43, 44, 45, 47, 49, 50, 51, 52, 53, 54, 55, 56, 57, 58, 59, 60, 61, 62, 63, 64, 66, 67, 68, 69, 70, 72, 73, 74, 76, 77, 78, 79, 80, 81, 83, 143, 306, 323
Lynch, Sgt. J., 96, 109, 111, 112, 116, 121, 125, 126, 130, 131, 140, 143, 146, 147, 157, 158, 159, 167, 168, 169, 171, 173, 174
Mageau, Carmen, 109
Mageau, Michael, 96, 150, 323
Mageau, Michael R., 86, 92, 282, 307
Mageau, Robert W., 110
Mallory, Officer, 135
Manson, Charles, 314
MapleStreet, 280, 311
March Air Force Base, 6, 317
Mare Island, 58, 62, 69, 127, 141, 151, 153, 154, 158, 159
Maritime Academy, 146
Markey, John, 170
Marsh, D., 140
Marshall Ranch, 25, 26, 31, 33, 38, 40
Mason Street, 328
Mc Kenzie, Robert, 291
Medeiros, Stella, 34, 36
Messages in code. *See* Cryptogram
Mexico, 185, 216, 247, 249, 273, 274, 275, 293, 327
Meyring, G., 75, 83
Mills College, 239, 240
Monez, Insp., 193
Montgomery, Ronald, 305
Morrill, Sherwood, 160, 306, 315, 320
Moskowite, Harold, 291
Mountain Lodge Prison, 266
Mr. Ed's drive-in restaurant, 24
Mulanax, Sgt. Jack, 150, 153, 163, 164, 175, 177, 178, 179, 181, 182, 184, 185, 186, 188, 202, 226
Munk, William, 208, 236
Murphy, George, 137
Najwoski, Sgt., 162
Napa Car Wash, 206, 230, 286, 289
Napa County Sheriff, 3, 204, 209, 218, 234, 236, 256, 283, 291, 294, 311, 320, 328
NAPA County Sheriff's Department, 204, 206, 208, 210, 212, 214, 216, 218, 219, 221, 222, 224, 226, 228, 230, 232, 234, 236, 238, 240, 242, 244, 252, 264
Napa Police Department, 131, 206, 209, 228, 284, 285, 286, 287, 289, 305, 312, 327
Napa State Hospital, 138, 143, 151, 228, 305
Napa, California, 158, 203, 256
Narlow, Det. Sgt., 205, 206, 207, 208, 209, 210, 211, 212, 213, 214, 215, 217, 218, 219, 221, 222, 223, 224, 225, 226, 227, 228, 229, 230, 233, 239, 240, 283, 286, 287, 288, 289, 292, 293, 294, 297, 299, 302, 304, 305, 310, 311, 312, 320, 328
Naval Schools Command Nuclear Power School, 144
Navel Sub-school, 144
Nawojski, 193
New London, Connecticut, 144
Nicolai, Melvin H., 178, 180, 256, 281, 282, 314, 315, 316, 320, 332
Nilsson, Sgt. Duane, 152, 154, 170, 196, 198, 200, 202, 226
North of Park Headquarters, 259, 285
O'Brien, Jim, 107
Oakland, California, 239
Ogden, Utah, 226, 302
Olsen, Raymond E., 256
Olson, Raymond E., 258
Pacific Union College, 204, 206, 207, 209, 210, 218, 219, 223, 227, 238, 239, 286, 287, 294, 295, 297, 298, 305, 310
Page, Capt., 297
Page, Capt. Joseph, 222, 223
Pancake House, 55
Peda, Frank, 278, 279
Pelissetti, Armond, 278, 279, 310, 311
Philadelphia, Pennsylvania, 226, 302
Phillips, James Douglas, 171, 172, 173, 175, 176, 177, 180, 181, 183
Piner's Ambulance, 206, 286
Pitta, Capt., 10, 12, 13, 18, 19, 20, 22, 24, 26, 27, 28, 29, 31, 32, 33, 34, 37, 39, 40, 42, 43, 44, 45, 47, 49, 50, 51, 52, 54, 55, 56, 58, 59, 60, 61, 62, 63, 64, 66, 67, 68, 69, 70, 73, 75, 76, 77, 78, 80, 81, 82, 83, 85, 141
Pope Valley, California, 220, 252, 295
Port Chicago, 146
Pythian Castle, 50
Queen of the Valley Hospital, 206, 208, 212, 222, 230, 236, 238, 244, 246, 248, 284, 286, 287, 289, 291, 297, 302
Ramona High School, 3
Ramos, S., 231, 233, 235, 237
Randol, Earl, 4, 6, 8, 256, 260, 262, 263, 281, 315
Raymos, Bobbie, 146
Redacted

Agt. Donald, 226
Andy, Jr., 92, 93
Archie, 284, 292, 293, 294
Aubrey Dwight, 262
Bassel M., 222
Bernard, 160
Bill, 151
Bob, 44, 68
Chris, 150
Clifford, 208
Clifton R., 289
Clinton, 201
Dalora Lee, 238, 246
Dan, 54, 83
Daniel, 51, 52, 66, 83
Danny Olon, 257
Darryl, 57
David, 135, 137, 138, 158
David A Bagano, 135
David Lee, 213, 214, 289
Dean, 218, 294
Debby, 56
Debra, 87
Denise, 252
Dian C., 57, 68, 74, 85
Diane, 62
Donald, 62, 85, 208
Donald Warren, 132, 133
Earl, 169, 206
Edd, 150
Edward, 238
Eleanor, 238
Ettore, 141
Fred, 138
Freddie, 155
Gary, 80, 125, 159, 238
George, 43, 85, 118, 119, 128, 257
George R. Jr., 162
Gordon Arthur, 144, 145
Griffin Raymond, 228, 262, 305
Gwendolyn, 238
Harold, 129, 223
Harry, 61
Homer, 24, 31, 33
Iris, 158
James, 27, 228, 305
James A., 49, 83
James Michael, Jr., 158
Jane Katherine, 169
Jerry, 87, 239
Jim, 207
Joe, 51, 83
John, 138, 139, 166, 223, 298
John Francis, 140
Judith, 209, 287
Judith Anita, 110
Judy, 207, 208, 209, 286
Larry, 57, 62, 77
Linda, 77, 127, 128, 218, 220, 252, 294, 295
Linda Lee, 221, 296
Madeline, 239, 240
Margo Blaine, 189
Mark, 55, 85
Mary R., 155
Melodie Ann, 199
Michael R., 195, 201, 202
Mike, 150
Mitch, 158
Norman Russell, 169
Opal, 228, 305
Othis, 58
Pat, 157
Patrick, 57, 146, 157
Patrick Dennis, 146
Paul, 159
Paul Eugene, 159
Paul V., 193
Peggy, 31, 32, 33, 83, 140
Perry, 143
Pete, 78, 79
Richard, 121, 150, 158
Ricky, 50, 51, 52, 54, 62, 64, 66, 67, 70
Ricky Allen, 56, 57, 84
Robert, 37, 39, 49, 83, 206
Robert H., 138
Robert Leonard, 166, 168
Robert M., 40
Roger, 87
Russell, 158
Santos, 135
Scott, 53, 54
Sharon, 50, 55, 59, 74, 85, 197
Shirley Irene, 183
Stan, 75
Stephen, 157, 158
Thelma, 186
Thomas Leonard, 262
Tom, 150
Vaughn, 142
Warren, 132, 148

Wayne, 252
Wes, 148
William, 117, 129, 160
Wyman, 170
Redwood Inn, 155, 156
Reynolds, Dan, 173
Rheem Manufacturing Co., 166
Riley, Lt. James, 135
Riverside City College, 3, 4, 318, 322
Riverside Police Department, 3, 315, 317, 320, 322
Riverside, California, 3
Robertson, Det. Sgt. John, 239, 241, 243, 245, 248, 264, 291
Robertson, Sgt., 264, 292, 295, 302, 303
Ronback, Eric, 230
Rust, Sgt., 103, 104, 106, 108, 117, 122, 125, 129, 143, 146, 161
Ryan, Phil, 228
San Francisco Police Department, 8, 170, 191, 276, 311, 312, 313, 320, 330
San Francisco, California, 2, 1, 8, 55, 96, 137, 138, 140, 143, 145, 147, 157, 164, 166, 168, 170, 171, 172, 176, 179, 184, 185, 191, 210, 254, 262, 264, 276, 282, 284, 287, 306, 308, 309, 310, 311, 312, 313, 315, 320, 328, 330
Sanford, Bryan, 306
Santa Cruz, California, 180, 181, 183, 185, 187
Santini, Donald, 302, 304
Schultz, Deputy, 278
Sears Roebuck, 157
Seattle, Washington, 158
Sharai, Dr., 107
Shepard, Cecelia Ann, 203, 204, 206, 208, 210, 212, 214, 216, 218, 219, 221, 222, 223, 224, 226, 227, 228, 230, 232, 234, 236, 238, 240, 242, 246, 247, 256, 260, 268, 271, 274, 281, 283, 286, 287, 297, 298, 304, 327
Shepard, Robert Hiland, 238
Shepard, Wilma Dolores, 238
Siebert, Dr., 306
Sims, Charles, 248
Slaight, Officer, 259
Slover, Nancy L., 91, 307
Snook, Det. Sgt. Hal, 212, 231, 233, 235, 236, 237, 256, 257, 260
Snook, Sgt., 212, 214, 219, 220, 223, 286, 288, 289, 290, 291, 295, 305
Solano County Sheriff, 16, 20, 26, 31, 32, 39, 42, 43, 60, 61, 62, 63, 66, 67, 78, 83, 85
Solano, Kenney, 162
Sonoma, CA, 76, 162, 166, 223
Southern, Tommy, 151, 152, 153, 199
Spanish Flat Coffee Shop, 213, 288, 289
Sparks, John, 187
Springmaid Textile Company, 158
Springtown Junior High, 148
St. Helena, Washington, 129, 210, 223, 228, 264, 287, 297, 299, 305
St. Salinas, California, 137
Stanford Research Center Menlo Park, 138
Stanley, Donald, 230, 289
STELLA BORGES. *See* Medeiros, Stella
Stiltz, Jack, 179
Stine, Paul L., 282
Stine, Paul Lee, 276, 277, 328
Stockton Police Department, 135
Straub, Dr., 224
Stuhlasatz, John M., 139
Suennen, Darlene. *See* Ferrin, Darlene E.
Suennen, Mrs., 171, 175, 176, 181
Suenner, Christina, 141
Sunnyside Road, Sanitarium, 220, 295
Sylvas Auto Wreckers, 58
Terry's restaurant, 144
Thompson, Capt., 139
Times Herald, 134, 143, 261, 282, 306, 308
Toschi, Dave, 311, 320
Townsend, Capt. Donald, 143, 158, 212, 219, 220, 221, 256, 288, 296, 311, 312
Townsend, Donald A., 4
Travis Air Force Base, 223, 224, 225, 226, 297, 302
Troutdale, Oregon, 204, 206, 286
Twin Chapels, 106, 107, 116
Union Oil, 195
United Pacific Builders, 162
USS Pelius, 193
Vallejo General Hospital, 12, 18, 306
Vallejo Jr College, 159
Vallejo Police Department, 87, 89, 133, 160, 162, 164, 166, 168, 169, 170, 172, 173, 174, 176, 177, 178, 180, 181, 182, 184, 185, 186, 189, 191, 193, 195, 197, 199, 201
Varner, Officer, 10
Washington Street, 137, 157, 162, 220, 226, 260, 276, 277, 278, 279, 280, 295, 310, 311, 328
Waterman, Det., 10, 12, 13
Watsonville Police Department, 173
Wesher, Bingo, 44
White, Archie E., 214, 216, 218
White, Elizabeth, 214, 216, 218

White, Sgt., 214, 215, 216, 239, 240, 292, 293
Yellow Cab Co., 278
Zander, Officer, 183

Made in the USA
Coppell, TX
07 October 2021

63594425R20190